To Ellie and Joe.

Little Warrior Brother

GABE KEITH

Edited by: Scott Waldyn
Edited by: Lara J Cox MD, MS
Edited by: Rebecca L Davis
Cover design by: Caleb Stauss
Copyright © 2017 Gabe Keith
All rights reserved.

ISBN: 0998662208
ISBN 13: 9780998662206

CONTENTS

DEDICATION

This is for two of my uncles, Doug and Rick. They understood me even when I didn't. There was a time when Rick was young, where he gave zero fucks and did what he had to do to get home, a long time before I did. When he got back, no one was there for him like he chose to be there for me. Doug has always been there for me and my brothers. For that and more, I'll always be grateful to them.

"So, I was thinking, Uncle Rick. I'm going to write a book about my time in the Marines. Maybe we could write our stories together?"

"Really? Not sure what to think of that. Are you sure you want your story next to mine? Because mine isn't what you think it is. I know we have talked a little in the past, but you don't know the half of it. I don't remember half the stuff that happened. It's been 40 years for me. What I do remember, I don't care to think about."

"Okay. I mean, I get that. Honestly, I haven't thought about a lot in years myself. But it seems to come back as I think about it these days. Maybe it could be the same with you, if we write down what you do remember."

"Yeah. But Gabe, maybe I don't want to tell a war story? Maybe I want to talk about inner battles and thoughts about the past. Who's going to want to read that?" ,

"I think whatever you want to say, you can put that in. And leave out anything you don't want in there, you know?"

"The war I've been fighting since I've been out is what's been on my mind lately. My story is different than what people see in the movies. It's embarrassing and awkward, not what people want to see."

"You should say that, then."

■ ■ ■

Her paws scrape against the road's surface as she slowly hobbles up to the back end of my post. My bunkered position rises from the middle of the road in a half-assed tower of stacked sandbags on top of boxes of sand wrapped in metal mesh and plywood. I pull back the heavy red blanket that serves as its back door to see who is approaching. It's our dog. She bleeds from multiple bullet holes as she climbs up the sandbag steps to where I stand, watching her.

She forces her way to the third step, turns slowly, and sits down, facing outward. Her body wheezes and shifts as she gazes as evenly as possible, stretching her neck so she can scan back and forth across the road. I want to touch her, in spite of orders not to. But her body is in pain. Petting her will only punish her more.

This is a memory, and I never trust memories. I blocked them out for years, and now they hit harder. I remember that pain, the way her face wore it. She looks out steadily with her nose tilted up, her eyes focused even though her breathing is forced and her body shudders in pain over and over again. I wonder if she knows she is going to die, her pups will probably die, and that will be the end. Riddled with bullets, she protects me still.

I can see the house in the distance where I have lived for the last couple of months and wonder how she made it back. I can't believe I'm mad at her. But I am.

I stand in the stuffy wooden box, encased in a sweat-stained shell of assorted gear held together by interwoven straps, buttons, and Velcro. My gear weighs down on my shoulders more than usual. It's been a long post. I let the curtain fall and return to facing the front. The smell of burning shit suffocates the senses. I listen to the wheezing creature as I ponder my options. I tell them she's here, they kill her. I say nothing, she lives until the next shift begins and my relief makes the call. I move her into the woods, she walks back over again.

My machine gun sits crookedly on the bipods with a belt of ammo resting on the can. The road beyond me disappears into the horizon, cutting through one-story houses with palm trees dotting little farm plots and an occasional lonely oasis. I'm currently on the outskirts of Fallujah. I'm in the Marines, in an infantry battalion, and we are on our third deployment to Iraq in less than two years since this thing started. We hold an area of large multi-story houses that stretch along the highway just outside city limits. Each house holds a full platoon, and each platoon has set up a perimeter to ensure the entire infrastructure is watched closely.

Since we replaced the last battalion here, it's been our job to manage the ebb and flow of traffic that enters and leaves the city. My post is the farthest out from the house my platoon inhabits on this side of town.

I reach for my radio and call in to command.

"Fisher?"

"Yeah?"

"Snowball is here, and she's sitting on my post. Looks like she's been shot up pretty bad."

"What?! Okay, hold on."

I wait. My squad leader, Corporal Fisher, must be checking with the lieutenant on what happens next. I look back outside at our girl, and remember how we got here.

Months prior, I was sitting among bunk beds that I shared with thirty other Marines. Some of us were coming off post, others were returning from the most recent patrol, still more were preparing for their turn in the suck. My squad was up for patrol. We checked our gear, cleaned our weapons, and made sure we had enough ammunition, water, and rations. Fisher checked our gear one at a time, moving from bunk to bunk. When he got to mine, I looked up.

"Well, Sweet-cheeks? Do we have everything?" he said with a half-smile.

"Yes," I replied. "Of course, if I do, Olsen will probably forget something."

Fisher rolled his eyes. "You guys are seriously going to give me a fucking heart attack."

He continued walking down the line, checking the squad. Twenty minutes later, we were outside and moving slowly across the road into the nearest neighborhood. Our gear was heating up and its weight burned into our shoulders, making it difficult to focus.

I sifted through notions of days long gone, of t-shirts and shorts. I thought about home. This could have been my thousandth patrol in Iraq, and usually nothing happens. When it does, it's over quickly and everything goes back to waiting and watching and wondering.

Our biggest problem was quickly becoming the dogs in residential areas. Unlike back home, people don't choose dogs here; it is the other way around. The wild creatures roam neighborhoods until they find someone's house and choose to stay and protect it. The homeowners keep them fed.

The dogs are wild and territorial. When anything moseys onto their property, like a group of Marines patrolling through town, they react aggressively. It wouldn't be an issue if we stayed to the main roads, but that creates a recipe for an ambush.

Sometimes we would shoot the dogs. Fisher picked one off one day and I felt the frustration build for all of us because it didn't feel like a viable solution. We were going to keep walking through the backyards of these animals and they were never going to understand.

Our leadership didn't have an answer. They told us to figure it out and follow the credo: "Adapt and Overcome." They never fail to assert recruiter taglines as useful guidance for very uniquely difficult situations.

One day, we were patrolling through a yard when a larger dog barked at us. I stutter-step toward it to back it off. The moment I moved it lunged, as if an invisible gate dropped between us. I grabbed at my machine gun, but it was too late. I reached for my Berretta instead. The dog stopped abruptly before me and I heard someone shoot into the ground a safe distance away. At least someone got his gun out in time. Or maybe, through sheer luck,

I was a foot or two off this psychotic mutt's perceived property line.

At night, the dogs would announce our every step. We wore night vision goggles and quietly moved through the neighborhood farming community. Before this particular problem began, sometimes I doubt people even knew we were in their homes.

One night, we found roof access to provide over-watch for a patrol while they slowly maneuvered through a moist field of churned ground underneath a moonlit sky. I stood in a living room and waited for the Marines in front to finish filing up the stairs and onto the roof. I watched as the family slept around our feet. We sweated silently and our gear creaked and groaned. A little boy shifted and lifted his head off the ground, staring at our dark shapes hovering overhead as we filed up the stairs and onto the roof. He cried, but as quickly as he started, a hand appeared from the person sleeping next to him, lightly resting on his head. Whimpering, he lied back down.

We tell the community there is a chance we will occasionally travel through their backyards and front doors. This message is lost on the dogs. Each house we approached kicked off new sets of animal sirens. Mario turned one night and walking back towards where I knelt, while I scanned the night, hoping our position wasn't compromised. We needed to be eyes here, and nothing more.

"Hey, fool."

"Hey."

"Fuck these dogs, fool," he said in the tone that served as his way of wanting to scream and throw shit.

"I know, man."

"Have you ever seen this before?"

"No, I haven't," I said. I thought back about how superstitious he was when we arrived in country and wondered if he still was, or if it was something he'd grown out of.

We sat in the back of a Humvee together, on an early convoy at what was the beginning of his first deployment and my third.

"Hey, Mario, what will you do if this happens?" I take a drag off a cigarette and simulate a sniper round smacking the back of my helmet, sending me back against the bench seat as I exhale to simulate the smoke from the blast as it exits my body.

"Don't do that, fool. That's not cool, fool. Seriously, fool, stop it!"

None of us thought much of the dog when she showed up at our house. She seemed content to sit in the front yard, panting and watching us trudging through our daily routines. She was a motley thing, with her belly loosely hanging in the dirt and ugly patches of hair interspersed with patches of hairless, wrinkled skin. Out on patrol one day, she followed us, moving among us at first. As we moved through town, she took the lead.

We followed her instead of sticking to the planned patrol. When she didn't recognize someone, human or otherwise, she would stop and growl. Quietly, we floated outward from the snaking, staggered formation. Some took a knee in a ditch, leaned against a wall, or crouched among trees, like we have so many times before on our own intuition. Then, we waited, keeping her in our peripherals. When she relaxed, so would we. When she moved, we moved, one-by-one getting up to resume the patrol.

She would meet other dogs at their property lines, growling or sniffing her introductions. They began to leave us alone. No more dogs died and no more humans were attacked. The nights became quiet again, even when our dog didn't follow.

After some time, another dog stopped by the house and stayed. He adopted the same habits as his female counterpart, and as Marines took turns leading patrols, so did the two dogs. Gossip spreads, and we made the mistake of telling others about the dogs. Command sent an order down: We aren't allowed to feed or touch the animals because they might be unsafe and diseased. Either command didn't know or didn't care how helpful the dogs had become. The decision was above our pay grade to question, but command doesn't say to stop working with them, so nothing changed.

Since I was one of the two Marines carrying a medium machine gun in my platoon, I was always assigned to the furthest outlying post that stood directly in the center of the main road. I don't like the feeling of being so exposed, but it usually meant that when it got dark, I shared my shift with another Marine, another kid to swap stories and rumors with throughout the night.

I got used to seeing the dogs on patrol, and soon the one that showed up first adopted a new role. She began sitting on the back of my post and looking out. If anyone approached she would growl. I would turn, brush back the red blanket to see what she saw. I watched her with a smile on my face as she sat in the front yard and watched me walk out to my post, knowing she was processing the scene before her and would decide to join me soon. I stood on post, smiling to think about how comical it looked with this creature sitting just outside the tent flap, like a mythical beast guarding the gates of an ancient stronghold.

I would talk to her sometimes, and I think others did, too. She was one of us, and it was beautiful. We fed the dogs what rations we didn't eat, but never touched them. We struggled with not reaching out and giving her a 'good girl' or two with a pat on the head.

In time, the animal that showed up looking sallow and unkempt turned into something well-fed and less bloated. She led a few less patrols one week. Her belly was growing again, but not in the sunken way it was before. She had pups. We built them a shelter so they would survive in the rain and sandstorms. Their fur was fine and thick, like American pets.

At night, they played outside. During the day, they sat in the shade. The fuzzballs tackled each other regardless of the hour. They were almost impossible not to play with or assign little doggy names. It was fun watching the little things bounce around. Days pass, and the pups weren't that old when we were given orders to kill them.

Command wouldn't budge, so a few Marines picked up the pups and their mom and drove them into the city in hopes of finding a nice family to feed them. That was our first mistake. We knew she had abandoned her pups when she returned.

Her belly is sagging for the third time now, this time pregnant with blood and bullets. Dirt from where she sat ground into the matted, bloody mess. She shakes and wheezes and looks on down the road. She must have been shot at by every post along the way, but she sits behind me like she has done so many times before, in spite of her bloody, wheezing frame riddled with bullet holes by our own guns and at the expense of her lost pups.

I stare out down the road in front of my post, listening to her labored breathing and waiting for Corporal Fisher to respond with instructions.

The radio crackles.

"Keith."

"Yeah, Fisher?"

"How bad is it?"

"She's about dead."

"Well, the L.T. said put her down, so go ahead and do that."

"No."

"What?"

"I'm sorry. I don't mean any disrespect, but I just can't," I say as my eyes begin to water.

The radio is quiet for a while. Time passes in a windy desert silence. The dog growls, and I turn to check it out as I've done with her for months. Fisher approaches, and I can't tell if he's mad at me or the whole situation. His face looks resigned and tired at the same time.

He walks up to the post and lightly prods the dog off the sandbags with the barrel of his rifle. Whimpering, she hobbles down into the street. Fisher starts shooting at her and she yelps, running off the road, and falling down the side of a ditch. He swears under his breath, following her there and shooting at her again. I can't tell if his shots are landing, but she scrambles her way out into the thick tree line and the backyard beyond.

Fisher looks at me and, for once, he doesn't say anything. We both know he shouldn't have had to come out here. He turns to walk away and I drop the red blanket back in place. I face forward again, staring down the road, waiting for nothing in particular. She is out of sight now, and we'll never see or talk about her again.

When people ask me how many people I killed, sometimes I think of her.

1

17 IN 2001

"So, you're telling me the symbolic nature of their role is more important than the fact that they didn't physically engage in combat, so they should be considered combat vets? Then I could tell people I was a boar hunter, even though the only time I went out hunting for boars with Uncle Doug I never saw one."

"I wasn't in the infantry either, and it doesn't hurt my feelings because I knew I was in a supporting role. Not everyone understands that their job was just as important, and getting close to that kind of ugliness affects us all in different ways."

"Look, I'm not searching for any greater truths or trying to refine how people look at certain social issues or hurt anyone's feelings. I plan to tell things the way I remember them happening. I think it will be nice to say what's been on my mind every day for about a decade now. I'm going to stand up for that seventeen-year-old kid who walked into a recruiter's office one day."

"Honestly, Gabe, I think there's more of a chance this will make a certain type of vet hate himself a little less. That's the kind of story I want to tell, at least. I want to talk about the kind of person who comes home with low self-esteem and a lot of bitterness. I want to help that person."

■ ■ ■

"I'm sorry, but you have a history of seizures, like you said," said the recruiter. It was May of 2001. I was 17.

"I checked with my command. Even though you haven't had a seizure in four years, the physical and mental stress it takes to make it in boot camp alone could possibly trigger an episode, so there's really nothing we can do at this point. Sorry, brother."

I drive home, replaying in my head what the recruiter told me in that broken-down strip mall in Roseville, Minnesota. It's my junior year of high school, and all I want is to join the Marines when I graduate. I pull up to my parents' house in Stillwater, slam the car door, and stomp inside.

Mom asks what's wrong as I speed-walk past her in the kitchen, running downstairs and slamming the door to my room. She follows me and asks what happened from the other side of the door.

"The recruiter fucked me!" I yell back, not caring that cursing was against the rules and unaware that Mom's next action, taken out of love, will be enough punishment for both of us.

She calls the recruiter, and he drives out to my family's house in Stillwater that day. By the time he arrives, I have dried my eyes and calmed down. He talks to my family in our living room. Mom and Dad sit close, listening to him reiterate what he'd told me when I visited earlier. I won't make it past the Military Entrance Processing Station.

Why did he even bother to come out here, then, if all he's going to do is tell my family the same thing he told me? This isn't what any kid on the verge of adulthood wants to hear, at a time in life when physical setbacks don't feel real.

I follow him out to his car. He stops in the entryway. We are alone. He says there's one more option. I can lie. I can just pretend the seizures, the narcolepsy, even the fact that I need glasses, never existed. A flood of relief washes over me and I thank him, feeling stupid for crying in the first place. At least now I have a purpose again.

Dad owned a construction company. It was called Northland Painting and Decorating. The business card incorporated half a pine tree in the corner that started with a brown streak at the bottom and looked like green steps walking up to the top left corner. Dad made company jackets for his employees, and gave them to some of the people from church as well. Others would ask if he had more and he gave them to anyone interested. He paid his employees what they were worth, regardless of what little they were expecting to earn.

The company began in our garage, and a decade later it had turned into something that ebbed and flowed throughout a giant warehouse. Around sixty employees walked in and out during the course of a day. Painters approached the warehouse manager for supplies, the office for a paycheck, or the loading dock to load or unload materials.

The building was an old cattle slaughtering facility, and it needed a lot of work when Dad brought his operation here. One of my earliest jobs was to paint a pipe red. It crisscrossed among other pipes and spanned the length of the ceiling. Dad set up a ladder that stretched all the way up to the ceiling and handed me a one gallon can with a roller, a brush, and a little grid inside. I climbed the ladder and began rolling out the paint, brushing it into the grooves. The building is occupied by many different tenants now, but the red pipe runs unimpeded past walls and company signs from different businesses. It's a road map to the past, so relevant in our lives then, and irrelevant now.

Back then, Dad threw Christmas parties at the four-star Radisson Hotel in downtown Minneapolis. He believed that playing hard was just as important as working hard. A live band serenaded during the meal, and afterwards people sang songs and danced.

It's all bittersweet snapshots now. Dad was standing in our front yard on Dayton Avenue in the nineties after a long day of work. Putting paint-dried fingers in his mouth, he whistled loudly, and wherever we were in the neighborhood we came running. We'd slam through screen doors on either end of the house, welcomed in by the irresistible smell of fresh bread and homemade pasta. Bundled up on the living room floor with my siblings around me as the fire burned and crackled on Christmas Eve, I stared at the dark, needled tree as the warm glow from the little red bubble lights and the smell of pine carried me off to sleep. Summer days held few responsibilities. Friends walked in and out with their parents for a barbecue or casual gathering. On cool days in the summer, we opened all the doors and windows, making sure to shut the screens to keep out bees and flies. Mom managed seven kids and an occasional renter. She cooked, cleaned, and organized all our extracurricular activities, then put on makeup in the small oval mirror above the bathroom sink. Once, I asked her why.

"Well, honey, I want to look good for your dad. He's had a rough day."

"Why, Mom?"

"Because you need to make sure, when you're married someday, to make more good memories than bad ones together."

While Dad seemed to care about physical things like working, taking us to church, or participating in his kids' sporting activities, Mom was concerned with how we felt. She listened when I talked about other kids and asked questions about the stories I shared with her after long days at school. She cared about the little plot points that weren't so little for me. We were close.

I'm not sure if Dad and I knew each other that well back then, at least not in that way. He coached my baseball team. Sometimes he showed up at school with my favorite sub sandwich. It was important to him that I knew he loved me. He told me this a lot and still does. His father never had. Mom and Dad knew about real pain, and they protected us from it.

That was the beginning of my life. My parents created a different world for us than the one they endured, like bowling with bumpers firmly in place.

Then high school came.

My grades suffered near the end of junior year, but I was passing. I daydreamed and procrastinated with the best of them. I began looking for other options. I became distinctly aware that I needed to pick a path. When seniors took turns sharing what they planned to do after school, I began to say, "Join the Marine Corps infantry."

I wanted to be taken seriously and this was a way to do it. I could be like one of the fantasy heroes I saw in movies or books. I could be Aragorn in *The Lord of the Rings*. I could be Ender in *Ender's Game*, the knight in *Dragon Heart*, or the prince from *NeverEnding Story*. I imagined staring out in wonder at the vast desert landscape next to Luke Skywalker, past my boring life and into the horizon of a dual sunset. I imagined the truth of things in the universe, past what my parents had revealed, while John Williams' score played slow and soulfully in the background.

I could be dangerous, heroic, and brave.

Since then, when people ask why I joined, my answers have been anything but consistent. It all depends on which version of me is asked. The seventeen-year-old version said, "I joined because I need discipline in my life, and the military will give me life experience and pay for college." The twenty-year-old version (or any version during my enlistment) said, "I joined because I wanted to slay the lava monster in the goddamn commercials." The person I have become simply says, "I think I just wanted to know."

I wonder if anyone really knows why no one talks about his service. Is it the pain or the judgment we all avoid? Most veterans don't want to tell a woman on their first date or an employer in an interview that they experienced horrible things. Then again, a lot of veterans don't want to admit they didn't see anything, even if it means quietly serving as the poster boy for combat-related situations everyone automatically assumes they experienced.

I'm always trying to avoid one question I'm often asked. I can see it in people's eyes even before they say it: "Did you kill anyone?"

It's never about the question; It's about what led the person to ask it in the first place. Will their opinions on this topic direct them to choose to question my character based on my response, or take my answer as an affirmation of strength? What if I answer, and they ask how it happened? I can never allow that.

Having been asked this question so many times, I have reached the conclusion that there are many different types of Americans. There are the ones that never stop wondering about the way things work, even if the information they find contradicts the path they are traveling. There are also people who look past their individual existence and care about others, embracing different perspectives.

Then, there are the annoying ones I try to avoid at work or family gatherings. These are the people that march into retail stores, intent on picking a fight with lowly sales reps to vent about corporate policies or business models they don't understand, related to products they don't value. They say things like, "In theory, I don't think it should be like this," or, "I own my own business, and I would never run things like this," even though their business is significantly smaller. And they never realize how quickly they all resort to using random metaphors.

But we all know those types. They don't get it. That doesn't make them evil. Just stupid. I really struggle with the gullible ones, the ones who don't realize they aren't taking the time to gather information while attempting to draw rational conclusions. Maybe people are just hardwired to pick a viewpoint and stick with it. I wish I could go back to my thoughts before I joined and look at that perspective now. I wonder what I would see, and with whom I would agree. Is this what it's like to slowly go insane over time?

Whenever anyone asks me questions about the Marines, an eighteen-year-old boy who has been sitting in the desert, playing with sand on a rock, stands up from this distraction and becomes present. It sounds silly, but he existed then. He looks at us, joining the conversation in his own way, keenly curious on what answer I'll use to ward off the question – an answer that will describe a place and time when I was someone else. He intently stares, as if he's waiting to see whether I will decide to awkwardly jostle words into the air, making a sad attempt to appease the person who asked the question while betraying him in the process.

What am I supposed to say to such a biased, pain-filled perspective? I've always found it feels better to deflect and move on. If I'm lucky, the boy inside my mind fades, leaving me to play out the scripted routine I've adopted since him. But then he judges me for my deluded memories of his life. He makes me feel uncomfortable, as if my answer was downplayed to hide the truth, or worse yet, embellished to increase the perception of my worth.

"You've forgotten the pain," he whispers into the billowing sand. I don't want to be one of those vets who lie. But then again, I also don't want to be one of those civilians who stop growing and gaining perspective.

September 11, 2001, is a time capsule for every single American. For me, it is a lazy day in my senior year of high school. Whispers of something happening have begun by the time I stroll into class. The TV is on, and the scene of the towers smoldering is on repeat, over and over. Students stand around the teacher as he stares at the screen, mouth open.

I ask to use the bathroom and walk down the hallway. Every classroom door is open, and every TV is on. The synchronized sound from thirty TVs playing the scene of the burning towers echoes down the halls. Images flicker of people hanging on for help or precious fresh air until they fall, straight down like the metal lines of the skyscrapers, while thick black clouds of smoke billow horizontally out into the cloudless blue sky. Thousands of innocent people in the middle of their lives were gone in minutes. Hundreds of thousands of precious memories involving final moments spent kissing kids, wives, and husbands good night, spent dancing or drinking or consoling or existing alongside. Time used as if tomorrow would be there safely, not there only in memory with never a new one. All of it eight months before I would be in the Marines.

Ten days after graduation, I stand on a pair of yellow footprints in Camp Pendleton in San Diego, California. Everyone remembers the footprints. Some look to the Marine Corps' official emblem, the Eagle, Globe, and Anchor, as the most iconic symbol of the organization. I think of the first picture taken as a Marine. Mine hangs in Mom's stairway.

We stand in a line and one by one walk behind a curtain where a Marine takes the top half of a vest, pinned with the only medal we earned upon graduation, and Velcroes it onto us from behind. The sleeves from the elbows, the waist, the chest, and the back are cut. The edges fray from the many arms continuously punching through the sleeves. Two strips of Velcro tighten and hold the sham together, creating the illusion of a well-pressed suit. Three different sizes lie on the floor, and one by one each recruit walks into the frame and gets the butchered uniform slapped on. He is anything but the man his parents and friends will see when they frame the photo and hang it somewhere warm and personal. The camera snaps with a flash, and the next one files in. The backdrop is similarly contrived. Three inches out of the shot and it's dingy, depressing, and colorless.

Sometimes I think I remember that recruit, my old self, standing there before the frame.

During the week between high school and boot camp, Dad's extended family planned our yearly Keith family campout. We met in June 2002 on a nature preserve. We stayed in tents, campers, and my parents' RV. I remember feeling very loved.

Aunt Mary was there. She wore her black shirt with red flowers. She sang the National Anthem to the tune of the *Star Wars* theme song. She played spoons on her knees and laughed with people she loved. She introduced me to some of the books I cherish more than anything. Aunt Mary wrapped a hand towel around my head when I was a baby, prancing around my parents' house, proclaiming to the world, "Zaltan, king of the gypsy babies, has arrived!"

It was a bright sunny weekend, and the only other kid about my age was one of my cousins. We stayed in one of the tents, playing cards and talking about our plans after school. Family members went on walks, returning for food or naps. Some grabbed towels and swimwear, exchanging shoes for flip-flops, stuffing fanny packs with sunscreen and granola bars. The adults talked about adult things with each other or threw a ball around with the kids. They asked about our future plans, imparting advice of their own. The younger kids ran to the lake or begged parents for change to spend at the park's little check-in shack where toiletries, knickknacks, and candy bars waited for them.

After the weekend was over and I had said my good-byes to the extended family, we went home. Boot camp was nearing, and I couldn't shake the growing sense of dread that I'd made the wrong decision. I was leaving all these people behind. I had signed up to become a warrior. And sometimes, warriors don't come home.

But the papers had been signed. I had already told everyone I was going to join.

I wish I could step outside myself then and find Mom and Dad, and quietly listen to them talk in the way a couple does when they are still together and all their kids have yet to leave home for good. I want to find my brother Jake and tell him I'll be there when he starts high school next year. I would find Tim out by the basketball hoop in the driveway, and let him know that even if he doesn't make it to the NBA he will still do something great someday. I want to hug Dan, Ben, Tom and Veronica. I wish I could find myself outside in the sun in May 2002, while I threw a basketball at the backboard in the lazy way semi-gifted athletic high school boys do. I would tell me that the Marines would only be a lonely, sad place and that everything Dad had built would be over soon so I should enjoy it while it lasted.

Every ten years of our lives, give or take a few, we become completely different people, living in completely different worlds than before. These different versions step seamlessly in and out of our lives until they all abruptly stop one day.

On the day, I left for boot camp, Dad called me into the office to give me the final talk a dad gives his son before he leaves home for good. I had my feet planted firmly in two worlds. I was lost in a land of make-believe, and a lot of things that were intense for my parents, like me leaving for the Marines, felt like nothing.

Dad spoke in a quiet, measured tone as I waited for him to stop. I had made it to the final boss in Final Fantasy X right before the camping trip. "If only I had spent more time leveling up, I might've been able to beat the last boss by now," was my most pressing concern. I didn't know I was experiencing the last time my family would be living in the same house, that my parents would be married, or that this house would be our home. I thought of video games while Dad was trying to reassure me that there was still a place for me here if I didn't make it through boot camp. He said that he would still love me and that everything would be okay.

Another voice from the past floods to mind. I was visiting a friend from school. His family loved four-wheelers and hunting. Good people. My friend was a big country kid, and his dad quiet and thoughtful. His son tells him, as we walk in one afternoon, "Gabe's going into the Marines like you did, Dad."

My friend's dad looks at me, and I nod.

"Don't do it," he says. "It's not what you think it is. They brainwash you. Treat you bad. It's not worth it."

He must have pussied out, I thought then.

When the recruiter arrives, I am sitting in my room, clacking away on the controller, staring down the TV. My backpack bulges with the things awkwardly jammed inside. One of my little brothers is sent for me. I turn off the system, walk upstairs, and hug the family. We say goodbye, and I climb into a stranger's car.

I wish I could go back and scream at myself to stop. I wish I could stand there and laugh in the recruiter's face as he puts his car in park, a deep guttural sound emitting from the back of my throat as I stare at him, slack-jawed and shaking from the hilarity or insanity or untruth of everything he represents.

When I'm a dad, I'll see this man come to my home for my kids and know. He talked about a lot of things. For me, what he said was hope. For him, it was a sales pitch. I was his sale.

I romanticize about going back in time. I would politely ask him to wait while I looked for a hammer. I would take it to him until he broke down and admitted the game he was playing.

Every day when we go to sleep, we die. Every time we wake, we come back to life and start over. These aren't things we understand, even though we pretend we do. One day I woke up with a family, and the next I left them forever.

This is my burden that I carry when I wake up and brush my teeth in the morning. This is the burden that sometimes weighs on me when I drive to work, when I meet friends for drinks, or play video games alone in my apartment while Mom tells me about her day on the phone. It's something I don't know how to define or explain, and it feels awkward to talk about in this place.

17 IN 1970

"I couldn't remember much of March 1971 until a few years ago. Most of the gunners and crew chiefs couldn't either. My gunner remembers it and still can't talk about it. I have been told what happened to me and the others by a Cobra pilot who took a pic of my A/C en route to the pick-up zone. He has since disappeared. What I found out was that a C-130 killed over 500 North Vietnamese Army troops preparing to invade our small, 150-man strong company area. They killed them just outside our perimeter. I remember hearing it go overhead. I had no idea how close we came to being destroyed until last night. Close only counts in horse shoes."

■ ■ ■

Cars infrequently pass by the old farmhouse and barn that sit off the main road running through the Grafton, Wisconsin countryside. It is a cold, cloudy day in January of 1970, and massive snow drifts curve inward where the packed earth recedes down the driveway. A school bus slows down as it approaches, its lone, noisy engine cutting through the frozen silence. Easing to a full stop, the doors rattle open, and I emerge, wearing an old coat that is about three sizes too big, ripped up jeans, and a poorly shaven bald head.

I'm seventeen, and I'm tired. That morning, I'd gotten up early before school, gone out to the barn where the horses lingered in their stalls, and filled up the troughs with the hay Dad had sent me to purchase. Smelling like shit, I changed into my old, worn out clothes and headed to school. This day had played out like many before. I meet my only two friends, and we stand in the hallway chatting a bit before running off to class.

"Hey, how are things?"

"Good. We've got to talk."

"Cool. What's up?"

"We're in our senior year, man. When are we getting the fuck out of here?" We hang around the lockers, looking at some of the girls who pass by and resigning ourselves to the inevitable wave of classroom double-talk. The English teacher will say that English is the most important subject, the math teacher will talk about how math is in everything, the history teacher will say history repeats itself and forms the future, and the science teacher will talk about life, but not mine.

"We need money. How much do you have?"

"I don't know. Seventy, maybe eighty?"

"Sounds about right on my end too. But my dad would kill me — and yours too, I imagine — if we dipped out."

"All right. Well, we'll talk later. See you in Third Period."

We've been having this conversation a lot lately, and so the day continues to take its usual course as I go from class to class until the final bell. We mill out of the school and onto the buses that will take us to our homes. I stare out the window, ignoring the other kids, who would only ignore me at best back then. The bus stops and I move past the rows of chatter until I'm standing in front of the driveway as the bus pulls back out onto the road.

Kids jeer, with arms wedged between windows and faces mocking from the openings, as the cold wind scurries the bus away, leaving me alone and aware of being home. I cannot get away from this place soon enough, for one reason. Dad is here. The girls would call him a monster. I would call him a fucked-up veteran from World War II. I don't think he saw any combat, because he was there in the end. He talked about using C-4 and dynamite to blow up buildings in Japan. People would spray out of doorways and rubble like panicked rats, traumatized from the Nagasaki bomb.

I walk down the driveway towards the house and the barn that shelters a small clan of Dad's horses. The barn door is open, and I decide to close it before putting on my uniform and heading to the factory for my evening job. I think back on how we put this ragtag group of animals together.

When Dad would buy a horse, he would go to the local slaughterhouse, and pick out the healthy animals who were set for death more for their attitude than anything else. He could buy them for pennies on the pound, bringing them home and locking them in the corral. They liked to strut around and rage. I'm not a cowboy and was never taught how to break in a horse properly, so I would jump on them and ride around until they would break or I would. Dad expected the animals to be tamed, so I took my beatings from them to avoid as many as I could from him.

As I approach, I realize there's no sound coming from the dark maw of the barn. I get to the large sliding door, put my hand on the worn, paint-chipped frame, and look inside. Instead of horse heads swinging comically over the short walls to greet me with dumb stares, the stalls appear empty. I approach and open one gate, finding a dead horse inside. My heart sinks as I look around and realize all the stalls are empty of life. I wonder how this could have happened, but the most qualified answer quickly threatens my sanity.

I run over to my favorite horse's stall and unlatch her top door, seeing nothing, then unlatch the bottom one. There she lies, whimpering a bit at seeing me, or maybe because she notices movement through the sick film over her fading consciousness. I sit down and caress her head, willing her back to life despite what I know is possible.

Tears roll down my face. Cradling her head in my lap, I ignore the feverish froth around her mouth as it smears on my jeans. I sit there crying in the barn while she finishes dying in my arms.

I can hear footsteps and know the sound of Dad as he approaches. He fills the door of the open stall where I'm sitting.

"How the fuck did this happen?"

"Dad, I'm sorry, I don't know."

He walks over to the hay in the stall, picking up a piece. "You gave them moldy hay."

"Are you sure?"

"What the fuck is wrong with you? Your poor mother and I feed and clothe you, and this is what we get for it? You don't even deserve the whooping I should lay on you. Stay out here, at least until I'm asleep."

I sit there alone again, thinking about the last time he hit someone. The day our old landlord pushed Mom.

We were poor and occasionally late with payments, but we always paid the big Polish man. Pounding on the door, signaling that he was waiting outside. Mom approached from the entry way, trying to smile like a polite hostess greeting an unexpected guest.

"George, how are you? Nice of you to stop by. We were just planning on bringing you this month's rent," she says.

"Yeah? This month or the next? Or maybe not at all, me think?"

"No. Frank and I were definitely talking about it just yesterday."

"Is your husband home now?"

"No," she lies, glancing back inside the house.

"Well, that's too bad. Because he shouldn't leave his wife here to answer for this. Give me my money."

"I don't have it here at the moment, because, you see, Frank doesn't tell me where he keeps it. And besides, it isn't due for another week."

"Don't lie to me!" shouted George. He pushed her, and she fell.

It's too late, she thought to herself, as footsteps from the living room approached.

"Take your glasses off," Dad said, who was there now.

Cicadas buzzed noisily amid the silence that followed. George paused before removing his glasses, then set them down and swung. Dad stepped back before moving forward, smashing the bigger man in the face, dropping him off the porch and onto his back. George's head bounced off the packed earth as his fists become transformed into feeble shields in front of his face.

Dad was on him and his punches were raining down. Grandpa must have heard Mom screaming for Dad to stop, because he ran out, and pulled his son off the man. I think my little brother and sisters were inside. If they were home, they would have known instinctively to hide somewhere upstairs or around the side of the house.

The next day, George's wife would show up and tell us we had to move. Her eyes would be black and blue.

I sit there in the barn, mad that I cried. Work will be wondering where I am right now, not that it matters anymore.

Dad's parting comment echoes in my mind.

"We are going to the slaughterhouse tomorrow. You caused this, so you're going to help me deliver them dead horses. We'll figure out how you will pay me back later."

The next morning at school, John and I skip out for the day. We head over to see Tony, who is older and not in school anymore. We ask him if he wants to take the day off and leave for Chicago with us. He's all for it.

We begin our trip by going east and don't stop in the Windy City. We go on to Cleveland, then to NYC, and then south to Florida. For two weeks in late January and early February of 1970, we travel with only a hundred and fifty dollars to our names, not stopping for anything but fuel.

Sometimes we feel uncomfortable, like when we drive through Manhattan. It's enchanting and foreign in both size and design. We leave the car, staring at old and tall buildings. I've never seen such heavily traveled roadways in my life.

We cross the top of the Gulf of Mexico, where our money starts to run out and we begin siphoning gas at night to keep on the move. We walk into grocery stores, stealing food, cigarettes, and beer. We run out of money completely in Louisiana, and the three of us begin begging for food in New Orleans' French Quarter. We score enough for a loaf of bread from the local bakery.

One night, I'm sleeping on a bench in the cold when I feel a hard nudge on my boot. Opening my eyes and pulling my coat down, I peer up at a cop who's not much older than I am.

"Are you from here?" he asks.

"No."

"Did you run away from home, or are you homeless?"

"Yes. I mean, I ran away from home."

"This is a dangerous place."

"I'll be okay."

"You might, but there's a lot of crime here. Dangerous people look for ones like you, alone without much they could do against a few. If you get caught by them, which will happen if you stick around, you could get hurt or even killed just for the change in your pocket."

The next day, I talk to John and Tony. We decide to make a go at driving home, stealing gas to keep moving. We stop at a gas station in St. Genevieve, Missouri, where one of us attempts to distract the attendant while another begins pumping gas and the third sits in the driver's seat anticipating a quick getaway. Someone in the back is watching, though, and a sheriff's squad car lazily pulls into the gas station lot, stopping directly in front of us before we finish our theatrics.

He's older and fatter than the cop back in Louisiana, and maybe a dad himself. Instead of arresting us or chasing us out of town, which has happened on the trip already, he brings us to jail and forces us to call our families. I don't remember much of what my parents said. They were angry. They wanted me home. Dad probably threatened while Mom cried.

We still have fifty dollars from my cousin Pete, who wired the funds to us from California while we were in

Louisiana, and so we drive on towards home again. John and I talk while Tony sleeps.

"Our dads are going to hand our asses to us."

"Yeah."

"So, why not join the Army? Let's take that aviator job the recruiter offered us the other day."

"I guess that makes sense. At least we would have a roof over our heads and food."

"Far away from home, too, which would be nice."

"Let's go in together."

"Okay."

"I turn eighteen in two weeks. Let's talk to a recruiter and see if they can take us then."

"Sounds like a plan. Good luck with your parents tonight. At least you didn't take the family car."

"I know. I killed the horses."

2

BOOT CAMP

"I want to talk about POGs."

"What are those?"

"Personnel other than grunt. I bet there are thousands of guys out there who never served in a combat occupation but collect disability for PTSD. You can pick them out online. They pose with their friends in pictures that are deceiving. They say things like, 'I'm in the artillery infantry,' when they are in the artillery, or, 'I'm an Iraq War Vet,' when they didn't have a combat-related job. Sure, in some photos they stand on a base in a safe zone with their guns and gear, smiling in the sun. But you know what? None of their gear is dirty. Everything is so clean. They look healthy, too. Well fed. They don't look malnourished from moving across long expanses of terrain for weeks, invading cities. They have things in the picture they don't realize wouldn't be there if they, in fact, had the job they claim to have had, like boxes of rations. No one carries boxes into combat. I wonder what guys from the unit that invaded Fallujah would think. Are there others out there who hate these tools as much as I do?"

"Well, I guess I'm one of them."

"No, you're not. You were in combat. I'm talking about liars like this one guy who talks about his combat experience from a deployment to Iraq he was on in the Marines. He has these podcasts, and local news stations reverently report on the demonstrations he organizes. But guess what? This guy was in Civil Affairs. He wasn't in combat. It wasn't his god-damned job. He did one deployment, then got kicked out when he got back — and not honorably. He can be proud of what he did, sure. But the moment he pretends to be some sort of war-fighting badass and uses that lie to corroborate his weak philosophies on the war, then he's what people should view as an asshole. It's mind-numbingly simple. If your job was stocking shelves in a supply room, that's what the fuck you did. I was in the infantry, but you don't see me going around pretending I was in Special Forces or comparing the job I did to theirs. I don't pretend I was one of those guys that saw a ton of combat myself. The moment I would do that, then I'm a liar and an asshole. This fucking guy. You know what, bro? There's nothing wrong with your opinion on the war in Iraq, but the moment you lie about seeing combat and use that information to make people feel more sympathetic to your perspective, it makes you a weak human being and a liar."

"We called people who weren't in the infantry or in a supporting role "REMFs." It's short for Rear Echelon Mother Fuckers."

■ ■ ■

The recruiter drives me to the airport. He's quiet, staring straight ahead with an uncomfortable look on his face. Maybe something is on his mind. Or it's just that the sales pitch is over.

We met over a year ago, when I was unsure about my chances of getting into the military. From my earliest memories, up to about age thirteen, I had seizures. The doctor said that if things ever turned for the worse, I would have to wear a helmet everywhere, might not be able to drive, and brain damage might even occur and keep me at home with my parents for the rest of my life. I was told that would probably never happen, but it couldn't be ruled out for sure. I spent time in the hospital and saw what real victims of seizures suffered. Some of them lived chaotic, violent lives. The condition stole their youth and robbed them of pleasant moments.

When I was in the hospital, I lived in a giant circular room with bedroom doors facing inward. At night, I slept with flowing cords glued to my shaved head. When awake, I either watched movies from bed or walked out into the middle of the room with the cords snaking out from my head. It was a magical place. We played all kinds of video games that weren't allowed at home for almost as much time during the day as we wanted. It was even more magical if we were conscious of that fact. Once, I noticed that one of the kids I was playing games with was positioned at a TV with his mouth open and body suddenly shaking. His mom sat there with a smile and a tear in her eyes. A doctor came over. This was their normal.

Another patient wasn't a kid. He was big and kind and slow. He lived with his parents, and had no issues with explaining all the little nuances of exploring the fantasy world of *The Legend of Zelda*. It was funny to him that I couldn't find the special swords hidden in remote areas of the map. His mom often followed him around. Many of the mothers did, always one step behind us.

One of the rooms stayed dark during the day, seemingly empty until a girl sat up, setting off a light beeping alarm. Some of us turned to watch a nurse shuffle over, whispering to her. Sometimes the nurse helped her out of bed, taking her for a walk around the room and then back. That was her life.

Cords crossed as patients moved about. We'd dance about to untangle ourselves. When my parents told me I was going back to this place, they didn't expect my excitement upon hearing the news. Between the video games and all the candy bars, it was a fun and caring place for me.

Sometimes I toured the hospital out of boredom, walking around with the cords glued to my bald head looped and connected to a pole with wheels. Families of other patients watched, horrified at whatever condition they could only imagine had led me here. I smiled as I walked by. I was here for testing. The ones fighting for their lives, that was different.

But that was all buried under a stack of documented lies when I stood in the recruiter's office. He laid out a bunch of little pieces of paper with a single word listed in bold on each and asked me to pick three that fit my reasons for joining the Marines. I think I chose discipline, purpose, and college. But that wasn't the point. He took the three words and applied them in a variety of sentences, making me feel like my goals were aligned with my curiosity about the military. He asked if I knew about the benefits. When I said no, he looked at me as if I hadn't realized all along how lucrative a move joining the Marines would be.

"Oh, yeah," he said. "You join, you get college paid for and medical coverage for the rest of your life."

Some left real possibility behind when they joined. Some passed on sports scholarships. One had a rich uncle who begged his nephew to travel the world with him. One kid, about to graduate, decided to decline a full scholarship to West Point. He chose a path that meant he wouldn't meet any pretty girls anytime soon. He wouldn't earn a first-class education. When he got out of the Marines, everything would be harder than it had to be. He would be someone that could say he fired a gun for four years before he began attending a university and squeezing in a part-time job. If he kept things cheap, maybe he wouldn't need to take out loans.

I don't think I would remember the West Point guy if I hadn't thought back once and realized that he couldn't accomplish a single pull-up. Recruiters need to hit their quotas, or they don't keep their jobs. Then their families can't live the lives to which they are accustomed. Whoever was this guy's recruiter didn't mention how unlikely it was that someone who could only do one pull-up would make it through boot camp. And yet once he enlisted in the Marines, he nullified his West Point scholarship for good. His recruiter bragged to us in front of him, "Tim here is passing up a full scholarship to West Point to be a hard-charging jarhead! Now that's guts, gentlemen."

I had never been particularly impressive in anything. I think that's the pool of people in society who join the Marines.

There's a commercial that has never left my mind as the single most effective tool the military ever created to increase recruitment numbers. Whoever was running the marketing department that day earned his promotion.

> [*A good-looking dude, known by some as Rifleman Johnny, Blast-off Ben, Hemorrhage Harry, Two-Gun Tony, or Pull-Trigger Pete, navigates through an obstacle course, climbing up to the top of a massive turret placed in the middle of a stadium packed with screaming fans. The scene is serenaded by music that pulls at my heartstrings in the way John Williams would in movies like Jurassic Park, Indiana Jones or Star Wars.*]

NARRATOR: It is more than a trial by fire.

[Hemorrhage Harry grabs the sword out of the stone.]

NARRATOR: It is a rite of passage.

[A glowing bridge appears, leading to another turret set across the stadium floor from the one where Two-Gun Tony currently stands.]

NARRATOR: A challenge to join the elite.

[As Blast-off Ben crosses the glowing force-field bridge, a lava monster erupts from the churning volcano that now fills the base of the stadium. As Ben approaches the center of the bridge, the man and beast start swinging away at each other.]

NARRATOR: And if you succeed, if you can master your fear, outsmart your enemy, and never yield, even to yourself, you will be changed forever.

[Pull-Trigger Pete rips his sword across the midsection of the monster, spewing molten lava outward in a brilliant rush. The creature breaks into a coagulated mix, sinking back into the lava. Pete begins following an iconic Marine Corps procedure to stand at attention with the sword, flourishing

the weapon in confident sweeps as he finishes the maneuver. The crowd erupts in a roar of approval, and finally he is transformed from a guy in a muscle shirt to a stoic Marine in dress blue uniform.]

NARRATOR: The few, the proud, The Marines.

The commercial didn't show the crooked but fierce smile on the face of Chesty Puller, or the stern look of Dan Daly on faded picture technology from another age, no less real. I'll learn about them soon. And others, Marines who did superhuman things in the face of death. There is a certain standard of a Marine that doesn't involve personal well-being. "Good night, Chesty Puller, wherever you are," is something we will scream over and over again at night while we lie face up on our racks, staring at the one above us or the ceiling.

If accuracy and truth were the most important aspects of marketing in the modern world, this is what I imagine as the direction of a Marines advertising campaign.

[A single note on a piano in a slow but consistent rhythm sounds off on the backdrop of a black screen, intended to clear the mind of the viewing audience. Every plunk hangs in the air as the face of an iconic Marine from a past time blinks into existence, staring back at the viewer. The face blinks out, then the image blinks to another face, stoically

chiseled expressions from the hammer of time spent enduring relentless hardship.

The scene transitions from the faces, running in order from oldest to most current, to Marines sitting in fighting holes in the dark, in the cold. Standing post in the jungle in the dark, in the cold. Dying on battlefields, killing on battlefields, winning on battlefields, and then coming home and standing in line at retail checkout counters, in traffic, or the DMV.

The last scene plays out and everything goes black. The Eagle, Globe and Anchor fades in. Underneath, words say, "Only if you dare."]

The recruiter and I are almost to the Minneapolis-Saint Paul International Airport, and he tells me I'll do fine and reminds me to focus on working hard.

Inside the airport, I run into Robbie Cross and Jedd Williams for the first time, along with a group of other recruits from Minnesota. Williams proceeds to tell the group about a couple of girls he knows. Each story involves one amazing account of sexual prowess after another. The guys around him listen and laugh. Cross cuts him off and begins telling a story about high school.

Cross comes from a family of Marines. His father and two older brothers both served, and now he is ready for his turn. He grew up in a small town southwest of the Twin

Cities, a place where dirt roads and corn fields separate the small downtown of Good Thunder, Minnesota from schools, farm houses, and a couple of random gas stations.

I never hear much of Williams' real past. He only tells those kind of stories. He enjoys comparing them to mine. At this point, I am a virgin and have never more than sipped a beer in my life. We board the plane, and I tell Cross to stop picking on someone. He looks me up and down and starts laughing, asking if I would rather get picked on instead.

We arrive in San Diego, and spend the night in a hotel. I look at my room key and listen to the Marine who tells us to make sure not to be late for the bus the next morning. I walk to the elevator, thinking to myself, "Finally, I can start my life and make this thing into something I always wanted it to be. And my parents can't get in the way."

The next morning, I run out to the bus with everyone else. We drive through the city, and I begin to realize everything is new.

When the bus stops, a drill instructor stomps up the steps, screaming instructions. The newness begins to fade. The bus continues, this time with our heads down and out of sight for the rest of the trip, and the drill instructor yells at anyone who flinches, coughs, or attempts to whisper to the guy next to him.

Let me paint a picture of the first six weeks of boot camp with one simple concept: We stand or sit for days. Literally, days. No sleep between checking in our gear, but we aren't moving either. Every moment is spent crammed into the back of the person in front of us, whether standing or sitting cross-legged. Nut to butt, they say.

We strain to stay deathly quiet without flinching. Anything sets off the roving drill instructors — a blink, a slight frown, or any hints of emotion in our faces. Drill instructors walk up and down the lines, exploding on anyone who fails to maintain a perfectly rigid form. Slouch an inch, and they swoop in to make us stand up straighter, stop drooping our eyelids in exhaustion, or pack in a little tighter on the next guy in front. We fail if we don't completely fight off the subconscious effects of exhaustion. This is discipline on a whole other level. Strain to maintain, and ward off punishment. Relax, and suffer.

A drill instructor stands in front of us, yelling as he demands to know how we will make our beds. They will be called racks from now on. He screams for a volunteer. Cross jumps up, already familiar with how to respond as he snatches one piece of bedding after another, screaming back the proper response to each command. They choose him for squad leader. Williams becomes the platoon scribe. I react to commands and watch, but this isn't what I thought it would be. I am overwhelmed beyond words.

Our first night of sleep doesn't happen for two days. During this time, we are issued gear, sent through a procession line for shots, and forced to sit or stand for hours as one disclaimer is yelled at us after another. How we are supposed to act and talk here would be intricate and difficult to comprehend, even if our bodies and minds weren't being pushed the entire time.

When our uniform packages come, we all tear into them voraciously. Instead of tricolor camouflage, we are faced with digitally printed uniforms. We are the first group ever to wear these. In the next couple of years, every unit will have cycled to the new uniforms, but for now our group of about two hundred recruits will be the only ones seen marching across the base in the new digital patterns until the next batch of kids start their thirteen-week course seven days later. If anything is going to set us apart as noobs for the first half of our careers, it is these ridiculously different and modernized outfits.

Marching around base from then on creates a distinct awareness that everyone who doesn't look like us will be done here before we are. With thousands of individuals wearing the symbolic tricolor uniforms, the notion is disheartening.

In that first night of sleep, I think frantically in the dark. I know now I've made the biggest mistake of my adult life. The airport is next to the base, and listening to thousands of lucky people flying away from here only makes it worse. Others whimper and sniffle, while even more must be sleeping harder than they ever have before. I'm sure Cross was fast asleep with the best of them. Riddled with feelings of regret and self-loathing, I fall asleep. The next morning a drill instructor flicks the lights on and begins screaming commands.

Everyone jumps out of his rack, scrambling to dress in unison. If we don't all have our left sock on when commanded, we are screamed at to take it off. This is how we don every article of clothing. We get close to being fully dressed, only to fail to finish in unison, winding up naked for it moments later. The intense dressing period is almost over as everyone is nearing being fully dressed.

I stand there. Naked. Unprepared.

Cross appears before me, fully clothed and concerned. He asks what the hell is wrong, and we both start dressing me as fast as possible with the intent of getting my clothes on my body without the drill instructors' realizing I have not followed the orders properly.

Later that night, after the lights turn off and the DIs retire to their sleeping quarters, Cross slinks through the barracks to where I'm sleeping. He shakes my shoulder. "What the fuck happened to you this morning, bro?"

"I don't know, man. I'm not supposed to be here," I whisper back.

"Well, fuck, man. The problem is, you are here."

"I guess."

"Okay, so you had no idea what you were getting yourself into. But, as far as I see it, you have two real choices. Tomorrow morning, when the lights come on and we are getting screamed at to dress, just repeat what you did this morning. Stand there naked and refuse to do anything. It might be intense, and you'll definitely get yelled at, but eventually they will have to kick you out for failure to adapt. When that happens, you'll go home and go to college or whatever. You'll forget you were ever here and life will go on for you. Your second option is to wake up and move faster than anyone else, yell the commands louder than everyone else, and forget about everything else until this is over. This is where you are now. It's your decision to make, but you have to make it. All right, have a good night, man. Good luck."

I was never sure why he chose to be friends with me. I think I entertained him with my reserved personality and affinity for all things nerdy. Maybe it was the Minnesota connection, or how comfortable we were being honest with each other.

That night I stare at the rack above me, thinking of home, but also of what awaits me tomorrow. I can't believe I put myself here. All the issues I've ever had were mere notional and deliciously desirable in comparison to this. I signed up for the Marine Corps infantry. Four years of this will be my life, and I've barely made it through day one.

I don't know where my mind wound up that night before sleep took me, but the next morning when the lights kick on I jump up, scrambling to the end of my rack, grabbing at clothes, screaming the commands back. I block everything out. I push back my urge to cry. I quell the desire to call my mother and father, to apologize for leaving them. I glance over at Cross. He smiles when he sees me, just as three drill instructors converge on him, screaming everything out of his mind as he drops to do pushups, periodically jumping up to run madly in place.

There's a narrative of soldiers involving packs with gear, hiking through the mountains, and M-16s glistening in the sunlight as helicopters fly overhead, blades whirling in slow motion.

It. Doesn't. Fucking. Exist.

That's nothing to do with the first six weeks of boot camp. We march everywhere, and stand or sit cross-legged between runs. Any movement not taught in detail by our drill instructor is considered a horrible error and triggers a set of painful routines. When I sniffle and crinkle my nose, they pull me out of formation, finger-pointing and shoving and screaming, forcing me through a physical gauntlet of pushups, burpees, and jumping jacks while being told to scream back, "Yes, drill instructor sergeant!" or, "No, drill instructor sergeant!" until lightheadedness dims my thoughts.

We all must be the same way now. It's like learning a new language overnight. The drill instructors begin to sound inhuman. They exist loudly and just three inches away from our faces, and they're slowly losing their voices.

Recruits piss themselves trying to figure out the new way to ask permission to use the bathroom.

"Recruit Keith requests permission to use the head, Senior Drill Instructor Staff Sergeant Hall, sir!" One wrong word or a hesitation in its delivery is all the DIs need to scream us back into formation with the others.

Everyone becomes sick in the first month. They call it recruit crud. I've never seen so much puking in my entire life. With a weak stomach myself, I barely handle it when one of the recruits jumps up, spewing a host of angry co-agulated food and stomach rot on to the ground.

Our platoon stays in a barrack quarters facing the parade deck. I stand in front of my rack, facing the window. I always look past the parade deck at the brown line of stucco buildings. On one of the buildings is a bright red door. I imagine walking through it, leaving this place and the impending years in this environment for good. I would walk past Sergeant Rodriguez while he screams at the recruits who dash about on the hot parade deck in the California sun.

Recruits are never allowed to be alone or unattended. A drill instructor might scream out a command, but in every version of the dream, I'm too close to the door. I get there in time to rip it open and find Minnesota on the other side.

I know it's hard to stop imagining guns and gas chambers and the tactical bullshit from video games, because I know that's what we see every time we reach back in our minds to recall what we know about the military. It's all thirty-second slots that have nothing to do with any particular job. These commercials usually show the most quintessential moment in every romanticized job in the military. When we see a guy running on the ground with his gun, flying a jet, dropping food from a low-flying vehicle, hovering into a landing zone while troops drop off into flat blown grass, and sitting at a computer directing a remote-controlled robot, we are seeing fleeting moments pulled from a multitude of different professions. These moments are sandwiched inside our brains between thirty-second slots of bullshit about hamburgers.

We stand in line at Church on our first Sunday. Most recruits attend the big Catholic or Protestant congregations, but there are high-level officers and enlisted men present there. I choose a random denomination where there is rumored to be just an old man in a room, one only a few recruits attend.

Unmoving and rigid, we wait in line outside the old man's office. The DI who brought us here is pacing. He raps someone's hand and screams out something about thumbs maintaining flat against the trouser seam. I pull my trembling shoulders up, resisting gravity's pull, to avoid being given hell over a slight slump or even the movement required to correct it.

The door opens, an old man nods to the DI, and we file inside. The door shuts, and I relax. I stop my fake expression and move my hands onto my lap. I decide against crossing my legs or extending them out from the chair, just in case this old man says anything once we leave. I breathe in and exhale, relaxing my face for the first time in over a week.

One night, we stand in front of our racks with arms outstretched. In both hands, we hold full canteens. The

DIs order us to drink. One canteen down. We hold it up-side down for inspection, then we're ordered to guzzle an-other canteen. Some puke. Others run to the head, trying to avoid puddles of undigested food and water.

The game continues, canteen after canteen. One re-cruit is ordered to stand in the center of the squad bay. The rest of us, having hoped the game was over after downing four canteens, are yelled at to run back to the sinks in the shower room and fill up once again.

We slide one canteen across the floor to the man in the center until a small hill of green canteens covers his feet and ankles. Ordered to drink until they are all empty, he opens one after another, drinking and puking until each new heave drops him to his knees. His arms struggle to push a container up to his lips. He knows openly crying isn't allowed, but tears of frustration and exhaustion mix with sweat as he fights to finish the im-possible task.

Another canteen down and no one seems to be hold-ing anything in anymore. A DI walks up and down the line. We run to refill the canteens. I avoid puking by pour-ing the water down my shirt in moments when the DI is distracted. Trickled just right, it mixes with sweat patterns and the trick works. That night more cry. Others sleep bet-ter than they have in a long time.

In the six weeks that follow, we start using our gear in the way it was intended. We hold M-16s for the first time. Some of us stay friends and find ways to enjoy small things that only kids would risk the world to experience again.

One night, Williams tells me he has something to show me. He's afraid of even mentioning what it is until later. We creep away, hiding in a shitter together. He pulls out Skittles and I look at him for an explanation, knowing the answer but still shocked that he thought candy was worth risking tonight's sleep in a place like this. We furiously chew on the Skittles. He waves me to stop in mid-chew. Footsteps come and go before we resume.

I'm mad that he brought me out here just for candy, but I appreciate the thought, since he could have done this alone. It does the trick. I sleep better that night.

Each platoon has three junior drill instructors and one senior. Of the three juniors, two have been in the infantry. I remember this because those two constantly put down the third, and in a group of kids forced to take direction from three people at all times, we pick up on their dynamic.

Sergeant Rodriguez was in the infantry. He is Mexican and short. When he moves, he prefers to career around with arms flailing. The general consensus is that he is the scariest. Then there's Sergeant Evans. Evans is tall, white, and reminds us of Arnold Schwarzenegger from *The Terminator*, more in temperament than in stature. Lastly, there's Staff Sergeant White. He's older and balding, but yells and runs around just as emphatically as the other two. What the other two dislike about him is that he outranks them but has never served time in an infantry unit.

The three constantly clash with each other in passive-aggressive ways. We are more than their slaves, we are their audience. The fourth man, the one considered the boss in our platoon's chain of command, is Staff Sergeant Hall. He is a thin and intensely well-spoken black man. He is harsh in demeanor, poetic in discourse, and yet somehow, he appears to care in a way. Hall encourages us when we believe we can't be broken down any further by his juniors. There is an intense rapidity to his movements and social engagement. He speaks quickly with as much meaning as possible packed into the smallest number of words necessary. We fear the juniors and don't want to incur their punishment. With Hall, we are terrified of his disappointment.

One day, he stands in the doorway to our barracks as we clean in silence. The first one to recognize his presence screams the command for attention. Cleaning stops. Stoic and quiet bodies wait as Hall walks past us.

"I just received horrible news, gentlemen," says Hall. "The kind of news that must be shared immediately, and can't be taken back or changed or questioned. It's the worst kind. The lead singer of the illustrious band Drowning Pool has died. If there was anything left for him to accomplish in this world, it is gone as well. As you were." He turns into his office, shutting the door. The song "Let the Bodies Hit the Floor," muffled by a wall, serenades us as we silently clean.

Every week, we are tested physically. We are always tired, and most barely pass requirements at the end of long days. Accomplishing three pull-ups before boot camp meant failing to do one after a day here. That's where most seem to struggle. In high school I did fifteen. I ran but stopped when I got tired. I did push-ups and pull-ups, working out in my parent's basement on a rowing machine.

I barely reach six pull-ups here. Those that fail to hit the mark are held back, and the rest move on. Some give up and stop training, resorting to pissing themselves and staring at the ceiling from their racks, not even flinching when yelled at. Whenever someone drops out, Sergeant Rodriguez strolls into the barracks in a calm rage, then looses a slow cackle. "Another one bites the motherfucking dust," he says.

I think back to the kid in the recruiter's office who passed up a full ride to West Point to join the Marines, but was unable to accomplish a single pull-up at the time. Did he make it through boot camp on schedule, or did it take him the better part of the year?

This is my biggest fear. If I fail to make the minimum run time, pull-up count, or sit-up time, I'll drop from this platoon and go back to another one where everything starts over. I will revisit every single moment of every single day I have survived up to now. If I'm injured, I will go to a place called the "broke bodies," where I'll heal up before starting again with another platoon and beginning the thirteen-week cycle over.

Some try hanging themselves with their belts at night to end the madness. The belts, however, are designed to hold tight around the waist but release when a recruit's full weight slumps against the pressure clasp.

Some admit to past medical problems they'd lied about to their recruiter and are sent home for good, the nightmare over forever. I find myself in this situation. It happens after I volunteer to become a pallbearer. This is my big break. Instead of more of this for four years in the infantry, I could work out, polish my uniform, and stoically carry coffins. There's honor in that, and a lot less pain. I am the perfect height, and I score high enough on a test they administer to get past the first level. Next comes the screening process.

I stand in a room with others, facing a man in civilian clothes. I don't know it until later, but he is a high-ranking officer intent on weeding out anyone with an undisclosed medical history such as mine. All I have to do now is keep quiet.

"Listen, gents," he says, smiling. "So far, you've made it through the process. The only thing left to do is explain to you how the background check will work. You might have made it into boot camp by lying, but it won't save you now if you don't tell us absolutely everything in your history. We are going to conduct a very thorough investigation, one that will go further than anything done on you before. If we find something you didn't disclose, you could be processed and sent to a military prison for a long time."

I'm naïve, so I tell him about my history of seizures, not realizing I've just signed my ticket back home. He leaves, and when he returns the smile is gone. I'm sent back to the barracks. Sergeant Rodriguez appears out of nowhere, slamming me into the wall. Grabbing my wrist, he twists my arm into a lock behind my back and drags me into a janitor's closet, where he throws me in a tight chokehold. He yells commands, intent on discovering why I was trying to get out of my commitment to the government. I yell back in response to his questions, telling him I didn't want to quit and that it was all a mistake.

Moments later I'm standing in front of Hall, who tells me he has two choices laid out before him in my case. First, he wants to know why I said what I did, and if I'm trying to leave. I tell him what happened. Struggling with military vernacular, I begin using phrases like, "This recruit lost his mind, sir," and, "This recruit didn't know what was going on, sir," until he orders me to speak plainly.

I tell him I didn't want to get kicked out and thought that if I was honest with the guy, maybe I could still work for the unit that carries coffins. Maybe I could pick something else instead of infantry.

"The nice man you were talking to happens to be very important in this place. He's a full-bird colonel. I now have orders on my desk to make sure you are standing in front of his office when you leave mine. Is that what you want, recruit Keith?" says Hall.

"No, sir." *Not like this,* I think.

"Well, then, my drill instructors and I are going to make a judgment call. We are simply not going to send you. With everything that goes on here, no one will miss one lone recruit not showing up somewhere. This will go badly for us if you don't go along with it, so you need to be very clear on your intentions right now. Do you want to be here, Keith?"

"Yes, sir."

"Then report back to your platoon, recruit."

Leaving the room, I'm relieved. But my smile is quickly smacked off my face by Sergeant Rodriguez, who has been hovering outside the door waiting to see whether I am going to be his again. He snatches my wrist, swinging me around with a lock and throwing his elbow into the back of my neck, screaming in my ear the whole time.

"You thought you would get out of the infantry! But now you are mine, mine, mine!" he cackles. We run up a hill the next day, where he finds me again, laughing and yelling as I struggle forward, "So, you thought you could carry coffins and leave the infantry? Well, Keith, looks like you will be hating your life forever now!"

Recruits are awarded positions as squad leader, platoon guide, and scribe. Those that held these positions are capable of getting promoted from private to private first-class or even lance corporal. The mock ranking system in place creates little dramas between us. As a squad leader, Cross becomes a monster, always yelling at recruits who slow down. Eventually, he will be demoted because of his penchant for getting physical with those who fail to react to commands with enough urgency.

Williams manipulates us without the use of force. As the platoon's scribe, he sets up the night watch schedule. While I am considered his friend and am able to get out of fire watch almost every night, others have to barter to earn full nights of unmolested sleep. Williams eventually loses his position when some recruits complain of standing post every night for weeks.

The entire base is maintained by recruits in their seventh week of the process. After an eternity, it is our turn. Instead of scrambling from the moment the lights turn on until the final moments before they are cut, one Marine turns the lights on, waits for us to get dressed, and escorts us in formation to working parties around the base. This is the midway point of our training. Soon we will head north to Camp Pendleton, where everything picks up a notch. That will be where we carry guns, hike into the woods, and go through iconic boot camp activities like land navigation, water training, the gas chamber, and finally the crucible.

Williams is still scribe and assigns recruits to different duty stations throughout base. He puts me and Cross with him in an office that has air conditioning and cubicles. Mostly, we sit around, unless someone needs the printer restocked or the refrigerator in the break room cleaned. Cross and Williams argue all the time about who outranks the other. We are friends, but Williams has been leveraging his role as a scribe to give Cross countless hours of night watch. Cross, on the other hand, orders Williams around when the squad leader rank allows and assigns him to extra duties. I maintain both friendships, but find their personalities pulling my loyalty back and forth throughout.

A Marine orders Williams and me to clean up a mess in front of the printer. We find ourselves on our hands and knees, picking up little pieces of paper one by one with our fingers.

I can tell today is different. Williams is silent and reflective. We whisper quietly, only stopping if another Marine walks by.

"Keith. You're the best friend I have here, man. But I've been completely fake to you and everyone else for a while now. I can't take it anymore."

I can't imagine what he's talking about, but I have the distinct feeling that he's about to say he's secretly in love with me.

"You know all those stories I told, about being the prom king and getting laid all the time?"

"Yeah." *Oh God, here it comes.*

"They never happened. It's all lies. I was home-schooled my whole life and I'm a virgin," he says.

I stop and look up at him.

"I'm sorry, man. I hope we can still be friends," he says. "I just didn't know what to tell people, you know?"

"It's fine, bro. I don't care."

We are all too young to realize that all of us are full of shit. Most stories are embellished, especially the ones about sex and high school. In the future, the ones about war will be too. Some tell the truth, but there aren't enough high schools in the country to harbor the number of prom kings and football heroes trying to survive boot camp at Camp Pendleton.

The next six weeks make the first six seem bearable. Instead of running and marching everywhere, we hike with packs. Hiking is called humps here. It's not a term many know in the civilian world, but it is the worst and yet most quintessential aspect of the Marine Corps rifleman's routine. They teach us how to grab the packs by the straps and flip them up overhead and onto our backs. Now, we run everywhere with packs. This feels more like the Marine Corps I expected, one where we carry guns and gear.

Hall leads the platoon down the range in the morning. The sun hides, turning the sky a barely lighter color than the dark tree line. We march in tandem with his chants.

Drill instructors start out their cadence in a rigid form. They begin with, "Yo left, yo left, yo left, right, left!" Hall's cadence begins like a song, intended to build. The syllables shake with potential in the cold air until they burst, set free to the sound of our rubber heels smacking against the packed earth. We repeat each line, singing louder when we start in on the part about mom.

> "Yo lay ohh righhhty laaay ohh!
> Yo lay ohh righhhty laaay ohh!
>
> I saaaay, Yo lay ohhhh ohh!
> Yo lay ohhhh ohh!"
>
> Mama, Mama, can't you see?
> Mama, Mama, can't you see?
>
> What this road is doing to me!
> What this road is doing to me!

Mama, Mama, can't you see!?
What the Marine Corps has done to me!

They put me in a barber's chair!
Shaved my head 'til it was bare!

Used to wear designer jeans!
Now I'm dressed in jungle greens!

Thought I'd get to have some fun!
But all I do is shoot my gun!

They took away my set of wheels!
Now I've blisters on my heels!

Up in the morning much too soon!
We're still marching after noon!

Standing tall and looking good!
We ought to be in Hollywood!

Ain't no use in going slow!
There are many miles to go!

Ain't no point in going fast!
We shall never be the last!

And if I die in a combat zone!
Box me up and ship me home!

Put me in a set of dress blues!
Comb my hair and shine my shoes!
Pin my medals upon my chest!
Tell my mama I did my best!

Mama, mama, don't you cry!
Marine Corps' motto is do or die!"

Maybe Hall knew what we were going through and wanted us to know it was okay to accept our pain, if we chose to push through it. I wouldn't see him again, after I left boot camp, until four years later, a few days before I got out. He was a First Sergeant then. He had been transferred to the same unit on the same base as me. I'll never forget our conversation, or how even though so much time had passed since I wondered about his nature, he still understood me.

The following weeks involve heavy amounts of hiking. We are doggedly tired and broken down. We begin to think and act differently. Some things are becoming habitual for us, like asking to use the head, while others, like responding to commands as one, are already muscle memory.

We finish a hump, dropping packs in front of an obstacle course. Recruits line up and take off in rows while simulated explosions and gunfire noises reverberate around us. I low-crawl through the mud past other recruits who are struggling to make it under the wire. Reaching the end of the course, I jump up and run over to Hall with my rifle. Standing in front of him, I yell the proper command to let him know I have completed the course. I relax the muscles in my face, slowing my breathing, all to look at peace. I can tell Hall is searching my expression for something, eyebrows furrowed in concentration. Then he stops and looks me directly in the eyes.

"I'm trying to find the boy that was there before, recruit Keith, but all I see now is a man. As you were, recruit."

"Sir, yes sir!" I yell as I run back to formation, feeling capable here for the first time since this process began.

3

SCHOOL OF INFANTRY

"Do you want to know what infantry primarily does? Two fucking things. We walk everywhere, and we fucking hike. We carry all our shit. Sometimes more than ninety pounds of shit. We carry it everywhere, and we carry it all the fucking time. But I get turned away for back problems at the veterans' hospital. Thank me for my fucking service? Let me go to a hospital where people search for pain and try to find ways to remove it. Instead, I go to a place where people use talk tracks to get me out the door.

"The second time I went in for my back, they gave me a stipend for six sessions with a chiropractor outside the VA. When I went, the guy showed me pictures of my spine. He said some of the vertebrae were pressed closer together than they should be. A couple of days later, he called and told me the VA denied the claim. He told me I needed months of treatment. But I couldn't afford it, and I didn't have private health coverage. I was right out of the Marines with no civilian work history and no idea how to move forward. I might as well have been a heroin addict who checked out of the real world after high school and was just going clean.

"I don't get it. I tried telling my friends and family. They don't understand what I did, so why should they believe I have back pain related to the military if the VA is telling me I don't have a problem? You know what another doctor told me recently? My last two vertebrae are crushed around my sciatic nerve. I'll need surgery. He said I'm young, though, so it's best to try physical therapy and other things like yoga and pilates and healthier eating habits. So I'll pay for the chiropractor adjustments and physical therapy I can barely afford.

"I was told I had medical benefits, and I don't. That's a "Fuck you." When they send me that text once a year, I laugh. When people carry signs saying they support the troops, I laugh. I know I'm supposed to thank them for thanking me for my service. And I know as far as feelings are concerned, they do care.

"Here is the truth, though. People don't value what I did. They don't understand it. They just feel bad for me. That's why I don't have any treatment for my back, but people thank me for my service all the time. I get it, though. I really do. If I saved the human race from an alien invasion of ass-raping dinosaurs, people would call me a hero, and it would make sense. But they know I'm not a hero and so do I.

"They give me two boxes. I can be the strong silent type that keeps it all in or the angry guy that vents it out, but only because he needs to learn how to contain his inner warrior. Fucking annoying. I'll never know where I went wrong. But I'll never sell out on that eighteen-year-old kid who didn't have a clue what he was getting himself into."

■ ■ ■

Infantry training begins after a ten-day break from boot camp. I get off the plane and find the shuttle that will take the other newly minted Marines and me back to the base. It doesn't feel much different than the first time, but now I have the haircut, the posture, and the C-bag as proof I have been through some of the process before.

I don't know any of the guys on the shuttle. I'm supposed to be a Marine, but I'm terrified yet again that I made a mistake. As we pass through the gates, the shuttle drops me off in front of a barracks. The atmosphere is chaotic. Young Marines like me run around in uniform. I feel funny in these new digital cammies, lost in a sea of yesterday's old school tricolors.

I ask someone where I can find the command, and I'm directed to a stuffy room inside the barracks.

"Yes, can we help you?" a sergeant asks when I enter. I've interrupted his chat with a few other Marines.

"Sir, yes sir."

He looks around at the others in the room as if sharing a tired inside joke. "I'm not an officer or drill instructor, son. You can call me by my rank now."

I begin to call him sir again, then stop.

"For fuck's sake," he says in the direction of one of the other Marines in the room. "Get this kid out of my sight before he makes it any more awkward."

One of them leads me into a squad bay where other Marines are sitting around, and I pick a rack near the back to put my stuff down.

"Go to the PX and buy a lock if you don't have one," says the lance corporal. "Oh, and don't call yourself a recruit. Or address anyone as sir, unless they are an officer."

"Thanks. I'll try to remember that, Lance Corporal."

"That's one more thing. Only address someone by rank if they are a leadership ranking. You don't have to use my rank because I'm a lance corporal. Corporals and above better hear you call them by their rank, unless you want to get your shit kicked in."

He leaves me there to dig for my lock and secure my belongings. I'm waiting with about a hundred other guys fresh out of boot camp for a unit to pick us up for the next school of infantry class. We sit in a room for two weeks as other recruits join us. We run in the mornings, exchange rumors throughout the day in the barracks, and stand in long procession lines for the chow hall.

After the first week, an entirely new company of Marines drops in from leave. I meet Branham Flynn for the first time. He winds up living on the top rack next to mine. He's also from Minnesota, and he's composed, not loud and obnoxious like so many others. About a year later, he will walk around one night while we train in the desert and find that anyone who doesn't recognize him in the dark assumes he is an officer and resorts to calling him sir because of his demeanor.

The two Marines who bunk directly below us are an interesting pair. Webb is tall and comes off a little snobbish. Washington is an aggressive Irish kid who hates Webb. He calls him Manboobs and tells him how badly he wants to beat his ass every chance he gets. Flynn and I like Washington and enjoy watching him go after Webb.

One night, Flynn and I are standing around the racks. Flynn decides to play a trick on Washington. I help him fold the bottom part of Washington's sheets in half and remake his rack, so it looks the same as it did before. Then we jump up into our racks and wait for him to get back from the showers, facing each other with barely contained glee.

The point of this is setting someone up to ruin their rack for inspection the next morning. Beds must be made perfectly, with square corners and precise folds, and no creases along the flat surfaces. Most of us sleep as carefully as possible under the blankets, so all we have to do in the morning is straighten out the creases in the big spaces and tighten the folds in the corners. The victim of a short-sheeted rack doesn't know it until his feet hit the folded sheet halfway down, forcing him to kick out the rest of the blankets and giving him twenty minutes less sleep in the morning before inspections to reset the display.

As Washington approaches, he's fuming. We hide under our blankets.

"So, Webb is talking shit again, like he could back any of it up! This motherfucker, man, and his fucking man-boobs. That's why I can't handle rich snobs. I can't believe I'm stuck with such a bitch as a rack mate!"

My rack shakes as Washington settles in on the one below. Flynn and I have pulled our blankets up to our bulging eyeballs, harboring a horrified glee as we wait for the finale. Washington's feet hit the sheets and he stops moving. "Oh good, bitches," he says, chuckling a little. We burst out laughing. He lets us know we will make his rack tomorrow or pay with our lives.

After two weeks of waiting, we are picked up by a company and begin infantry training. It's the same three-week course for everyone before we choose the particular job we want to have. Cross chooses 0311, which is rifleman. Flynn and I choose 0331, which is machine gunner.

As machine gunners, we have a lot of bookwork ahead of us on how to operate the different types of guns. We sit in our squad bay, taking apart specific sets of machine guns we've pulled from the armory so that we can learn everything we need to know about them. Cross is with the riflemen, and they are stuck out in the field a lot longer than us, not able to enjoy most weekends. They practice assaulting and flanking maneuvers. We practice laying down support for their movements.

The bookwork doesn't end there. We learn more about Marine Corps history, and the responsibility on our shoulders to live up to the Corps' reputation as the most efficient military organization on the planet. They teach us about two hundred years of undeniable courage in the face of death. Dying is an option. Failing to do our job is not. They show us pictures of generals and heroes from the past. They remind us that we dared to step into their shoes.

After running in the mornings and training throughout the day, we look forward to the weekends. Most of us don't have cars yet, and the ones that do don't have them on this particular base, since after the school of infantry we will all be sent somewhere else for our official duty station.

On the weekends, I take the shuttle to Oceanside. One of my favorite things to do is to go to the pier where a restaurant called Ruby's Diner overlooks the ocean. Ruby's is a fifties-themed burger joint, and it is the closest I get to home. The girls are pretty, the service is nice, and most of all it reminds me of the family diners back in St. Paul.

It is the fall of 2002, and I am almost nineteen. I sit in the diner and watch the families on the pier. If I knew how to talk to girls, I think this would be an excellent place to meet one. If I could stay in San Diego, that is.

One day, I call home from a payphone. My little brother Jake tells me he found a half-written letter that our sister had left open on the computer, an accusatory letter to her ex-boyfriend. I can hear Jake fighting back tears on the phone as he apologizes to me for not going after this guy. I remind him he's only fourteen and tell him that it's good he told me instead.

I buy a ticket for home on Thanksgiving weekend, even though Minnesota is far beyond the two hundred miles from base that we're allowed to travel. At the airport, I feel what I've felt each time I've been here, waiting to go from one place to another. It's a surreal exchange of realities and perspectives.

On one side, I'm a poor excuse for a Marine. I'm just starting out as an adult, an awkward first attempt. On the other side, I'm the oldest brother, already a man.

Now, I'm coming for Dan. This fucking guy. He uses words like "chillaxing" and dresses like a gangster, but lives in the same privileged neighborhood as everyone else in my town.

When I get home, Jake and I stand in the living room. He saved the letter in a file and pulls it up so I can read it. I don't know where Dan lives, and I know Sis won't tell me. The next night, after Thanksgiving dinner, I approach her friend, Jen, who is spending the holiday with my family. We argue for a bit, but then she agrees to show me to Dan's house. It's around midnight when I drive my parents' black SUV into West Lakeland. Jen points out where to turn. "Okay, that's it," she says, as I pull up to the curb just past the edge of his mom's property.

"Sit in the driver's seat. If everything goes to shit or the cops show up, can you drive? I know you don't have your driver's license yet."

"Yeah, I guess."

"Well, get out of here if anything happens." Her dad will kill me if he finds out about this.

I get out and walk towards the door with the letter in my pocket, a little nervous. Walking up the steps, I pound on the metal screen door and wait. Behind it, the front door opens. It's Dan.

I stand in the glow of the single rusted front door light, talking earnestly through the screen. I bicker with Dan about coming outside and answering for what he did. Dan's mom, rumored to be sleeping with her cousin, has come up behind Dan and tells me to go away.

Done with conversation, I reach for the screen door and pull. Dan holds onto the other side, yelling, and his mom screams as I rip it open. They run from me into the dark house. Dan yells that he's going to get his samurai sword. I take a few steps into their living room, then look at Dan's mom, who is holding the phone and screaming that she's talking to the cops. Realizing what I've done is illegal, and more than positive I don't want to deal with Dan and his sword, I run out the front door and back to the SUV.

When I get home, I walk upstairs to tell my parents what happened. I say the cops might be on their way. Then, I go to my room in the basement. I lie in my old bed and stare at the ceiling, thinking about the trip back to base and how it would almost be nice not to wake up in two days to all the annoying training routines and stressful physical testing. I could tool around a military prison for a while instead. I could come back home eventually and go to college like I should have done in the first place.

But the cops never show up. I've done what I can with the little time I have. The next day, I fly back to California.

As the two-month training evolution is wrapping up, rumors of where we will be sent keep running rampant through our unit. The worst of them wind up being true. Some of the guys will stay here at Camp Pendleton, but the rest of us will be heading to the desert, to a base located next to a town called 29 Palms that's buried in the Mojave Desert about thirty minutes away from Palm Springs, California.

29 Palms is the largest live-fire base in the world, which means it is one of the few places in the country that allows live ammunition during training. Units from all over come here once or twice a year to spend weeks doing exhausting desert training, known as combined arms exercises. When they finish the exercises, they get to leave. For anyone who finds this place their duty station, though, the desert is right there in the backyard and that miserable training never ends.

It is considered such a miserable place to be stationed that command decides not to tell us our assignments on the last day of training, which is a Friday. They believe that anyone who is scheduled to be stationed in 29 Palms and has a weekend to think about it might not show up to formation on Monday.

The school of infantry ends a lot like boot camp. This time, though, only those who signed up for the reserves are celebrating. They laugh and tell us to have fun for four years. Some Marines are even more disappointed than the

rest of us to realize that they signed up for six-year con-
tracts when they could have chosen the bare minimum of
four.

Some families arrive to pick up their sons, husbands,
or friends. For the first time, but certainly not the last, I
imagine my mom driving up in her blue Ford Expedition.
Somehow, magically, the passenger door swings open and
her hand stretches out to me. There is a smile on her face.
"Get in, son. We're going home."

4

THE BASTARD BATTALION

"I definitely chose the wrong job when I went in. I would love just to have a good back. Every day it aches and burns. People keep asking me what happened, and I don't have any answers except to mumble something about carrying stuff in the Marines. I've been to the VA. They asked me if anything happened while I was in that would cause my back to go out like this. They took some x-rays and sent me home. I was well within the time post-discharge when I was supposed to have full medical benefits. Three weeks later, I received a letter in the mail informing me that they found no proof of anything wrong with my back.

"No proof. I wake up feeling like someone took a bat to my spine, even though I'm only twenty-two and look like I'm in great shape. How can I tell them that, yes, something did happen. I was in the Marine Corps infantry for four years. Why isn't that enough?

"One time, we went to a place called Bridgeport for training. The whole time we hiked up and down mountains. I remember one day we woke up before the sun came up and we were still hiking when the night set in. We stopped around midnight. Well before that point, people were burnt out, swearing, and yelling. I started carrying my gun by the barrel, letting the rest of it drag in the dirt. People were so spread out and tired that no one even said anything. When we finally stopped, you know what happened? Our captain showed up from base camp.

"He hadn't been with us all day. But he showed up now, rested and ready to go. He ordered us back into formation, and we continued in the dark, our legs and backs giving out from exhaustion. He ended up taking us on this loose shale path that went down a hill. People were falling and yelling more than ever. Tears were running down my face. I was pissed but in a desperate sort of way. We were breaking down.

"The next day, our company was rendered combat ineffective because there were so many Marines in the sick bay with stress fractures in their legs. Something like a third of the unit. There was an internal investigation, which of course is just so a company can protect itself. But that's the kind of thing I went through for four years. How did it happen? The question betrays ignorance. It's almost as if there's only help there if you're about to lose your shit."

"You're about to lose your shit."

■ ■ ■

I peek around the corner and look down the hallway. I'm on the second floor of a brick apartment complex with concrete walkways. Last night I arrived in 29 Palms to report to my unit. The guys we'll be working with for the next few years are in the middle of training somewhere in the desert, so Flynn and I are alone for the moment. Now, I need only find his assigned room.

Last night, our group from boot camp was separated for a third and final time to go to our different units. Cross, Flynn, and I went to Third Battalion, Fourth Marines. From there, Cross went to Kilo Company, and Flynn and I found ourselves in Lima Company.

Our battalion has an interesting story, from a historical perspective. Our unit was the only one in the history of the United States Marines that was known for surrendering the American Flag. Well, technically surrendering it, at least. In World War II, the unit was surrendered by an Army General during the Battle of Corregidor Island in the Philippines. They were marched over a long stretch of land, but before they were captured the unit's flag was cut into little square pieces. Each one was handed out to a Marine with the idea that if there wasn't a flag to capture, the horribly dishonorable act of surrendering it could be avoided. After the march, not all of the pieces were recovered. Many Marines had died along the way, and their bodies were left on the side of the road, harboring those little pieces of cloth.

They disbanded the unit shortly thereafter. When the Vietnam War kicked off decades later, it was reinstated. This time, it was sent out of the Fourth Marines and placed in the Seventh Marines Regiment, earning the nickname "The Bastard Battalion." It's also known as Darkside, which makes every Star Wars fan in the unit happy beyond words. It has become known as the most deployed unit in the history of the Marine Corps.

I look both ways, head toward the room I think is Flynn's, and knock on the door. Though he mirrors my look of apprehension as he opens the door, he seems glad to see me.

"What's up, man?" he says.

"Nothing, want to head over to the PX?"

"Sure, but come in for a minute. I need to grab some stuff."

"So, what do you think so far?" I ask, walking in and shutting the door quickly behind me.

"I don't know, man. We just got here. Did you see those ugly mountains outside?"

"Yeah. This place sucks."

Flynn finishes putting on the rest of his uniform, and we walk down the steps to the sidewalk and start heading towards the PX. It's the military's version of a Walgreens, but to anyone stuck with only the options that exist on base, it feels more like a Super Wal-Mart.

"Dude, this is crazy," I say. "I can't believe we are here now. What do you think it's going to be like? I hope nothing like boot camp. Fuck SOI. Thank God, we are done with that place! The desert. Of all the places they could put us, why the hell did we wind up here? How bad do you wish we had never joined in the first place?"

"Shut up," he says, sighing as he squints to see how much farther we have to walk together.

"All right. What do you want to talk about?"

"Nothing, man. Shit."

"Hey, at least when the unit gets back it will be Friday. So, we'll get the weekend off, too, which is cool. You know? That's like four days off in a row!"

"Do you smell that?"

"Yeah, it smells like shit."

"Like waves of shit."

We find out later that the smell comes from Lake Bandini, just across the main road that separates the fence from the rest of the base. New Marines are encouraged to take a swim in the flat, man-made body of water. Their seniors explain the years of tradition behind the ritual while trying not to laugh.

The lake is attached to the septic cleaning system, which sends bad water from the sewage there and funnels it through a cleaning process before sending it back into our barracks and other buildings within the compound. When the wind catches the top of the lake just right, which it does on and off all day, the entire base smells like the inside of a giant outhouse.

At the PX, we buy sandwiches and Gatorade, then head back. The next day, we hang out in one of our rooms or the other and watch movies on a portable DVD player to pass the time. Friday morning, I wake up to the sounds of marching and yelling. Then, the clatter of boots and people seem to fill every hallway and stairwell outside my door.

Getting up, I throw on my uniform and wait. I hope they like me. Maybe I'll finally learn what the fuck I'm supposed to do here. I can't fuck up like I did in boot camp and SOI.

The door flings open.

"Who are you?" says a gaunt, soft-spoken private first-class. He doesn't sound weak, just quiet. He keeps most of his meaning implied in the air, watching the thoughts of others as they jump out of mouths and into life before us.

"I'm Gabe Keith. Nice to meet you."

"Jeremy Bryant."

"Sorry, they put me in here. There weren't any other rooms."

"Keep your things in the corner. This is a two-person room."

Bryant is from Missouri, and we don't particularly care for each other. That's a pattern among Marines. We either get along well or not at all. There really isn't much of a middle ground when you're eighteen and among strangers.

Matthew Olsen is Bryant's roommate. They were in boot camp together. He's from a small town in Wisconsin. He doesn't know why he is here either, but like the rest of us, he's along for the ride.

We meet Phillip Preston later. Stereotyping Preston is automatic for anyone who meets him. He's an entitled rich kid from Dallas, as best we can tell, and he talks shit more expertly than anyone I've ever met. But to understand him, you should know why he joined the Marines in the first place.

After partying and burning his bridges with family and friends while in college, Preston found himself in court. He was facing charges that could send him to jail or rehab, and in either case, his family might completely disown him. At best, they'd never respect what their son had become. The judge overseeing the proceedings said his only other option was the Marines. No matter how bad things got while we were in, it was a second chance for him, so he was happy even when it got bad. It was evident whenever he asked me if I was having fun yet, or if I would rather be somewhere else.

We are the new guys. The ones who will be carrying the heavier guns, the ones assigned to the majority of the working parties, and standing post at night. Half of my squad is new to the Marines, and we are therefore assigned to work with a group of Marines who have been together for a couple of years and now are in charge for the first time.

The guys in this group begin with Corporal Moore. He's tall and capable. He runs the entire section of machine guns. Since he isn't a part of an actual gun team or squad, he serves an almost purely administrative role in the section. He reports directly to the platoon sergeant and is responsible for the three squad leaders who run the gun teams.

Corporal Pickett runs First Squad. He's from Texas, and casual conversation for him involves talking shit and threatening people. When he laughs, it is because he knows his audience doesn't know whether he's serious about wanting to hurt people. His team lead is Corporal Green. Green is the most physically imposing and laughs a lot. He enjoys putting us in painful scissor locks with his legs, crushing our torsos and laughing while we tap out or yell in pain.

Corporal Miller is the second squad leader. Physically, Miller is the weakest of the group, and it's something that becomes painfully self-evident when he fails to climb the rope every time the battalion runs through the obstacle course. Miller loves to quote the book *On Killing: The Psychological Cost of Learning to Kill in War and Society,* by Dave Grossman. He recites it as if the quotes were from his personal thoughts. Preston is the only one educated enough to pick up on it and tell us later. He points out statements that are direct quotes from the book, like, "The bravest are surely those who have the clearest vision of what is before them, glory and danger alike, and yet notwithstanding, go out to meet it."

Other times, Miller quotes the book in an attempt to give us mental tools for possible killing situations. "The basic response stages to killing in combat are concern about killing, the actual kill, exhilaration, remorse, and rationalization and acceptance." He believes it is important to think about these things to avoid falling into the mental trap of failing to pull the trigger when it matters.

On the first night with my new platoon, Lewis bursts through the door. He is far more concrete in his approach to conditioning us for whatever is waiting out there. He generally doesn't speak of the future and focuses only on what he sees in front of him.

"You Keith?"

"Yes, Corporal!"

"I heard you're from Minnesota. Is that true?"

"Yes, Corporal."

"I was given the first pick of who to put in my team. I'm going with you over Flynn, so you better not be a fuck-up or a pussy. We're in Miller's squad, and I'll let you in on who the fuck else will be in Second Squad when I find out."

I'm tired of finding reasons to be afraid. I know something he doesn't. He should've picked Flynn over me.

Jon Hayes drops into our unit and is put into my team. Lewis likes Hayes even less than he likes me. He sizes us up. One country kid from Texas with a big front tooth, and one mild-mannered over-privileged kid from Minnesota. When he calls for us, it is often by the names Snaggle-tooth and Candy-ass.

Hayes has one massive front tooth that twists sideways in his head. It didn't start out big. He went to the dentist for braces when he was young, and had the tooth enlarged with a material that would allow it to withstand the pressure of the braces that would turn it over time into its rightful place. Once his twisted tooth was made twice its natural size, though, instead of Hayes getting braces, his dad lost his job. Hayes was stuck with the enlarged tooth indefinitely.

Sometimes he smiles, and when his upper lip curls back over his tooth it doesn't take long for others to give him reason to stop smiling. When we share fighting holes together in the dark, I listen to his dreams like he does mine.

"Once the Marines fix my tooth, I'll find a girlfriend and everything will be okay because I won't look like a fucking freak anymore."

They outfit us with gear, and we begin training. I will operate the 240G and provide covering fire for line platoons. In school, I fired it once. Now it's mine to carry.

Every morning we get up while it's still dark and shuffle out to the parade deck with our gear. Placing our packs and flak jackets in organized rows, we take turns watching the gear while the others head off to the armory to check out their weapons. As the light comes up, we hike into the desert and around the mountains that surround the base towards firing ranges where our squads practice maneuvers all day.

Every job has its primary function. In the infantry, gun teams run gun drills. The team consists of three individuals. The team leader holds the tripod, and the other two follow him. When the team leader drops down where he wants to see his gunner set in, he drops the tripod in the sand.

The gunner is behind him, holding the M240G, a medium machine gun weighing out at 24.2 pounds. The gunner runs up and drops down on top of the tripod, locking in the gun and popping up the top to expose the ammo tray.

The ammo man drops in next to the other two as they scan for targets, dropping the ammunition between the team leader and gunner. The team leader grabs the ammo and slaps it into place, and the gunner drops the top down and finishes sighting in. The ammo man holds the rest of the ammo and the bag with the spare barrel in case the primary barrel overheats. He runs back and provides rear security, or posts up alongside his team.

The team leader yells to the squad leader, alerting him that the team is prepared. The team leader makes sure the gunner shoots effectively at the correct target. The squad leader coordinates between the two teams he operates.

This is the cornerstone function of a machine gun team in a line platoon. Our squad leaders time the process to see how quickly each team sets up the gun. As the light starts to leave, we hump back to base. On the way back, we drop our packs off at the barracks. Then we turn our weapons in at the armory, but the day isn't over until our command releases us for the night.

We return by seven or eight and then stand outside our officers' building in formation in the sand. Hours pass. They often make us stand there in formation until midnight or one in the morning before they eventually send us back for the night. A few hours later, we are up and out the door for training again.

We sit in the room one night. Olsen has been lying in his bed since we were released a couple of hours ago. He's feeling sick and doesn't want to talk about it. I'm listening to my CD player when Olsen pukes all over himself. Bryant gets up from reading on his rack and orders Olsen to go sort things out in the bathroom. Olsen obeys. It's silent for a moment, and then Olsen comes out of the bathroom, stopping short in the doorway, blinking and looking at us without any expression on his face. He throws up all over the floor, washing a reddish-brown mess up against the garment bag and gear that I've stacked in the corner.

Back in the bathroom, Olsen pukes his brains out in demonic waves, over and over again. The next day, Bryant is sick and puking as well. That night Lewis comes to our room. He tells me to get my gear and meet Flynn at the armory. We were both volunteered for guard duty on the Humvees in the motor pool.

I walk with Flynn to the armory. We stay quiet, thinking about any number of things. Not least of these is the fact that we worked all day, will stand post all night, and then work all day again tomorrow. We draw two M-16s and a magazine of ammunition apiece. The motor pool has Humvees and amphibian assault vehicles lined up in a gated enclosure. Since there are no keys or locks on the vehicles, they must be guarded at night when no one is around.

We strut around a bit, conscious of the added weight of loaded magazines that we have become accustomed to carrying empty. A fence cuts the motor pool in half. Flynn is on one side; I'm on the other. He suggests we sneak up on each other so we can get an idea of what it will look like if someone tries breaking in. Holding onto the links of the fence, I watch until Flynn appears back in the dimly lit area. He gets up close, then we switch back and forth between roles until we get bored of playing soldier and decide to talk through the fence instead.

"Did you see me, Keith?"

"No, not at all. At least, not until you were almost on top of that row over there." I point to a vehicle, relatively closer than the majority of the parked Humvees and 7-tons.

"Well, fuck it, then," says Flynn. He sighs and breaks away from the fence to walk the perimeter.

I take a cue from him and begin walking around as well, trying to breathe in the night air and wish away the nausea that keeps getting worse. By the morning I am ill, doubling over to dry heave uselessly next to a Humvee.

When the Marines running the motor pool show up, Flynn and I give them back the ammo and return the guns to the armory. There's an hour left before formation and I'm in the bathroom, sitting on the toilet with both the room and stall doors closed, clutching my stomach and praying the nausea leaves. Bryant tried telling me to get out to formation, but I've never worked through feeling sick before and don't plan to start now. Especially not when it feels this bad.

I hear the barracks door slam open. Corporal Lewis stands outside the bathroom. "Get the fuck outside, you piece of shit! I don't care how sick you feel! Stop being such a fucking pussy, get your shit, and get the fuck out to formation!"

"Corporal, I can't. I'm sorry, but I'm sick."

"I don't give a fuck what you are! We have the gas chamber today, and I'm not going to let you pussy out of it! Get the fuck out there right now!"

I tell him I need just a moment, and Lewis is replaced by our section leader, Corporal Moore. While Lewis screamed and smashed about, Moore implies all that and more in his barely repressed passive-aggressive tone. "Keith, believe me when I say I will have you charged for unauthorized absence and sent to the brig if you don't get your shit together and get the fuck out here. And that will be after we beat the shit out of you."

Shaking, I pull up my pants and open the stall door. Moore smacks me in the head and yells at me to move faster as I struggle to wash my hands and grab my gear.

As we hike, I fall back. My head starts to tingle, and I start losing focus on the man in front. Falling in around me, Pickett, Lewis, and Moore scream and yell to move faster, stop embarrassing them, and "stop being a fucking pussy." Lewis pushes me, and I drop to my knees. Pickett tries grabbing the back of my pack to pull me back to my feet, but I fall forward and manage to crawl back into formation.

I stumble. My chest feels heavy.

They take the gun, which forces one of them to carry something for once in his career and only makes them rage harder. Before, they were angry, but now they are motivated by a self-righteous hate. It is as if I am doing this because the terrorists we were learning about in training had whispered in my ear one night, telling me that the way to undermine the American infidels would be to fall out of tomorrow's hump.

It will be brilliant, I imagine the terrorist whispering. *Your leaders will be forced to carry a heavy gun for once, something they've avoided thus far. They will be so mad. They won't know what to do. The terrorists have won.*

"Put him in the truck!" a welcomed voice of reason yells out. It's Sergeant Ward, and he's not happy, but he can see this is going nowhere. "Oh, and Keith! You're not getting out of the gas chamber. I don't care if you are sick. When we get hit with gas, and you don't die because you know how to operate a gas mask and suit, your mom will thank me!" he says as he runs back to the front of the platoon.

Sitting in the back of the Humvee that follows the hikers, I close my eyes as the vehicle winds its way down the dirt road. The rest of the company arrives at the gas chamber, about five miles out from base in the desert. I get out and stumble over to a shaded area next to the building.

The different platoons are milling about as they shuffle to find their places in the formation. Each team, squad, and section have specific rows to fill versus the others in the company, as does each platoon. I'm ordered to join my platoon, and I run over and stand in formation. Each platoon takes turns going into the gas chamber. Eventually, it's my squad's turn. I struggle to get my suit on and pull the gas mask over my face. The suit is suffocating and hot, and my body starts to tingle. I feel light headed. We head toward the gas chamber. They let me keep my mask on, though I struggle to breathe through it as it is. The Marine who augments the training fills the room with a substance that feels heavy and glistens in white sparkles in front of our faces.

Anyone who knows anything about the Marine Corps in 2003 knows about the palpable fears of chemical warfare. Even the job description given to the Marines who augmented all our training in this area sounds sinister: CBRN, which stands for Chemical, Biological, Radiological, and Nuclear.

Blinding light floods into the chamber. A door cracks to let Marines pour out. Walking in a crooked circle, we remove our masks and mill about to let the air burn away the painful chemicals. We cough and battle the urge to rub the chemicals further into our burning faces. Mucus drains from our faces and runs like soup down our shirts.

I hobble out of the circle and dry heave on the sand. One of the platoon commanders asks if I'm all right. He's not in my immediate chain of command, so I lie and tell him I'm fine. No bite. He orders me to grab my pack and head back. I get my stuff and hobble over to the Humvee that brought me here.

The PX is still open when we return, so I head that way as the evening approaches. My uniform is covered with sweat and the crystals from the gas chamber. My face is swollen and red from not sleeping in days, not eating, and being sick. As I walk up and down the aisles of miscellaneous items, someone says crackers and 7-UP might help.

At the register, a big black woman scans my items and puts them in a bag. She looks up. "Are you okay, honey?" she asks. She's so sweet and welcoming that for a moment I consider closing my eyes and reaching for a hug.

When my unit arrives back from the long day of training, Corporal Lewis shows up, pounding on my door to get out to formation. He's mad I missed out on training and lets me know it. I can barely stand in formation. We are called to attention by our company commander and then parade rest. I try standing there with my arms behind my back. My platoon sergeant notices me weaving and trying to choke back the urge to vomit.

"You better not break rank, Marine!" he says. The platoon commander from this afternoon returns, pulling me aside to stop me from moving in formation. I stand off to the side as the rest of the company faces the lights from the adjacent building, going through the last bit of formality before they allow us to sleep for a couple of hours. The sleep never lasts.

5

OPERATION IRAQI FREEDOM

"What kills me is that most veterans who don't see war wind up promoting it because it represents an extension of how they see themselves. It wasn't their experience, but if enough of them claim it was, then it creates a public perception of war that evolves into accepted beliefs and then into the most dangerous commodity on the planet, universal truths. That's why when people start telling me their opinion on the war, I always ask them if they would go. Not just go, but sign up for the infantry. The answer is always no.

"I think about the guys who replaced my unit on the outskirts of Fallujah. They were the ones that went in. I remember when we came back to take their guns and send them home. I'll never forget their faces or the way they moved around in pairs, hugging the walls, when they walked to the head or the smoke pit. They looked like rats just released from a cage. Their uniforms were dirty. They looked feral. Their eyes scanned continuously. It felt serious.

"They had taken over a schoolhouse before we arrived. One kid told us a story I'll never forget. We were standing in the courtyard at the center of the school when he told us how bad roadside bombs were becoming. They didn't just blast some shrapnel into the vehicle. They took entire vehicles out, killing everyone inside. He said he watched the vehicle in front of him blow up. He said it was such an intense explosion that he knew right then all eight friends inside were dead. That's what we were facing. Yet the leadership gave us the shitty Humvees.

"That was the first time I started smoking. I stood there and stared at the brand-new Humvees lined up next to the building. Those weren't the ones for us. Instead, I got directed over to the skeletal frame of a vehicle. I jumped up in the back where my gun would mount. Whoever drove it before wrote on the frame 'The Doom Buggy.' So, I'm expected to take this thing out every day of my fucking life here, and the people in charge who never see shit or leave the safety of the compound get brand new armored Humvees. And I have to try ignoring the fact that if I look down in mine, I can see the goddamn ground moving beneath me.

"But, hey, that's just misplaced anger I should let go, right? That's something that doesn't matter anymore. Of course, it definitely doesn't matter for more than a few of those kids, who can't stand here and talk about it today."

■ ■ ■

Captain Potts doesn't waste time telling us not to become too lazy over the weekend. His job is to make sure we do ours — a task infinitely more physically demanding than his, but you wouldn't know it from the way he talks to us. We are leaving for either Japan or Kuwait soon. He emphasizes the need to resist all of our urges to ruin our military careers before we can finally become useful to the United States.

Captain Potts is replaced by a monster. Platoon Sergeant Morgan is a bald little man with a beet-red face, round and shapeless from wear. His tone is one of pure rage, delivered in a coarse, rapid torrent of words. He paints a brutal picture with those words, further destroying my preconceived notions of the ideal soldier I anticipated meeting and becoming.

When he talks, he starts out looking like an ordinary human, a short one with maybe a few harder years than most. As he continues to rant and the words flow out, his stature increases. He isn't a little man anymore. He is a monster, a hulking brute of anger bursting at the seams of a human wrapper. But he always invites any Marines in his platoon who don't have family in town to join his family for Thanksgiving.

"All right, listen up, you bitch motherfuckers. Don't mistake a single fucking word your bastard ears will no doubt block out like your mother's cunts should have blocked the insignificant, twisted, little faggot cocks of your fathers. Make no mistake; we are going to be fighting a fucking war soon. Japan would be nice for pantywaist pieces of shit like you, but that's not what's in store, maggots. My daughters as the cunts, the little cunts they are, could do better than I've seen out of you. Motherfuckers, you better pay attention and train hard, because shit is going to get real now. Enjoy your fucking weekend, and don't lose your fucking mind by fucking me with your stupidity."

I spend the weekend sitting on my rack, watching DVDs I bought at the PX and eating pizza. Sometimes I wake up in the middle of the night and reach under the bed to grab at the pizza boxes cluttered there, then down the cold pizza with an open two-liter bottle of soda. I don't leave the bed for the entire weekend. I'm just glad I don't have to move and hope I'll feel better soon because I don't think I can handle the reputation of being a quitter.

Lewis stops by to tell me how mad he is that he picked me and not Flynn for his team and that I better man up.

None of the senior Marines who are in my direct chain of command have been enlisted longer than three years. This deployment will be the last one for anyone from their group who doesn't reenlist. They aren't the sort of fearless leaders people imagine, like John Wayne or Captain America. It's hard to explain that, against the alternate reality of all those commercials and movies that play behind our eyes every time we think of camouflage uniforms and assault rifles. But these guys aren't military strategists or monster-slicing legends. They are kids, most no older than twenty-one, and they are in charge of us.

There is one leadership spot that hasn't been filled yet. Out of the one section leader, three squad leader, and six team leader positions, they're one man short. This leaves them with the task of choosing someone from the new Marines. In each team are two other positions that the rest of us will fill. One guy will carry the machine gun and the other the ammo bag. Those of us not in the running to be the guy who leads the team are stuck trying to be the guy who carries the gun in order to avoid being the guy who carries the ammo.

At the top of our group is Phillip Preston, the rich kid from Dallas. Ricardo Luvs (not his true last name but the closest most got to pronouncing it correctly) drops into the unit next. He's Mexican, adopted, and from Florida. He is a nice guy, more or less, but an opportunist. I consider him a good friend. At the same time, I know he will do what he has to do to climb the ranks. Though people criticize his motives, they're very simple. He is good at managing Marines, and he knows it. He grew up in a solid middle class family which provided a stable base that guides his actions. Unlike many others, he usually makes the right decisions.

There is Lonnie Fisher. Eventually he will be my squad leader, but at this moment he's just another new guy. Fisher is a country kid from a small town in Illinois. He prides himself on this fact, and proclaims how much he hates pantywaist virgin Yankees like me until someone reminds him that Illinois is also in the North.

Jason Hensley is an enormous man by appearance, though a little man inside. He towers over all of us and is the least socially adjusted. When someone asks what time it is, he twists his wrist upwards to shove his watch directly in their face.

Corporal Pickett found out Hensley was a virgin early on. One night, he pulled Hensley into a room. A girl stood naked in the center of the room while other Marines drank and laughed around her, taking turns fondling her vagina. Every so often, one of the Marines mustered the courage to get up and walk over, bending her over to bang her in front of everyone. The rest laughed, made jokes, or played with her nipples and stuck fingers in various orifices.

This girl seemed to be hanging around the barracks almost every night. I never talked to her, or saw her except in passing when she walked around the catwalks looking for rooms to give blowjobs or have sex in. My friends thought she was retarded. They said she'd been in a bad accident and suffered from brain damage. I don't know if any of that was true. I wouldn't have believed she was going around having sex with everyone if I hadn't seen it myself.

Her father was one of the top sergeant majors on base. She made friends with a group of other girls who stopped by to let Marines run trains on them. We called these girls "barracks whores," though prostitutes would have at least tried to make a little money. These girls never did. They lapped up the insanity of it all, although they never seemed to smile.

Years later, Hensley will tell me Pickett said to him that he might die overseas and he'd never know what it was like to be with a woman if he didn't do this. Pickett told Hensley that if he didn't have sex with the barracks whore he would be disobeying a direct order. He said they would respect Hensley if he chose to make a man of himself that day.

The other Marines made Hensley sit down naked on a chair and instructed the girl to climb on top. Hensley had no idea what he was doing and was too nervous to let things play out naturally, so Pickett got up and put his hands around the girl's waist, moving her up and down. In our future conversation, Hensley will admit he wasn't aroused. But he went along with it because, in the end, what kind of a Marine is a virgin?

In the barracks, I'm horrified at the story as Hensley finishes it up with a nostalgic look on his face. "Now they respect me, I think. Now that I'm not a virgin," he says.

Before I can shake off the eeriness, he's off to tell Pickett that I'm also a virgin. Pickett approaches me that evening and asks if I've ever had sex. I admit that I haven't, and he laughs and says it looks like he'll have to teach someone else how to have sex by the numbers. I tell him I won't do it, and Pickett simply nods and walks away.

They never respect Hensley after that.

Bryant and Olsen come next, then Flynn and me, who are the first guys sporting the new digital camouflage gear in the entire unit. Then there is Hayes. A couple of weeks later, Caleb Wagner arrives.

Wagner is a big guy. We call him Big Dub. He is soft spoken and a country boy, a few years older than the rest of us. In part because he is older, and in part because he is a devout Christian, Wagner isn't swayed by anyone's opinions. Out of all of us, he is the gentlest and the most dangerous.

Hayes never wanted to be a machine gunner when they pulled him from the assault men, but he's here now.

The others seem to like Flynn, who is silent, but sure of himself. There is an enigma lurking in him and no one is clever enough to find it.

Preston gets the last team leader spot. He is the only one of us that has been out on a full-scale training evolution. Most of us have only taken day trips out to the desert immediately surrounding the base to practice gun drills in our squads before sauntering back.

The mortar men and assault men have their drills, and so do the machine gunners. Getting up early, we shuffle out in the dark in green shorts and shirts, coughing and cursing our way to the parade deck. We stretch in a circle and start to wake up. As night shifts towards lighter shades of gray, we get in formation and run up the road towards the empty desert at the foot of the mountains. Marines take turns singing cadence next to the formation, and we yell back, in time with our shoes as they slap the packed earth.

Back from the run, we shower, change into our uniforms, and eat at the chow hall. Then we head to the armory to draw out weapons for gun drills. Everything is competition-based. All the drills are done in rows, with each team competing against the others. We practice setting up the gun and loading it over and over again.

Whether we provide over watch for patrols or covering fire for troop maneuvers in combat, or we sit on a checkpoint in the middle of the road, the basis for all our activities is the gun drill. We spin around until we are dizzy and then complete gun drills. We practice in the rain and the mud. We practice blindfolded. We start out lying on the ground or hiding behind a wall. The result is the only thing that matters, and yet after all the drilling I have no better idea of what this very basic function will look like in combat.

Tired after each day of drills, we head back in formation as a section to drop the weapons off at the armory. Once there, we clean the guns until they're spotless. A big dunk tank with used solvent is the first step. We dump the guns' mechanics into it to dissolve anything that has crept its way inside, threatening the functionality of the weapon and therefore our entire purpose.

Once we get the guns clean, we return to an uninspiring set of one-story buildings. Other platoons return from their training evolutions and we all stand there, at first hopefully but eventually breaking rank and milling about, waiting for hours to be released for the night. Every day we train and return here, waiting for command to let us off for the night. Every night they leave us outside without any explanation until midnight or even later.

Rumors circulate. We know our schedule for the next month or so, and have been told we are going to Kuwait. Even so, no one knows if we will invade Iraq, or if we'll go no further than the border before we head back to Kuwait City Airport.

Each squad is known for its varying degree of intensity. First Squad is the worst. Pickett is a terribly simple and brutal human being to work for. He smiles and hazes his Marines every day. When he speaks, it is between clenched teeth, armed with sarcasm and hate.

Third Squad is the best out of the three. They come in last place on most gun drill competitions, unless Wagner is involved. His athleticism makes up for anyone else's lack thereof. The squad leader, Perry, is known to some as "the drunk Indian" because he is Native American and fond of alcohol. He isn't a monster like Pickett or selfish and insecure like Miller. His team leader, Boothe, had been demoted prior to our arrival in the fleet. Some of us lesser mortals watch a movie in Boothe's room soon after we get there. He treats us like normal people when his friends aren't around.

Corporal Diego is the leader of Second Squad. He yells at us like his peers, but he is an idiot. He isn't trusted to accomplish much beyond backing up his friends who are in charge.

One day, we head out to the backyard, an area in the desert directly behind the mountain range where plywood rooms were built to simulate a town. New barrels are handed out that turn our rifles into paintball guns. Breaking up into teams, we take turns rushing through the plywood corridors of the tacky, house-of-cards style set-up. We are looking for the designated bad guys while trying to avoid shooting designated good guys.

In our first match out of the mandatory three that day, part of my team begins laying down covering fire as a few of us run forward, hitting the wall of plywood. I peek around the corner, then jerk my head back. Pickett is there. I pop around again and shoot him in the flak jacket. He realizes I've hit him and that's that, and stands up, shooting me in the Kevlar helmet before walking off the training environment to the sidelines.

I hit the wall with my team and circle into the main hallway, rifle up and pointed forward. We're trying to float along and pie off the make-shift windows and doors, scanning through the openings and shooting at movement here and there. As we get to the main room, I see Sergeant Burrows with his hands in his flak jacket and take a couple of shots before realizing he's not one of the designated bad guys. He grabs my flak jacket, whipping me around until I hit one of the plywood walls.

"What the fuck, Marine? If I had been a little kid or a woman, you would have just committed a war crime!" He walks out of the room in disgust. I look down another hallway to see Lewis, Miller, and Moore converging on me, screaming about how many people I'm going to get killed and all the innocent people I might slaughter now that I've proven I am capable of murder.

I stumble out of the labyrinth of wood and tarps and walk back to an area designated for anyone who has finished the training exercise. Corporal Rollins walks up. He was on my team during the house-clearing drill.

"Hey, Keith, don't worry about it. Those guys are idiots. It's just a fucking game. How were you supposed to know a big bald Marine was a good guy and not a bad guy? Don't let them get in your head. Those idiots are only

going to give you a complex that might actually get someone shot if they don't let up on you guys."

In my third and final simulated gun fight, I see Pickett
approaching again, wearing his patented shit-eating grin.
He doesn't see me until the last second, but I hesitate. I
take one in the flak jacket.

6

GAS MASK WEDNESDAY

"I stayed angry way too long and it fucked up my life. I thought everybody else was fucked up and I couldn't understand why they thought the way they did. When I heard about Tom Brokaw calling the World War Two guys the 'Greatest Generation', it just pissed me off, because the 'Greatest Generation' didn't stand up for us one fucking bit. They said we didn't fight a real war, and statistics prove that we fought a hell of a lot more battles than they ever did and we lost a lot of people. So, them telling us it wasn't a real war just irritated the living piss out of me and everyone else I know. Getting thrown out of the VFW because I was 19 years old and — well. You know, I had my uniform on, and I was still pissing Vietnamese water. It gave me a real bad attitude about the Greatest Generation.

"Tom Brokaw? Fuck him. I'm still mad about it. That's all part of the rejection that the American forces suffered at the hands of our own people when we got home. Have you ever been kicked in the ass? It hurts! It's insulting, isn't it? The Greatest Generation didn't stop demonstrations. They didn't slow them down. In fact, they were in on it. So, when we got home, my whole generation of guys were treated like fucking monsters. People said, 'Do not talk to them.' The VA was in on it, too. That's why in the 90s we all started to snap and break down. You know, go nutty from the Gulf War kicking off, which brought up a lot of shit we had been repressing for a long time. We started to get together. A lot of people went to school and became therapists after Vietnam, and they knew we were all fucked up from PTSD and that we needed help and that there were no programs in place.

"The Greatest Generation let us all down. They didn't control their kids who didn't go to war, and they didn't support the ones who came back from one. How can you go to places like Normandy and Guadalcanal, but not support your own boys? Instead, you call them baby killers? Who the fuck would do that? Who would kick us out of a VFW? I mean, really. I got invited to go back to the VFW by one of the guys I knew recently. He said it's all different now. He said we run the VFW. If they're doing some things to help our boys now, the ones coming back from Iraq and Afghanistan, well, that's good. Do I sound bitter? Yeah, I'm a little bitter. If someone had helped me adjust to civilian life in my twenties, I don't think I would've been so mad and pushed so many people away over the years. I think I would be a happy old man, with a bunch of happy kids, a bunch of happy grandkids bouncing around. But no, that's not how it worked out. Yeah, that's an issue for me. Of course, it's life, and shit happens."

■ ■ ■

Gas mask Wednesday arrives, and we file out of our rooms in the morning with our gas mask cases secured to our hips. Standing at the beginning of the line of machine gunners, Staff Sergeant Morgan checks one Marine at a time along the catwalk. Corporal Moore is with him.

"This is Keith. He's in Corporal Miller's squad," says Moore to Morgan.

"Well, Keith, are you ready for a gas attack?" Morgan responds, with the tone of someone who has asked this a hundred times by now.

"Yes, Staff Sergeant," I say. Morgan reaches down and pulls back the Velcro flap that holds the gas mask inside its case. He looks up at Moore with a smile on his face and raised eyebrows.

"Keith!" says Moore, as he grabs my gas mask from its open case, "How the fuck do you plan on putting this on if it's upside down?" He emphasizes the mistake by slapping me in the face with the mask. I can hear Preston laugh and then abruptly fake a choke and go silent somewhere further down the line.

"Well, Keith? Your section leader just asked you a question," says Morgan.

"I don't know, Corporal." My eyes tear up a bit, and my voice chokes slightly.

Moore exhales and looks up at the ceiling of the catwalk above. When he looks back down at me, he's calm. "What are you doing here, Keith?"

"I don't know, Corporal," I reply.

Barking a laugh, Morgan continues down the line. Moore mouths the words, "You're paying for this," as he walks by.

Lewis screams at me later: "Good, Keith. Glad to know you want to embarrass me in front of the platoon sergeant and section leader. You better stop fucking up and get your head out of your ass, you worthless fuck!"

Life is not a voyage over a sea of connected experiences that we travel from one to the next. It's a single moment, played over and over continuously until there are no repetitions left. Consider all the moments that would have to happen to lead to the one where a gas attack occurs, and everyone dons the suits and masks, waiting for the wind to clear the deadly toxic gas. How will we know the air is clear? Someone will have to take their mask off, breathe in the air, and walk out into the wind from whatever hole we huddled in during the attack. But everyone is a little different in density, design, and genetic capability. How can we be sure it's safe? The weakly articulated plan forces one person from each race to take their mask off first to check the air and allow the mission to continue quickly, with the greatest number of survivors possible.

For Flynn, this plan isn't something he will forget. It guarantees his mixed heritage would lead him to be singled out if there were to be a gas attack. Sitting there, he would look up and see that most of his platoon had turned in his direction, a faceless sea of masked individuals waiting for him to test the air.

When he returns from Iraq and goes to check in his gas mask, he will find a rip inside the frame. He'll realize that, not only would he have been expected to be the first to take off his mask in the event of an attack, but that it wouldn't have mattered. He wouldn't even have made it to that moment.

Checking the boxes. That's what it's all about in the Marines, checking the boxes to make sure that our training has been augmented thoroughly and evenly across every unit. Each officer has a checklist, and every enlisted leader as well. Did we run them today?

Check.

Did they go to the range and rehearse gun drills?

Check.

Was there a room inspection?

Check.

Shots at the infirmary?

Check.

Drug test, check, run, check, clean guns, check, obstacle course, check, more of everything all week?

Check. Check. Check.

One of our humps is updated to include wearing the gas masks. The morning of the hump, we wake up and file down to the grinder with all our gear. We place it in our platoon's designated place and take turns watching it as the others walk to the armory to draw their weapons. When everyone is assembled, complete with heavy packs and guns, the hump begins. We start filing out in two rows, up the road towards the desert portion of the base.

We get to the first stop and drop our gear, hopeful that we won't have to wear our masks. Maybe we can just complete the hump. Tragically, as the rest period ends and the command to gear up is given, another shout echoes down the line. "Gas! Gas! Gas!"

Along with the hundreds of other Marines along the two lines on either side of the road, I pull my mask out and secure it to my face. We suck the air in and force it out in a way that forces any possibly tainted air to leave so that only filtered air from the mask can return. Then we tighten the straps and wait for the hump to continue.

We begin moving and I resist the urge to rip the mask off my face. Two Marines walk back and forth among us, looking for anyone without their mask or with slightly loosened straps. I try to block out the pain and focus on the burdened Marine in front of me, plodding along in agony like the rest of us.

I stretch my jaw and focus on trying to break the seal to let the precious air from outside seep into my mask. Drenched in sweat, the mask sticks like a giant leech. Just a momentary brush of free-roaming air would be nice, but my efforts barely work. As I struggle to breathe, I pass Marines who are now falling back. As usual, the weak ones fall back quickly, forcing the rest of us to move around them and continue at the pace set by our battalion commander. He is unmasked, with only a pistol and a light day pack.

My mask is fogged up completely as we reach the next stop. I peel it off, shutting my eyes to let the sweat burn in a cool rush. I inhale sharply and relax the pained muscles in my face and throat. Sitting on my pack, I grab my warm canteen of water and drink, washing down the coagulated saliva and moisture.

Cracking the Velcro on my flak, I let the air catch my sweat-soaked cammies and lean forward without the rigid form of my protective gear to inhibit the motion. Resting my arms on my knees, I stare at the ground, glad to exist without pain for a moment. I move the dirt around with my toe. Everything is pleasurable in the breaks between the hump.

"Keith! Push out for security!" yells Lewis.

"Yes, Corporal!" I leave my gear and the two lines of Marines on their packs and jog out about fifty paces. I drop down into prone with my gun facing out, angled up a bit by the bipods off the front of the barrel. Resting the lip of my helmet on the front sight pops its seal, leaving a stripe of red, angry skin on my forehead that can now begin to cool. I look down, allowing my helmet to sit on top of the gun. A little ant meanders over the little creases in the sand I've made by lying down. I'm completely content. I think about pizza and video games, this weekend, and calling home at the phone center.

Ten minutes later, yelling and movement cue me to return to the columns on the road. As we gear up again for the rest of the hump, they yell the universal sign for a gas attack again. We keep moving with our masks on. Marines begin to fall out more rapidly this time, and with the gun, I'm barely keeping up with the man in front of me. Then I realize he has fallen back. With about fifty meters to make up, I struggle to muster the strength to pass him. My legs don't react to the command in my brain. Without the ability to move up to the man in front of me, I hold the distance I've lost, willing the command to let us take off the masks and give us back the air. No one is passing me, so at least there's that.

At the last stop, we take the masks off and are told to put them back in the baskets at our waists. We've been issued syringes, three to be exact. There are two to counteract any toxin we might breathe in, and one long one with morphine to shut down the nervous system and hopefully stop any convulsions from snapping our spines.

During training and on the hikes, some of the syringes succumb to the aggressive motion. Marines randomly pass out on the humps or after running a drill because the needles are poking through their packaging, then the mask, then the leg holster. Eventually, they poke into the unknowing Marine's leg, causing his system to shut down.

Especially on the humps, the needle pricks aren't something easily noticed until it's too late. Flynn once noticed blood on his camouflage pants. After inspecting further, he found the needle punctures and saw how far the needle had traveled to get to his leg, It's a testament to the level of intensity involved in training, and to the degree of stupidity that is sometimes involved.

When it is time to sight in the guns, I find out I'm not necessarily going to be the gunner on my team. I am competing with Hayes for the spot. The section heads out to the range one day to train together for the last time before we will officially be training with our designated platoons for the upcoming deployment. When we get to the range, Lewis calls for Hayes and me. "Candy-ass, Snaggle-tooth, get over here!"

"Yes, Corporal," we reply, hobbling over to where Lewis waits with all our gear.

"Okay, Keith. If you want to keep your spot as the gunner, this is your last and final chance not to fuck it up. And Hayes, if you want to avoid carrying the ammo bag for the rest of eternity, shoot better than Keith today, and you can pass it off to him for good."

This is the first time I've officially shot the 240G. I've sighted in and pulled the trigger at targets, but without live ammunition. I'm terrified I'm going to fuck up and be forced to carry the ammo bag. Hayes is equally determined, and he seems to thrive on competition.

When it is our turn to shoot at the beat-up car in the distance, we conduct a mock gun drill to simulate a combat scenario. Lewis runs forward and drops the tripod in place. I drop down almost on top of it as I run up behind him, snapping the gun in place. I make sure to pop the cover open as Hayes drops the ammo on the tray. I slap it in, sighting in on the car down the range.

"Fire!" says Lewis, and I pull the trigger. The impacts fall way to the right of the car. Smacking my Kevlar helmet, he yells, "Adjust ten degrees to the right!" I make the adjustment and pull the trigger again and again. I'm missing the target. Miller is overhead somewhere. "Lewis, engage the target!"

Smacking my helmet, Lewis yells at me to move. Hayes takes my place. He does better. In the end, he's given the gun and I the ammo bag. We pass by the rest of the section, and they look at us. I can read their thoughts as I adjust the ammo bag over my shoulder, not used to the unfamiliar mechanics of carrying it. I feel like a tool now, more than ever.

Back at the barracks that night, I walk around the catwalk in the dark. It's quiet, and people are sleeping off the day of training and preparing for tomorrow. I can't remember the last time I was at peace. I start daydreaming about home again. It's nice to think about a time when everyone around me cared and somehow invested in my life. Most Marines come from meager backgrounds. Most didn't grow up in a big family, with parents who were fairly well off and a community that spent their lives engaged with each other.

When my parents were a young married couple, half of their church's congregation decided to move into St. Paul, Minnesota from rural Wisconsin. They picked a three-block radius in the city, and everyone bought houses in that area. They rented out space in a church that met every Saturday, allowing us to hang a banner over their name on Sunday when our church had services.

I grew up with friends whose parents had known my parents since they were kids and whose parents had been friends before that in most cases. My two closest friends from the community were Jon and Wendel. On Sundays, we hung out in the back of the church. We listened to the service but mostly tried to get away from our parents. As a child, I'm sure I was shielded from a lot. It was routine for us. Not much changed. Most stayed and few left.

If someone needed help moving, the community would meet them at home. All the men with trucks and trailers picked up the kids who were old enough to carry boxes. The women helped move or cooked food. Everyone pitched in, in whatever way could be useful.

The most interesting aspect of living in that kind of community was how everyone's highs and lows were lived out in front of us, in brilliant or faded colors.

I remember, when I was really young, there was a cute girl who had been diagnosed with something that would kill her soon. The entire community surrounded her and prayed for her. She was always laughing and hugging everyone. At one point, she hugged me and kissed me on the cheek. I remember telling my friends how gross it was, not knowing my mom was listening the whole time.

She grabbed my arm and whipped me around. She told me not to say things like that because the girl was about to die and was just trying to experience life and people for the short time she had left on this planet. She explained that the girl wouldn't have any time to date boys or get married or have kids of her own like I would. I'll never forget that conversation. My mom was wearing a bandana on her head as we both sweated a bit in the kitchen on that warm, muggy day.

Another young woman from my community married a man who had a disease that would kill him while he was still young. Everyone prayed for him. While the women from our community brought food to their house, the men put money together so the tragic couple could spend more time together than would otherwise be possible in their day-to-day working lives. The young man never stopped exhibiting a passionate love for his wife, or for all the people in his life. He didn't seem afraid of dying. He believed he was going to a better place when it all ended.

In the last memory I have of him, he sat in the living room at my pastor's house, barely able to hold his body upright in a chair. His head was bent over from the effort to maintain a very simple human position. Did he bend further to pray harder, or was he struggling to sit up as much as possible in the face of his failing body that slumped a little more each day?

People sat in chairs, on the couch, or knelt within touching distance. Everyone was pressing lightly with their hands or reaching out if they were too far away. They operated as if they were a part of a single functioning organism. The room was quiet, the silence broken only by intermittent words of prayer or encouragement.

In the winter, we met on a lake. The adults drove their vehicles out onto the snow-packed ice with all the gear necessary to recreate our little community packed into a couple of big green canvas tents designed from scratch. Inside the tents were heating tanks, and extension cords ran from them to generators placed in the cold to cut down on noise. Inside the tents, the men built rows of flat surfaces out of wood and plywood, the upper levels reached by wooden ladders. On these platforms, we threw our sleeping bags, like worms piled in rows on top of and around each other. During the day, some ice fished, others drove snowmobiles, and even more sat around in their snow gear and socialized.

I wish I could remember the soaps my mom bought then. Each room carried a scent, and a set of furniture intended for a different type of social function. We turn days of our lives into years of memories, and I could live in these for an eternity.

That was one world; and this is another. Instead of protecting each other with words, we use them to break each other down and increase our own self-worth. Our leaders act more like drill instructors. While there I was taught about the importance of living for a higher cause and treating people compassionately, here I'm told not to be a pussy, and to be sure to pull the trigger and not miss because people could die.

I thought being a warrior meant being a part of a community like the one where I grew up. The picture the recruiters painted was different from this reality, and I guess I ran with it. I thought I would be surrounded by the kind of warriors I read about in books and saw in movies. I thought they would build me up, and eventually, I would become one of them. We would face death and live through it together. And when we got out, we would never be afraid of anything ever again.

Now, when I put on my uniform, who I am is irrelevant. My story is gone. In its place is over 200 years of tradition resulting in a suspension of individuality. In its place is something designed to move as a coordinated whole, putting bullets in moving targets, until four years has passed and someone else steps in.

I lean over one of the railings and look out, thinking about how tomorrow will only test and expose me. This isn't anything like I thought it would be. This isn't the world my dad told me about.

The next day, I go to the PX and order new dog tags. Under religion, the words "No Preference" are inscribed.

7

HUMPS

"I need to find a way to remember how it really was, at least one more time. I think people have an idea about what I did in Iraq that's different than what happened. I can't stand all the metaphors. It's like I'm forgetting how it was. I've been out for ten years now, and I've learned one thing about people. We are expected to constantly lie to each other. We do it for all kinds of reasons. We don't talk about how we feel. We sit around and think about how we believe we should feel. It happens every time someone finds out I was in the Marines. It's this bullshit attempt at creating an objective perspective. But people pick and choose what they want to believe.

"I'm getting sick of hearing people say shit that is completely inaccurate about war and the military. I want to talk about how a recruiter told my family I would receive medical benefits and job opportunities once I got out. I want to talk about that one text I receive every year, thanking me for my service, and only getting a single gym credit for college from going through boot camp, of all things. I want to talk about that eighteen-year-old kid who couldn't tell the difference between lies and more lies. I want to talk about all those moments people call me a hero and tell me they can't imagine what I've been through. They never ask what happened, and they don't realize they all say the same thing."

"If I had written a book ten or fifteen years ago, it would be a scathing attack. But now I have a different perspective. Sure, I don't get people. That's why I stay to myself on this ranch in Florida. It's like I told you, Gabe, when you got out and you were mad all the time. We were sent out to the edge of the town to fend off the wolves. In the process, we stopped being a part of the town's people. When we came back, they didn't recognize us, or we them. We became more like the wolves."

"I don't know if that's exactly it for me. I can see the disconnect, but I don't understand why it exists. Why do we all lie to each other? None of us are happy, or none of us really care."

"People care. They just don't understand. Most of us don't understand each other."

■ ■ ■

I stand in my room on a Thursday afternoon, staring at a list of supplies intended for my pack in tomorrow's hump.

I set it down and begin collecting my gear and organizing it on the ground to ensure that when I pack everything, it will all be there for inspection after the hump. If I'm missing something from the pack, they will take my weekend. If I fall back during the hump, they will take my weekend.

I need to maintain my job as the gunner on my team. I didn't come here to carry an ammo bag into a combat zone. If I fall out of the hump, they take my job. There is always a lot riding on making it through these things.

My gear is laid out neatly on the ground, covering most of the space between the racks. I get to work, putting everything together in the pack and systematically creating as compact a shape as possible. At the end, I put on my flak jacket, then my load-bearing vest. I grab the straps of my pack and pull.

I can't get the pack off the ground or up any further than my waist with any sort of coordination. It's too heavy to lift, and a deep sort of fear sets in. I let it thud back to the ground, then grab the straps again and pull it over to the rack. I'm able to squat and lift it high enough to lean forward and ease it onto the mattress. Then I turn the ugly thing so that the straps are facing outward, the weight dragging my blanket and sheet into a swirl.

I loosen the straps, turn, and squat down, easing my arms through until the straps hang over my shoulders lightly. Tightening down on the straps until the pack moves fluidly with the turn of my shoulders, I remind myself that too much momentum with that motion could throw me to the ground. I ease the pack off my rack. As the weight settles on my back, I squat my way up to my feet. The joints in my knees are shaking from standing in place. I think of how my canteens will be filled tomorrow, along with my camelback. Then I'll be adding a twenty-five-pound machine gun as well.

This is what I will face tomorrow for hours and hours, at a pace set by a man with a pack weighing no more than a few pillows on his back, carrying only a light M-16 to give him the appearance of being one of us. It's always an officer, someone a couple of years older than myself who went through some random undergrad program before joining. Someone who strolls out of his truck with all his gear, the lie apparent by the lightness in his step.

He smiles and yawns, looking up and down the lines of infantry that he will be leading out on the hump, not realizing they all hate him for moments like this. He doesn't see that even though he looks like us, stands next to us, and talks the same as us, he can never be one of us. If that were the case, he would see what we saw in him and know. I've never carried the burden of leadership. Is it this heavy?

I don't sleep that night, anticipating the next morning. Even before the light hits the blinds, I hear yelling outside. I know it's time to get up and grab my gear and head out to the grinder. I think of the older generations, and wonder if this is what it was like for them as well. Maybe, but maybe not. Maybe I'll ask someone someday.

I do know that this is the heart of why infantry scoffs at all the others. When other Marines wonder why we look at them and laugh, shaking our heads, it's because we are jealous. They will never know this sort of pain. Same uni-form. Same commands and procedures. Different level of training. They go on their morning runs and hang out on the weekends, unburdened by the knowledge of the impending Friday hump.

After spending this evening stumbling around the barracks, all of my joints and appendages misfiring from the strain, I will pass out into a deep sleep. Then I'll suddenly wake up in the middle of an intense cramp, letting out a scream as I roll and fall off the rack. I'll writhe around on the ground until the troublesome muscle relaxes, and the pain fades back to a dull throb.

The beginning of the hump is always a struggle. I lean forward and let gravity drag me down but forward as I stumble on, using the locking motion of my joints to carry the impact and hopefully saving my muscles from burning out before the end. I stare at the pack on the shoulders of the man in front of me and try not to break the rhythmic pace set by whoever is leading this thing. I am carrying the gun again despite Hayes outshooting me on the range last week. Lewis gave it back this morning, almost grudgingly. I think he hates me slightly less than Hayes.

As one of two hundred people in a tight single file line, it's important not to fall back even a few feet. If you do, the man behind you has to slow down, breaking his concentration. The perception that you are falling out becomes a fear for everyone. The key is to stay right on top of the person in front of you. That way, when he lifts his foot, you place yours in his sandy step. Giving up creates a whole other level of difficulty, since everyone behind you won't put up with falling behind as well. Therefore, you step to the side and struggle to plow through unpacked sand as the unit passes, one troubled soul at a time in a single-file procession.

Sometimes I hike and stare at the person's feet in front of me, only to realize the pace has slowed. On looking up, I see that the person I thought was hiking along at the right pace has fallen far behind the procession, forcing myself and the people behind me to curse and stumble around him to get back on track and catch up. This is dangerous on a hump, especially if it's a long one.

I am carrying about ninety pounds, spread out over a load-bearing vest and a flak jacket. A twenty-five-pound gun hangs from the top of the pack. My arm goes numb from holding the gun, and the straps burn and sting relentlessly into my shoulders like razor blades. My back and hips and legs scream over and over again. The heat creates sweat, and the sweat saturates the gear. Sweating is dehydrating, but drinking interrupts breathing, interrupting blood flow, so a mindless determination sets in. The incentive is to earn the weekend free of harassment or working parties or more runs. More importantly, everything builds, so falling out now leads to an even more difficult mindset to overcome because the next hump will only be longer and involve more weight.

It always begins with something small. Let's say my right ankle will start to hurt this time. I will begin favoring the ankle, which will force my left leg to compensate for the weakness on the right. Eventually, the left leg will become burnt out, and I will start wobbling back and forth as the right tries to compensate for the left. Like a broken wagon, the task of overcorrecting creates more problems.

I will begin slowing down, falling slowly behind from the man in front. Someone in my section will take my gun to avoid me completely disgracing myself and my unit, since a high-ranking official is walking behind the formation and will take whatever squad-based weapon falls his way. He'll make it an example of a situation where Marines should police their own and never surrender their weapons or persons. As I would continue to fall back, I would be forced to accept that my weekend off is now in jeopardy for falling out of the hump. I'll realize this was only a 10-mile hump. The 12-mile is next week.

Every Marine is aware that his journey is a story, something he will look back on in the future. Will the script reveal a coward or a hero? Falling out of a hump creates a tragedy, and surviving one ensures at least one more day of acceptance. It allows the hope that someday these moments will be celebrated, not regretted.

Training is a progressive cycle, starting with a three-mile hump and progressing to twenty miles or more. Some Marines become conditioned to falling out every time. They hit a certain point where they mentally break, a familiar place for them. It's almost like a decision they make, but it's one they can't avoid allowing to creep in and take hold. "Goddamn it, Thompson!" or "What the fuck, Jones?" rings out as people grunt and breathe heavily on these marches. Looking up from a sweaty, tired haze, I see the drama unfold as someone from another platoon on the march passes us by, on the way to being ordered by the commander to drop his pack and get in the Humvee. There, he will sit and shake as a Navy Corpsman prepares an IV for his arm.

Stopping every three miles for a blessed couple of minutes, we line up our packs in a neat order next to each other. Some of us are ordered to push out about fifty feet to lie in the prone on their rifle or gun. The point is to simulate a combat situation whenever we train, so expecting an ambush is our primary concern. The rest of us sit on our pack, our bodies drenched in sweat. Our tortured brains and bodies relax as we prepare to push on for another three miles until the next break.

The key to making it through the hump also involves the way I wear my gear. It might feel better to strap the pack around my waist, but the constant tugging and pulling overworks my hips as they force my legs to dig into the sand. Once my hips go, I won't last. If I strap the pack too high, my center of gravity becomes too far from the ground for my body type and I fail to last the distance.

Carrying the machine gun creates other problems. Carrying it in front of my body eventually tires the arms: Placing it on top of the pack tires my back, angling it sideways so that the butt stock hangs far enough off the pack for one hand to reach up, balancing it out, creates an uneven pace. Everything comes back to the overcorrecting wagon scenario.

I never fall out of formation or drop back a foot. Sometimes an 0311 rifleman passes by, and I see that he had only been responsible for carrying a rifle. Here I am, with a gun equaling the weight of three of his, and I'm moving forward. It's encouraging to realize I'm not weak. Or maybe the feeling is more reassurance than encouragement. In those moments, I realize hope exists in the idea that I am strong enough to make it out of here someday.

We stop again for a few minutes, and in the blissful relief my mind wanders to the night before.

It's dark out. Lewis and I sit in a fighting hole that Hayes and I dug with our e-tools during the daylight hours. This is unusual for two reasons. First, Lewis never stands one minute of post or stays up one minute past the time he is able to sleep. Second, he never talks with Hayes me or. He yells, chastises, mocks, and goads us for reactions.

"See those lights out there?" says Lewis as we sit in the dark, looking out at the lights of the base in the desert night.

"Yes," I reply.

"What do you think you would do if this was Iraq and that was Baghdad, and we would be invading in the morning?"

"I don't know," I say as I shift on the ground, moving my weight from one knee to the other. I choose to lean against the wall of the hole and stare out into the black silence. I keep an eye on Lewis, in case he snaps and grabs my chin strap to jerk my face around or jumps up to kick me in the flak jacket. He is unpredictable that way.

"That's my fucking problem with you, Keith. You don't have a fucking idea why you're here. I knew I should've picked Flynn instead of you when I had the chance."

"If you're worried I won't pull the trigger when I have to, I promise that won't be a problem. I might be a virgin, but I don't plan on dying one," I say.

"Good, motherfucker," he says.

Our fighting hole is only one of myriad of dark places spread out in a giant half-circle to either side of us. Some Marines are walking in pairs back from the shit trench or from conferring with command, back in the tent that sits at the nucleus of this network of holes in the sand. I can vaguely make out the silhouettes of people moving around in the dark. They talk and walk quietly, a tactical compromise between command and the knowledge that this isn't real yet.

My flak jacket and neck protector fail to block the wind, so I scrunch my neck down to make the two materials press together. Two Marines approach from just past our position, and Lewis points at them. "Do you know who they are, Keith?"

"No, it's too dark."

"That's Jacobson and Peters from Third Platoon."

"How can you tell?"

"After training for as long as I have, you start to get to know what people look like in the dark. Everyone has characteristics that give away who they are, even at night.

That ability could save your life someday. Now, your turn," he says as two others walk past.

"That's Hensley over there," I point out quietly.

"Too easy. He's the only one in the entire unit that's tall and waddles like Big Bird."

I smile, and he tells me to guess again. "Okay, there's Moore."

"Good," says Lewis as he gets up to leave the fighting hole for the sleeping bag positioned about a hundred feet back next to Miller. "Have a good night. Don't forget to wake Hayes up for his shift, or both of you can kiss your asses goodbye tomorrow. Oh, and tell that motherfucker if I hear any more candy wrappers wrinkling in the night I will shoot his ass. I'm trying to fucking sleep, and all I hear is him unwrapping Jolly Ranchers. Drink water. If either of you falls out tomorrow, you're fucking done."

"Up, up, up!" someone yells. The neatly packed lines of stacked gear on either side of the road become jumbled as Marines throw on packs or assist others with the routine. We start out again, and the pain hits my legs, back, and chest as if it had been waiting just outside of my consciousness. It's like a blanket of spikes, hovering out of reach until it descends past my weak attempts to create a mental blockade. I hate that pain. I would cry, but that would take energy. I would yell in rage, but it would zap the little strength I have left. I would look up at the unrelenting glare of the sun, but the beating yellow orb would only cause vertigo and I would fall. I would question God and the universe, but then I would forget to focus on my breathing and my stride.

The next three miles creep by in a string of agonizingly thoughtless moments. We stop again, and this time I almost career into the Marine in front of me. Someone on the other side of the road must have run into someone. The formation creaks and stumbles to a halt.

"Get the fuck off me!" someone yells, as two Marines try to fight with packs on. Others run in to break it up. I struggle to unclip the straps that are burning into my waist and chest. As I drop the pack, fresh air I didn't know existed in this hell rushes in, cooling the hot sweat on my chest and back.

Three more miles and I can sit in my room for the weekend, I think to myself as I begin analyzing my condition. Some Marines are great for hiking, while others excel at running. It's all about mental conditioning and body type. Some fall out of hikes all the time. Others carry two machine guns, never missing a step, but struggle to keep up on runs. I'm somewhere in the middle of the pack.

My hips are burning, and I know that in the last few miles, I'm going to be pushing my body further than it should go. I know if I start hunching over to relieve the pain in my upper back, I'll put more pressure on my legs and burn them out. If I stand up straight and lock my legs to avoid using the muscles that have resorted to a numb sort of flexing, I risk twisting an ankle or breaking a bone.

Panic starts to rise in my chest and threatens my sanity. With the last leg of the trip in front of us, I know this is the time to burn out everything, if I can make it onto that goddamned grinder. But that brings up something else that can cost a Marine the hump. I can't think of how close I am to failing or I will fall out. I block everything out as we stand and struggle to get each other's packs onto our backs for the final three miles.

Moving again, I lose track of time. An animalistic acceptance settles in. As the last mile begins, I experience the crooked wagon wheel effect. My right ankle burns, so I sway heavy on my left foot. My left hip screams from the added pressure. My back swerves to the right to offset the loss of control from my left hip and leg. Heaving the gun off my burning shoulders, I struggle to hold the 240G against my chest. I know my arms only have thirty seconds of strength left before I have to toss the gun feebly back into its place on my shoulders, or I will miss out on the opportunity to have enough strength for the motion altogether.

Hayes has made it this far with the tripod and ammo bag but begins falling back past the formation with tears in his eyes. He's weighted down even further than I am. Lewis yells at him as he drops past us, Lewis' tripod becoming the deciding factor in his failure to finish out the hump.

As we turn the corner around a big rock, the base appears in all its glory before us. Hope floods in, but I know we can't just move towards it. There are roads and buildings in our way.

Just a little bit further, is the last coherently-formed thought I have left. People are falling back left and right now. I can hear some of them screaming in rage and frustration. Or maybe it's their team and squad leaders? It doesn't matter. Nothing matters and no one cares.

We make it back onto base, and the pace slows. I could cry from relief in the moment that the platoon in front waits for a car to pass by on the road, forcing us all to slow to a stop before turning onto the parade deck. Filing into three rows, we count off to see who made it to the end, and who is in the medic's Humvee and will need to be accounted for.

For falling out, Hayes will be showing up for a run on Saturday, or maybe other extra duties in the future. No one points out that Lewis made the two of us stand watch every night and forced Hayes to carry his tripod the entire hump, or the fact that he drank our water and ate the hardiest parts of our rations.

That night I pass out into a sort of death-like coma.

The next day Flynn and I walk to the Subway on base. We are tired and sore from training. It usually takes the whole weekend for us to recover. We pay for our food, then walk to a booth far away from the few others in the seating area. We sit down to eat.

"So, we had no idea what we were getting into in boot camp, right?"

"I sure didn't," I say.

"We had no idea how awful the school of infantry would be, either. Once we were in the fleet, we thought things would settle down. Instead, they're clearly getting worse."

"Yeah. Fuck this place," I say as I eat my sub.

"We don't even train efficiently. We haven't been on a single real training evolution yet. We're stationed on the largest live-fire base in the world, and we haven't shot more than 50 rounds through our guns. Even that has only been to sight them in. I came here to train with the best our country had to offer, but instead of world-class training, we draw lines in the sand like that's going to help if we ever have to secure a real building. What kind of a shit show did we stumble into?"

"One where we all die in the end," I say.

"What if this is nothing compared to what we'll be dealing with overseas?" continues Flynn. "What if we go into Iraq and have to kill people in cold blood and watch our friends die around us? What if it's just some ungodly horrible shit and we have no idea right now? What if this moment will be in the past soon and we'll be in a living hell?"

I stop eating and think about what he said. "I think if I have to kill someone, I'll either shit myself or throw up uncontrollably my first time. Maybe both."

Flynn nods, taking another a bite from his sandwich.

8

GUNNY MORGAN

"I would put in a claim just to show people trying doesn't really matter. It's been a decade since the first time I went in for my back and got denied. Now I finally have real health insurance. I'll just use that. At least the doctor I'll go to will look for the pain and attempt to fix it. Fuck all the Americans who think they care. It's not the VA; it's all the people who wake up every morning and only send that little text on that one day. It's the people who say they support the troops but not the war. I get how I have issues from it. I don't know if I can go there."

"Well, it's a bureaucracy, dude. To do anything, you've got to go through their bureaucratic rules. It's just the way it is. But once you get in, it's worth it. You are a productive man in your life at this point, and you want to continue being one. But you're knocked out of the saddle with your bad back, and you need to go in and do something about it."

"Well, you can keep the bureaucratic process. I'll use the health benefits that actually work. I have to make things happen before I get to the point where I'm crippled."

"You know it even makes it difficult to find the right women when you have issues? I think you're fucking up. Focus on getting your back better. Focus on getting your head right. Tell them you need to talk. They will take you seriously. Start focusing on the things that will really matter. The crisis hotline will talk you off a cliff, but you aren't on a cliff yet.

"That really is my best advice, little brother. There are people out there who will advocate for you. And it doesn't cost you anything. You could go down there today and you could tell them you need to talk. And if they pass you off to someone who was never in combat, then tell them you need to talk to someone who has been there and knows what the fuck you're talking about.

"It's a real positive and productive thing to do. I wish you would go. You'd be heading in a direction instead of just sitting there. That's what everyone needs to do. Your back might not feel any better, but your head will."

"Funny. I wonder how much better my head would feel if someone helped with my back."

"Right. Well, talk about that when you get there."

■ ■ ■

"One week of leave, you fucks," begins Gunny Morgan in his heavy-handed evening brief, spitting out words like an angry pit bull. "That's how much time you bitches get to work your finely tuned killing machines, paid for by the United States Marine Corps, back to the worthless god-damned bodies you puke pieces of shit fucks were when your mothers …"

I zone out as other groups of Marines cluster around their platoon sergeants on the parade deck, chanting in unison in affirmation or when they're given an incentive to respond with 'yut yuts' or 'oorahs.' All the companies begin in formation together until the battalion commander releases the unit for the weekend. Then the company commanders release their companies.

Finally, our platoon commander releases us to our platoon sergeant, where we are now. Morgan is ranting on about what we should expect if we forget we work for the United States Marine Corps as someone laughs in the back.

"You will shut shut shut the fuck fuck fuck fuck up right now in the back before I come back there and end your life before you go home and fuck the holes on your little whores to make other little whores. I motherfucking dare you to allow your fat bodies to get worthless, motherfuckers. And wrap up your little faggot twisted fucking cocks. Your job is to exterminate life, not create it."

His reddened face is wearing a comical expression. He looks like he is finally choosing to release some internalized pain and hurt everything and everyone around him.

"All right, listen. You're detaching to the platoons permanently when you get back. First Squad in all sections will be with First Platoon, Second Squads with Second Platoon and Third Squads with Third Platoon, et cetera, et cetera, motherfuckers. But don't think for a fucking second I won't be there to catch you fucking up if you so choose, you pieces of shit. And make no mistake, it won't be pretty when I'm done with you and your mangled worthless bodies."

One of the other platoon sergeants begins walking over to talk to Morgan, and the tirade shifts to him. "Get the fuck away from me, bitch, when you see me talking to my platoon, motherfucker!" The platoon sergeant stops and turns abruptly, then walks away as if nothing happened.

"See?" continues Morgan, "Motherfuckers know I'm no one's friend here! And don't think for a fucking second, they can protect you from me if they can't even protect themselves. They all know I'll put my goddamned boot on their fucking necks if they interrupt my mental calmness. And just imagine what I would do to you then!"

I spend the weekend in my room, reading or listening to music. I think of home while watching movies on Flynn's DVD player when he's not using it. It is difficult to move around as a new Marine without attracting negative attention. Walking around in the digital cammies like a pixelated asshole, I might as well slap a giant sticker on my chest that says, "Hey guys, I'm new!"

Graduating boot camp means nothing here, where everyone else has done the same. Those who are on the final two years of their first four-year enlistment make sure the rest of us know it. Walking to the PX, I make sure to salute when crossing the path of officers. I squint to properly identify the number of bars on higher enlisted Marines so I know what rank to acknowledge as I keep moving.

At the PX, I call home and Mom picks up.

"Hey, son, how are you?"

"Oh, I'm okay, Mom. How is everyone?"

"We're good, just getting ready for dinner. We're two hours ahead of you, so it's getting dark here now."

"That's nice."

"We miss you."

"I miss you, too. I don't think I'll be able to come home before I deploy. I used up all my days after boot camp, and I haven't been here long enough to gain more in time for deployment. But they say we might be coming back soon, if nothing happens after we get to Kuwait."

"Is that all they are saying right now?"

"That's all they are telling us."

"Are you afraid?"

"I'm really tired, Mom. Just really tired."

"Aww. I wish I was there right now, son. I wish I could be there for you."

"I know, Mom. Me too." I look around the tacky military convenience store's phone center, searching for words.

"Well, I've got to go. I'll let you know when I find out more."

"Okay, son. Thanks for calling. Love you."

"Love you too, Mom."

Hanging up the phone disconnects me from that place, bringing me back to another. It is tormenting, knowing my family is where I want to be, but I have put myself in this place away from them. Just like I intended. Just like I deserve.

Monday morning, we fall into formation with all our gear and weapons from the armory. Cursing the cold and shivering in the light material of our uniforms, we can't wait to begin moving. At least we'll be warm then.

We throw on our gear and the company begins moving out towards the desert, where we draw lines in the sand to simulate buildings and roads in a very imagination-driven combat scenario. Running forward and dropping down with our squad, we conduct one gun drill after another. I hit the ground over and over again, sighting in and yelling commands back and forth.

The routine is becoming second nature, and yet it couldn't feel any less realistic. Each time I drop and sight in, grinding the butt stock into the crook of my shoulder until it feels like an extension of my being, I'm scared this won't be enough to prepare me for anything that's out there waiting for us. I aim at targets and am instructed to imagine them as men with guns. I run around lines in the sand, and they tell me to picture walls with roofs over them. We circle around a hill, and they say we are flanking the enemy, but I still can't imagine what they are talking about.

At the end of every day, we hump back, turn in our weapons, and wait outside for command to let us off for the evening. We stand there as the evening light dilutes into darkness, waiting for hours and once again wondering what could possibly require us to stand outside in the cold for this long. People start pushing or milling about out of boredom until the leadership yells for everyone to get back into formation.

"Or else what?" someone yells out, to a warm round of "oohrahs" and "yut yuts."

"You going to make us stand out for more than 24 hours in a day?" The voice yells again, as corporals start yelling at PFCs to shut the fuck up and face forward in formation.

With only hours left for precious sleep, Staff Sergeant Morgan or the Lieutenant come out from the building, releasing us for the night. It will be like this every day until we are released on leave.

Flynn and I can't go on leave because we used up all of our days between boot camp and the school of infantry. We look forward to everyone else leaving. We'll finally get a few days of peace.

Everyone leaves for ten days, and Flynn and I are alone. It is nice. We still have to sit in uniform all day in our rooms, but at night we take a cab off base to watch a movie, play video games at the computer center, or go to the Denny's in town.

On the way back from town on our final day off, we are quiet as we pull up to a barber shop in 29 Palms with a few others. It's time for military haircuts all around; then we're back on the road towards base. Flynn refers to it as a fluorescent throbbing virus eating away at the mountainside.

The next day, everyone is back together in formation. Almost everyone has returned from home without incident. But in the Marines, it's famously said, "There's always one." If you mess up in the civilian world, they charge you there and then you come back and face the music here. There's no such thing as protection from double jeopardy. It comes back to that giant contract we signed.

Corporal Perry didn't make it past airport security. They asked him a simple question. "Sir, do you have anything to disclose at this time before boarding the flight?"

"Yeah, I got a pound of smack in my ass and a gat in my belt."

Perry experienced his first cavity search and interrogation by airport security that day. When he returned, everyone was laughing and asking him questions about the intimate moments he experienced with his captors. He didn't lose rank or his squad; only his dignity.

A few days before deployment, the electricity goes out, taking the lights and the hot water with it. We stumble around in the dark with candles and flashlights.

I take a cold shower in the dark and read with a flashlight I bought at the PX. Underaged Marines stand around, bored and alone. Some hide in their rooms and drink hard liquor straight from the bottle, dreaming or talking about the past or the future but never the present.

On the night we deploy to Kuwait, I'm walking back from the PX. There are two hours left before we will find ourselves waiting again, this time standing on the parade deck with all of our gear until buses arrive to take us to an Air Force base a few hours away. As I approach the steps at the base of my barracks, I can make out Preston's silhouette leaning against the ledge, a paper bag in his hand.

"Hey, Keith, we're about to go to Kuwait," he says, laughing.

"Yeah, I know."

"Want some of this?" he asks, reaching out to hand me the bag.

"Sorry, I don't drink."

Jerking forward off the ledge, he throws a finger in my face and says, "You better not fucking tell anyone, you hear me?"

"Yeah. No, man, I wouldn't do that. I'll see you later."

Laughing, he slumps back against the wall. "Do you think it's a good idea I'm drinking right before a deployment, Keith? Huh? Well, do you? Do you, mutt?"

Preston continues to laugh and mumble to himself as I walk away and head up to my room. I run into Luvs in the walkway an hour later.

"Hey Keith, were you with Preston earlier?"

"No, but I ran into him. Why?"

"He totally got busted drinking, and he's getting his ass kicked right now by Pickett and the others."

"Holy shit! What was he thinking?"

"I don't know, but I guess his team leader spot is mine now," says Luvs.

I go back to my room and lie down on the bare mattress, waiting for the yelling that will signal time to fall out onto the parade deck. It begins, followed by voices and the sound of doors opening up and down the entire walkway.

Donning the gear and pack, I walk out of my room to join all the other bodies milling towards the stairs. Preston walks by Pickett, who whispers something in his ear. Forms move past in the dark as Preston starts laughing aloud, and Pickett backhands him across the face, sending Preston to the ground.

"Get up, you fuck," says Pickett under his breath.

Running over, Moore helps Pickett grab Preston. They fiercely whisper for him to stop acting drunk as they pull him into a side room. Pushing past others who are jostling to see what's going on, I make it to the stairs and head out to the parade deck.

Transporting over a thousand men with all their gear is a drawn-out process that can only be compared to funneling cattle through a slaughterhouse. We stage our packs in tight rows according to our platoons and take turns heading to the armory to draw our weapons. Back in formation, we count off to make sure everyone is accounted for. Buses show up. We load into them and head towards the Air Force base. Once there, we stand in a long line to unload our gear, one pack at a time, and toss it from one man to the next all the way down the line.

Green is laughing and throwing the packs as hard as he can at Hayes until one of the bags mashes Hayes' fingers. Hayes screams and drops the pack. Green thinks it's funny and continues to throw packs at Hayes, who concentrates on catching what he can and trying to ignore the insults when he can't.

When all of the gear is accounted for, we huddle in cold groups, like penguins pressed up against each other for hours in the night. If we need to use the head, we go inside one of the hangars. There is more than enough room in the hangar for all of us to get out of the cold, and eventually, the Air Force personnel allow us to clamor inside.

Time passes. We are instructed to file onto a plane, where we strap into seats on either side of the fuselage. These moments in transit from all three of my deployments blur together. It takes days. We switch planes continually. Sometimes we shuffle out into a tent and lie down for an hour, then are funneled back onto a different plane.

We land at an airport in Kuwait City and board buses with weird fabric upholstery and oddly shaped seats, close to what we would have in America but slightly off. The buses leave the base and soon pass out of the city. The highway begins to run through more rural environments with thinning houses and gas stations until the city ends and the desert truly begins.

We turn off the main road onto a poorly worn trail in the sand. It feels as if we are floating along at sea as we drift up and down the sand dunes. A massive man-made wall of sand materializes in the distance, and it becomes clear that we are driving towards it. Someone at the front of the bus hands out ammunition as we approach the base at the edge of the Kuwait/Iraq border.

Nine-millimeter rounds are dumped into my hands and I struggle to put them into the magazine. I've never carried a loaded handgun in my life. Lewis yells at me to hurry up, and Miller makes Luvs load the rounds for me since we are pulling onto the base. We finish the trip in silence.

Once on the ground in Kuwait, they shuffle us towards a place where we pick up all our gear, then move towards a series of tents. I'm standing in a line of hundreds. One by one, we file into one of the tents. This is how they make sure everyone is checked into the base as quickly and efficiently as possible. The line moves slowly. After some time, I get to the tent flap and see the rest of my unit inside, snaking its way in a compressed zigzag back and forth towards two Marines sitting behind desks at the far end. One of the guys begins mooing, and another starts humming circus tunes. Tent after tent, we continue the check-in process.

The last tent is the one where we finally put down our packs, the one where we will be sleeping for the foreseeable future. Though it is tedious, I don't mind most of this process. In between brief moments of activity, I have been left alone to escape into dreams of home, of kinder places and people.

VIETNAM

"I remember walking into the hooch with my gear after a long day and seeing the brand new tiny black and white TV sitting there, all of the guys sitting around it. It caught my attention, you know? I had not seen a TV since I left home. I stopped for a minute and my heart sank as I realized what they were quietly watching. The antiwar protests were violent. The signs they held were mean, heartbreaking, and aimed at us. I stood there for a minute or so, then moved along to my cot, threw down my gear, and sat. All of us felt the same way, I imagine. Some weird sense of betrayal. Nobody said a word. Their eyes were glued to the screen. The protesters' signs said it all. The violence with the police only added to the message we were seeing. I put it out of my mind. So did the others. We were in that place whether we liked it or not, agreed with it or not. We had our missions, our jobs to do, and our duty to perform. There was simply no choice but to move on, and I did. We all did."

■ ■ ■

Basic training and Aviation School happened, and I learned a few things. Boot camp was a slap in the face. Aviation School started off intense but then ended just as quickly as it began. Reinforcements were needed in Vietnam.

So now I'm on a plane, flying to a place I didn't even know existed until recently. My orders are to join a unit planted in Vietnam. The soldiers packed in next to me are complete strangers. We are deploying together, if only for a moment. Once we arrive on base, we will split up and join our units, meeting more strangers and never seeing each other again.

I spent basic training with John through the buddy program, but he isn't here now. It looks like we won't see each other again for a while. It's quiet on the plane as we fly for twenty-four hours, all the time we have to adjust from the world we are leaving behind to the one where we are being transported.

No one knows each other, so no one talks. Most sleep, sometimes getting up to use the bathroom or flip through an onboard magazine. The airliner begins to fly low as we approach our destination. From my seat, I look down through thin clouds and can see the rotor blades of three helicopters turning below us, en route to somewhere. Is that going to be me someday? Suddenly the huge airplane noses over to make the landing. For an instant, it feels as if we are going to crash, then just as suddenly the tires touch down. We are here.

The Captain talks over the loudspeaker.

"Okay, gentlemen, this is your last stop. We have arrived at Bien Hoa airport. When you debark, stay together in one place. There will be personnel there to escort you onto the base. Good luck, and godspeed."

This feels like being on the bus to boot camp. I have no idea what will happen. When the door opens, I half expect a drill instructor to stride into view, screaming and yelling at anyone in sight, but there is only the nice flight attendant signaling us to get up and leave one row at a time. I file out behind the men in front of me. We walk from the doorway of the plane into a scene that that is totally unfamiliar.

I don't know what I had been imagining, so I suppose that anything would have been equally as unexpected. The muggy heat hits my face, nothing like Wisconsin. The thickness in the air catches in my lungs. It's a foreign feeling, like landing on the moon. I didn't know until this moment that we were going to the tropics. I never even thought of it. I didn't think period.

The trucks are there already, and we all get in. The heat doesn't let up, and the smell of the place is all around us, engulfing our senses. It overwhelms my understanding of physical boundaries until I'm almost unsure where the sweltering moist air leaves off and my sweaty skin begins.

The feeling of oppression isn't helped by knowing that the trees are said to hide a relentless enemy force of little Asian men that won't stop until they kill us or are killed themselves.

I look around and wonder if anyone will be a friend here, or if they will all hate me, or if I will never see them again. Driving onto base, we receive stern commands from the two men who brought us here. There isn't much room for personal decisions. Probably for the best. I'm scared, everything is new, and I have no idea what I'm supposed to be doing or saying. We stay here only long enough to be trucked to another reception center in a place called Cu Chi.

This is where we really get our first good look at Vietnam. The dirt is red clay. The green is as dark and as green as it could be, and there is a lot of green to see. I can't recall the names of the villages that we drive through on our way to Cu Chi, but they are just hamlets made up of small shacks with roofs made of tin or reeds and palms. I feel like I am part of some action movie, surreal and over-whelming and sensational all at once.

After a week of orientation about Vietnam and its people, new orders come down. I am assigned to an assault helicopter company in Tay Ninh, which is further up the road. As I am handed my orders, the guy says, "Good luck," before calling out the name of the next guy in line. Good luck? That strikes me as odd.

A day or maybe two later, the few of us going to Tay Ninh are told where to be in order to meet the helicopter that will take us there. I notice it right away as the huey lands, and so do the others. There is a big Crusader shield painted on the nose of the helicopter. I find out very soon that this is the name the company has chosen for itself. I am going to be a Crusader.

We pile our new gear onto the floor of the huey, climb in, and sit on the bench seat as it lifts. I am awestruck as we fly north, no higher than a thousand feet off the ground, very fast. My eyes are glued to the ground, then to the pilots up front, and then the crew in back. The crew chief and the gunner are both just sitting there like us, watching the world go by through that big open door.

This place is an almost-abandoned base camp in Tay Ninh, close to the bottom of an extinct volcano near the Cambodian border. It's a shell of sorts, a skeleton meant for a larger beast. Now, it holds only my aviation unit. I later find out it was once a thriving, bustling place, complete with a hospital, PX, and all the amenities of a full Army base. By the time I get there, all of that has disappeared and our company is all that is left. The unused buildings have been flattened and are gone, only big empty cement slabs as proof they were there in the first place. Whole areas are roughly cleared of trees like someone would clear a person's mouth of teeth with their fists.

Our uniforms are solid green, olive drab in color. I don't have much gear, just a metal canteen, a pistol belt, and a steel pot helmet. It's the same stuff that was issued to soldiers in World War Two and the Korean War. They give me an M-16 once I get to my unit, but there isn't much in the way of web gear. I don't need the normal grunt stuff. I have a toolbox that will stay on the helicopter. There is no need for anything else. The guys on the ground wear jungle-style boots and green jungle fatigues, which after a couple of months become faded and dull. In the flight platoon, it is all flame-retardant Nomex flight uniforms and leather jump boots for safety reasons. Fire is the biggest fear we have, apart from bullets.

The first assignment I am given when I get to the company is mechanic work in the maintenance hangar. All of us who are school-trained helicopter mechanics go to the hangar. There are some who work their whole tours here, and they seem to like it. They are really talented. They act with confidence and can be seen jumping up to grab at different parts of the engine or directing others to unaddressed issues. They keep people alive, and they never let anyone forget it.

There are different shops in the hangar. There is an engine shop, a rotor and tail rotor shop, and a sheet metal shop, all manned by seasoned men who have earned everyone's respect. The hangar has three walls of corrugated steel panels over a steel beam frame and a corrugated steel roof. The front of the hangar has no door. It is open all the time, and it is unbelievably hot inside. I really do not like it here at all.

It is not long until I am comfortable in my hooch, which I share with the others assigned to the hangar. A couple of the guys work on sheet metal repairs. Some are radio repair, and some are helicopter mechanics like me.

They are all good guys, and getting to know them and become friends is easy.

I am sitting on a buddy's cot one day when he opens a package from his mom and dad. All of us are excited when we get a package from home, and just as excited to see what others receive. Sometimes they share cookies or some other treat. In this case, he has some canned elk, a big package of crackers, and other assorted goodies which he generously shares. I find out that his father is a professional fur trapper in Alaska.

Near the hooch are bunkers, lined and buried with sandbags, reached either through a hole in the wall or by a short walk. Inside the bunkers, people from multiple tours before mine have lined the walls with empty rocket boxes. In one bunker, someone took a torch and lightly browned the wood so that the grain can be seen. It makes a nice place for late night card games. It's also a good place to hide when the mortars or rockets come into our area from outside the perimeter.

The first time I experience an incoming mortar is on my first day here. I have checked into the company and been assigned a bunk in one of the hooches. The sidewalks are made of long narrow planks held a few inches off the ground by wooden blocks.

I am sitting on a plank with another new guy, bemoaning our situation, when suddenly there is a very loud explosion behind us. It is close enough that we are instantly up and sprinting towards the opening of a big bunker situated between two hooches.

A massive dose of adrenaline hits me. I see men running out of hooches and flat out into the bunker in what seems like slow motion. By the time I get there, two or three others are stuck in the door because they've all tried to go through at the same time, not willing to stop and wait for the others to get in. I hit them at full speed, forcing them through the small door and onto the floor with me, all of us ending up in a pile with the guy behind me on top.

The explosions stop. We have no time to sit here, no matter how stunned we all are. There are more coming. There will always be more coming. I will run for the bunkers more times than I can count while I'm here, hitting the ground as flat as I can to avoid shrapnel. After the mortars stop falling, everyone gets up, dusts off, and goes back to what they had been doing. I do not sleep very well anymore.

As a new guy, desperately wanting to get out of the hangar doesn't win me any points with the others. But I want to be in the flight platoon. On the flight to Vietnam, I got to know one of the guys who sat next to me on the plane. He had always planned to be in the Army as a helicopter mechanic. He was excited and enthusiastic the whole time. As things turned out, not only did we share a row of seats on the crowded plane, we went to the same reception center, and from there were assigned to the same assault helicopter company in Tay Ninh.

After I've suffered for a month or so in the hangar, he drops by to say hi. I ask him to help me get into the flight platoon.

"Luke, please help me get the hell out of this fucking hangar!"

"What's wrong with hangar work?"

We talk about it for a minute, and he tells me he will put my name in when an open slot comes up. That gives me a little hope.

9

LINE OF DEPARTURE

"One of my guys wrote an angry book. I tried to read it. It was so angry it made me angry, so I never finished it. He didn't sell many books. He had a great title and a great cover and all that, but he was livid mad when he wrote it and it didn't read well at all. I mean, he was a good author, what he said made sense. But even though it was well-edited, it was still a shitty book. Because he was angry."

"Maybe I'll go through and add some more reflective pieces so it will read like more of a full circle thing. I don't know. Maybe I'm fucking weird."

"Gabe, listen. If you're not angry, you're not normal, okay? Not after what we've been through, and not after trying to readjust to civilian life and all that bullshit. You know, I was angry and I could let myself get mad again. But it fucks me up. It makes me stay mad. Boy, I hate that.

I just hate staying angry all the time. It alienates you. It's an ugly emotion. It isolates you. That's all it does."

"Yeah, it is. You hurt other people or yourself. I get that. But I was never that type of guy. I might isolate myself but that's about it."

"Oh, it's even in your general fucking demeanor. You know what I mean? The way your face is expressionless, or it gets mad. Everybody can see that. It's fucking normal for us. The military wants you angry while you're in combat. It makes combat easier. Did you know that?"

"Yeah, I heard something like that once."

"Probably heard it from me. When I got out of Vietnam I stood on the porch of my parents' house and didn't know who I was. I couldn't fucking believe where I was standing. The first thing that popped into my mind was that I had to get a job. I went and got a job, and I never stopped working. I always worked hard enough to prove I was worthy of a job. I never treated any of the issues I had. I just worked. Trying to forget by working. Am I making any sense? Then, years down the road, the stress of working started to get to me really bad. I eventually had a mental breakdown. Do you know what they call it? Delayed onset of PTSD. I had it all along."

■ ■ ■

The sun beats down. I'm buried under a warm blanket of sand. I open one eye inside my helmet and push myself up into a sitting position, watching the sand slough off.

Looking around, I see other lumps in the sand where the rest of the squad is sleeping. Miller and Lewis are across from me, and Hayes, Luvs, and Preston are a little to the right. Organized rows of tents spread out in the distance. We have been training harder than ever before. We run in the morning, conduct gun drills throughout the day, and spend the rest of the time working combined training exercises with Second Platoon. We've been training for a month. Today, we walked out into the desert and found a place to sleep.

People joke that this place looks like 29 Palms and it's just another version of CAX 2003, one of the major training evolutions back on base. It's February first. We are cold at night. Sandstorms occasionally batter the tents. Ours begins to collapse one evening, and some of the guys run outside to reinforce the stakes. Marines inside push out where the tent is imploding, while others pile more sandbags near the base on the inside and the ones outside pull on the ropes and reset the stakes. Those outside get yelled at for leaving the tent flap open. This allows billowing clouds of dust to rush in, making it difficult to breathe. The dust covers everything, including our guns. It is a constant struggle to keep them clean and mechanically fluid. People cheer when the tent is successfully reinforced for the night.

We don't have time to write to our parents. Our squads keep us training. First Squad is out the latest. They walk back when everyone is asleep. We pass each other in the desert at times. We still compete, squaring off with other teams and racing into the sun through the sand. We are intent on setting up the gun faster than our counterparts. We rush to take the thing apart, scream for approval, then rush to slam parts back together, finishing the drill with a clean rack of the bolt to prove it is assembled properly. We practice to improve everything we do. We practice with blindfolds. We even practice at night in the tents while the 0311's sleep, until the platoon sergeant yells at us to stop. Nothing is good enough for Miller and Lewis, and we are pushed further every day.

"Looks like cat shit in a sandbox," says Lewis, who is now sitting up himself. "Get up, Candy-ass, and get your boyfriend Snaggle-tooth up, too."

I shake Hayes. The others start to shift and materialize as the sand falls away from where they were sleeping.

I reach down slowly to grab my gun, still a little tired and beaten down from the run this morning and all the training up to now. Lewis walks over and kicks me in the side, sending me crashing back down into the sand. I stand up and look at him, hoping my face doesn't betray what I'm thinking.

"So, just because Miller and I let you sleep, you don't think you have to call me Corporal or move fast? You think you're special now that you're on your first deployment? Listen, motherfucker," says Lewis. "You think you know what it's like to be on deployment? You think you're salty now because you've been overseas for a month? Don't forget; you haven't shot this gun at all yet. You don't know shit until you've been on a full pump to Okinawa."

I think back to when we first arrived. Hayes and I were the only ones who didn't have our ID cards in our left breast pockets. We had packed them in our packs instead. Lewis began screaming at us as we ran back to the tent to dump our packs and scrambled to find the IDs. At first, I started shakily digging into the pack, praying I would stumble upon my driver's license near the top. Lewis pushed me aside, grabbing the pack and dumping it everywhere. Eventually we found what we were looking for. Lewis didn't stop screaming until everything he had dumped out was repacked and we were back in formation.

"Yes, Corporal," I mumble.

"What's that, bitch?"

"Yes, Corporal," I say louder.

"Keith, why are you such a fucking pussy?"

I look back up at him and wish I could say half the things I would like to say. But I know better. I would like to think I could kick his ass. He's short but definitely more aggressive than I am. Miller, on the other hand, is shaped like a pear. He can't even climb the rope bridge on the obstacle course, which has never stopped amazing me.

Even though I hate him more than anyone I've ever known, I can't help reminding myself I might be relying on him soon enough. He's in charge, after all. So I keep quiet and wait for Lewis to finish feeling better about himself at my expense.

"Don't make me give Hayes your spot as gunner. He did outshoot you, after all. Do your parents know they raised such a pussy, huh, Keith?"

"No, Corporal," I say. I look at him, hoping he dies soon and I'm there to see it happen.

The base where we are located is hardly a base at all. Massive dirt walls surround a cluster of tents. Our regiment's tank battalion arrives, along with more vehicles, adding substance to our position. It still feels like a sad joke, hardly something that could be considered ready to invade another country.

It is hard to miss the AAVs. They are amphibious assault vehicles, big metal boxes on tank treads with mounted fifty-caliber machine guns or automatic grenade launchers. Their sides are covered with metal sheets that have been folded like an accordion. When we leave Kuwait, it will either be on a plane heading home or over the Iraqi border inside these metal monsters.

We meet with one of the track commanders shortly after they arrive. He's a tall and imposing figure, speaking plainly about these vehicles and how they will apply to our lives if President Bush gives the call to invade. "See this steel room, gents? It can fit an entire squad, with enough supplies and water to last for weeks. It's designed to traverse all manners of habitat and environments. See the jagged metal sheets on the sides? Those are designed to let us take blasts from anything, from small arms to anti-air artillery, and keep moving. The idea is that when a round hits the side, it will impact at an angle. That deflects it so that it doesn't wind up penetrating the fuselage - or more importantly, any of us - in the process."

He waves at us to follow him to the back of the big wagon, and we walk around to where its back wall has dropped down as a sort of bridge into the guts of the machine. Walking up the ramp, he continues. "Inside, you'll sit on the benches on either side. Squeeze in and see how it works."

We file in and sit across from each other. Preston is looking at me from his seat on the other side. He smiles and winks, saying, "Oh, Keith, is this going to be fun?"

"Shut the fuck up, Preston," says Miller.

"All right, gentlemen," continues the track commander. "This is how it will look when you are riding with us. One of my men will be down here with a radio headset, while I or another of my section leaders will be positioned in the turret. We will be in communication with the other tracks carrying the rest of your unit, relaying commands on troop formations and battle strategies. Think of it this way: we transport you around, providing cover fire from our turrets, and in the event it gets heavy, we drop the back door and let you hard-chargers out the back to engage whatever enemy is out there. Any questions?"

"Yeah," says Luvs. "Where are our packs going to go?"

"That's yes, sir!" Moore cuts in.

"Calm down, Corporal. And don't interrupt again. Your packs will be strapped on the outside of the track with rope."

"Do we know what type of missions we will be going on?" Miller asks.

"No. I know as much as you gents. But I can tell you how this whole operation will look, if and when it kicks off. All of our tracks will be placed in rows facing the line of departure. When the phone call comes down from command, you will grab your packs and run out to your assigned track. Hopefully, after a lot of practice, you will be good enough at stringing your packs along the side of the track that you can be inside and ready for the unit to move across the border within a matter of minutes. To that end, we will be combining training for a while, until we are proficient at working together to coordinate how you will exit and enter the track if the need arises in a real combat scenario."

I learned, over time, that being attached to a line platoon of 0311s would never be fun. They had trained for months before squads from weapons platoon were assigned to them. They are a clique, and we are a smaller one. But unlike other elements attached to this platoon, ours is left alone. Our corporals treat us like shit, but given the opportunity, they treat others worse to prove a point. The platoon sergeant, Staff Sergeant Kelly, kept all of us in line.

One day, Kelly asks Miller to assemble his squad for the morning run and let the other elements attached to his platoon know that he would appreciate the same courtesy. We stand in a big circle with Kelly in the middle. He begins directing a mass stretching exercise before we form up into our two lines to begin a run around the base. As Kelly commands one stretch after another, Bryant is laughing with some of his friends. Kelly finishes with the exercises and gives us a little speech. "All right, gentle-men. We are here together as a complete fighting element for the duration of this deployment. Keep in mind, re-gardless of the officer in charge of you before or directly in charge of you now; everything comes back to myself and Lieutenant Oliver."

Bryant begins laughing louder. Kelly doesn't bother raising his voice. Instead, he runs at Bryant, getting in his face and yelling as he pushes Bryant back with his chest. Both men are rigid and staring insanely into each other's eyes as Kelly shouts and Bryant represses shame and rage at the same time.

When Kelly returns to the center of the circle, there's no more talking.

"We will have decisions to make in the next few months," he says, emphasizing the point by repeating it louder and clearer. "Decisions we will make, in moments we will be alone to make them, in a place no one can un-derstand and where no one will stand with us. If you are thinking about what it might be like to stand in front of a court of old men who will break down a mistake you made in three seconds over three hours of deliberation, under-stand this. I need you to make that decision. In the end, gentlemen, we all have to make the same crucial decision. And personally I - well, I would rather be tried by twelve than carried by six."

Walking away from the center of the circle, he takes the lead as the rest of us form up in two rows. He calls the platoon to attention. "I've made my decision, and if any of you haven't by now, you will soon be forced to. Now, fall out!"

We begin our jog down the packed dirt road past rows of tents as Humvees and an occasional seven-ton truck drive past and the morning breeze cuts unimpeded through the air. We yell cadence back and forth as other units go about their daily routine.

At night, I write home before the lights turn out. I listen to music on my CD player, playing certain songs over and over again. The Dixie Chicks song "Traveling Soldier" is secretly one of my favorites. I listen to the lyrics, imagining that there is a girl waiting for me to come home and wishing I was with her.

I dream of meeting her at a place like the restaurant on the San Diego Pier. In the dream, I am sitting in a booth and looking out at the beach as the sun sets and she approaches to take my order. She has curly hair, and she stands there in a summer dress, smiling despite the sun in her face. She is somehow happy to see me, as if we knew each other all along. We will always remember the moment everyone else became them and we became us.

She will sit across from me, and I won't tell her anything about the Marines or Kuwait. She will never know what a canteen is, or an ink stick. She won't know about barracks whores or bigoted jokes. Maybe I will meet her right when I get out, and I can simply tell her I have been in the Marines so she can be proud of me. I will tell her nothing else, so she won't have to be ashamed like I am now.

Some talk about banging strippers and getting shit-faced, but I bet they also fill their dreams with gentler moments. When I laugh along with their crude jokes, inside I always picture holding hands with this girl as we walk and talk together. I don't imagine much beyond these first moments when I know I'm not going to be alone anymore. We will be happy and in love, and she will miss me when I leave. She will wait for me to return. When I am with her, no one else will matter, and she will feel the same. We won't have sex for a long time. When we do, I won't mess it up like I keep messing up here.

We put all our gear on in the morning and patrol out to an area in the desert where we begin digging fighting holes. The sand disguises a strong, twisted sort of dirt and rock that doesn't give easily, and I weakly chip away at the packed ground in the heat as Lewis sits there. Hayes is next to me, chipping away at the other half of the hole. When we've dug three feet down, we are ordered to shift locations by fifty feet.

"Probably an order from some piece of shit officer," says Lewis.

We keep digging all day. That night, Hayes and I sit in the hole together, looking out at Kuwait City's lights in the dark.

"Hey, Keith, do you guys have malls in Minnesota where you take your girlfriends?"

"Oh yeah, bro. We got the biggest mall in the world. It's called The Mall of America. Well, actually, I think it's the second biggest. I heard there's something in Canada that covers more space."

"Is it like a Super Walmart?"

"Oh my God, man. It's way bigger."

"Can you show it to me someday?"

"Of course. You can visit me in Minnesota and I'll visit you in Texas, after this whole thing is over."

"I would like that. You're one of my best friends here."

"We're each other's only friends here, I think."

"Yeah, that's a good point." Hayes unwraps a piece of candy, taking his time in the dark to ensure it won't fall and be wasted in the sandy hole. "How many kids were in your class?" he asks, now with a candy-induced lisp.

"In high school? We started out with seven hundred, but I think it ended up dropping to about six hundred by the time we graduated."

"Wow. That's more kids than there were from K through twelve in my town." It sounds like he is attempting to put another candy in his mouth next to the first one. I squint my eyes and wait for the obnoxiously extended foil-wrinkling session to finish.

"Well," I say, adjusting behind my gun and looking over at his shadow under the helmet next to me, "I think you will like it in Minnesota. Except for how cold it gets in the winter. You should visit sometime in the summer so that you won't hate your life, and I'll visit Texas in the winter in case I can't handle the heat."

"Yeah, well. You won't have much of a problem with Texas weather after this shit."

"After this, I don't think I'm going outside ever again."

"Hey, Keith, do you think there's a bunch of hot girls over there?" Hayes says, nodding at the lights of the city.

"Yeah. I'm sure there are thousands of them."

"Do you think they would like us?"

"I don't know. Maybe some of us."

We fall out into formation for a run just as the sun begins to crack over the desert plain. It's cold and miserable. This time, instead of having one person stay and watch the guns, we bring them. We are wearing our flak jackets and day packs. The packs are small but weighted down with gear. Morgan appears and starts us out on a light trot away from the tents. He is carrying only a rifle. The pace picks up, and soon we are struggling to keep up with him. After twenty minutes, my body is screaming as I'm running as fast as I can. The 240 is hanging over my shoulder. My arm goes numb from trying to keep it balanced on my back. My consciousness becomes a singularly focused burning orb, only aware of the snaking jingle-jangle of gear and the jumbling shapes in front of me.

I look up and realize the person in front of me has fallen back. I'm forced to step out of formation and pass him. Soon, I'm right on top of Morgan, but my mind and body feel like they are going to give out. My fears amplify in these moments. I didn't come here to be weak. That can't be my story. Not here. Not now. If I fall out, Lewis and Miller will keep me up all night digging fighting holes. Or maybe they won't let me write home to my family. I can't keep fucking up.

Carrying this weight, my legs can't pump any faster. I slowly begin to fall behind Morgan. I turn to see who will pass me, but the entire section is spread out, trailing behind myself and a few others. We must look like a group of individuals running a race, though this is supposed to be a uniformed and compressed routine.

We turn back to the tents. This time, we stop in front of ours. Some of us are throwing up; others are spitting or swearing. Usually the runs are the worst when leadership gets involved. They always make us carry enough weight to make it impossible for us, even if it's easy for them. Slowing my breathing, I relax the muscles in my face. Miller and Lewis don't need to see any weakness if I can avoid it.

One of the 0311s in Second Platoon is Corporal Gibbs. He is easily the strongest and loudest. He is generally liked, or at least tolerated. When everyone is back from training in the evening, green sleeping bags cover every square inch of the ground inside the tents. It is important to pay attention to where Gibbs has sprawled. He lies in wait like a crocodile hiding just underwater, throwing out a hand to catch a passing Marine's leg. He drags him down slowly, amidst the laughter of everyone else in the tent and the victim's emphatic but completely useless threats and curses. Pulling the man down until he is completely wrapped up in a death clutch, Gibbs whispers incoherently in the hapless Marine's ear while making humping motions.

When we finish training in the evening, the chow hall line forms up in two rows that snake down from the tent where the cooks run the hot food service. They arrived weeks after we did. In line, Gibbs laughs and sings and talks to everyone. People know him, and he enjoys being seen.

The two Navy Corpsmen assigned to our platoon are terrifyingly immature for two grown men who are responsible for keeping everyone patched up and healthy. Jackson calls himself a warrior poet. He believes he is a dangerous killer and says as much to anyone that hasn't figured out he mostly lives in his own head. He walks around like he is about to invade an alien planet with his bag of Motrin, water, and IV packs. One day, he leaves a letter that he was writing home to his parents sitting on his pack. Some of us read it quietly in a corner, completely entertained by the valiant narrative he is carrying on. He talks about the different way of life he's living and refers to himself as a warrior with his gun. There isn't even a war yet, and he only carries a pistol.

The other Corpsman is Cox. He is a little more out of touch. Under religious preference on his dog tags, it reads "Shamanic Druid." I remembered reading about those in fantasy books. They seem to have abilities in kind to wizards, but it is his medical expertise we will rely on, mystical powers aside.

One night after training, Cox tells Preston and me about his ability to focus our chakras and realign our internal spiritual core. "Now, lay down on your stomachs," he commands.

Preston laughs and looks over at me to see if I am going to join him. We get down on the ground and Cox walks around us, pushing at different areas on our backs while telling us to breathe in certain ways. Wiping his brow as if he had just completed a dangerous medical procedure, Cox says, "All right. Now, it's important you don't move for at least ten minutes so that your chakras can realign, or you will experience a seriously metamorphic variance."

Preston starts to ask what a metamorphic variance looks like and is cut off. "Don't move! Do you think I was joking when I said that you could seriously hurt yourself if you don't stay completely immobile?"

"Get the fuck over here!" Lewis yells at us.

"Yes, Corporal!" we reply, jumping up and running over.

"Stay away from that creepy motherfucker, or you will be standing post for half the platoon tonight," he says.

We weren't allowed to take many personal items with us on deployment, so the little we had with us mattered. Some held onto little trinkets that reminded them of their wives or girlfriends. Others used religious symbols. It was rare for someone to not have something, however small, to remind him of home or to give him a little release from the mental anguish.

I had a piece of paper folded in my pocket. Before we left, I had picked up some of my favorite books, looking for little poems or phrases that would help when I felt alone. I wrote them down to carry with me. Whenever I had a moment to myself, I would pull out my paper to read the words, or just stare at them, trying to block out all the bullshit.

It sounds melodramatic, maybe. But in my own way, I was no better than Cox or Jackson. I was a lost child living in a fantasy land. I listened to my CD player, daydreaming about girls or spending time with my family. Every night was a relief. Every morning was a painful series of ritualistic moments, stranded with these strangers in this strange world. Dreaming of home was the worst thing to do when I had to wake up here.

At dawn, we roll our sleeping bags up and pack them away, inspecting our weapons if there is time. Then we fall out into the desert to run in the morning, train during the day, and at night roll out our sleeping mats and bags again. Training has evolved from random gun drills in the desert with our individual squads to full-blown platoon reenactments with the tracks. We practice loading and unloading, always hitting the sand in an arc around the vehicles as if we were ready to attack or defend. The AAVs are positioned near the line of departure in the long rows described by the track commander.

Each group of Marines assigned to the tracks conducts a very specific set of movements. First, we strap the packs to either side of the vehicle with ropes. Then we run around to the back of the track, piling in as quickly as possible. The whole time, a couple of Marines post up with their guns at the ready on either side of the track, providing covering fire. During moments of downtime, our section runs relentless gun drills.

Luvs and Preston hate each other and never really seem to get along. During one drill between the two teams in our squad, Hayes and I move a little faster than the other team. Lewis and Miller sit and jeer, letting them know they are failing. The drills continue like this for hours, until Luvs walks over to Preston and shoves him with his foot, saying, "Why are you so worthless?"

Stumbling to his feet, Preston grabs Luvs as they lock up, careening around in a tired, angry dance. Hayes runs forward, trying to break it up, as Lewis yells for them to stop fighting. Then Lewis runs over and pushes Luvs down, warning Preston to stay back and yelling at me for not helping Hayes break up the fight in the first place. I shrug my shoulders, too tired to care.

The entire unit has stopped to watch. Morgan demands that everyone show complete obedience towards his leaders regardless of their actions. As punishment for losing control, Preston is ordered to dig a fighting hole that night, and Luvs is ordered to dig it with him so that they can learn how to work in a team without resorting to physical violence. I imagine them sitting there quietly all night, two kids with nothing in common, forced to share an already too-small space. The next day, Miller tells Preston that Luvs will be team leader now since Preston should have controlled himself the day before and Luvs had at least chosen not to fight his gunner in front of the entire company.

Morgan shows up one day to conduct a brief and to check up on his squads who are attached to the line platoons. We can tell the possibility of invading Iraq is becoming closer to a reality. Morgan assures us that our Commander in Chief didn't sign a big fucking check to cart our sorry asses out here for nothing. The plan, according to the generals and commanders in charge of this whole operation should we invade, is set in place.

Falling out one morning, we report to a full battalion formation. After lining up in massive rows in front of a large section of tents, we finish the formalities and are told to fall in around the battalion commander. Those in front sit and those a little further back kneel down. The rest of us stand in back. Like a giant funnel of desert camouflage, peppered with the dots of our upward-turned gun barrels, we wait to hear our future.

"Oohrah, Marines!" begins Rhodes.

A chorus of 'yut yuts' and 'oohrahs' erupts in response to his greeting.

"It's come down to one phone call. We are one moment away from invading Iraq. Make no mistake, it will happen, and it will happen soon. Our unit did very well in training back in the States, and since we have illuminated ourselves as the best battalion in Seventh Marines Regiment we will be the tip of the spear in our offensive against Saddam's army.

We will move up, securing each town on the way to Baghdad, securing every bridge and major roadway along the most direct path to the city. The Army will push through the desert on the western side of the country and invade Baghdad from the west, while we will invade from the south. We take Baghdad; we win the war. Stay strong and remember our credo: we will adapt and overcome. Semper Fideles, Marines."

10

TANK BATTALION

"We have a hospital down here that was built for all the guys with spinal injuries and head trauma. I walked in there and saw a mother pushing her son around on a stretcher. He was dressed normally, but he wasn't home in the head. He wasn't there anymore. He was just alive. And I stood there and watched her while we were waiting for an elevator, and I looked at him, and I looked at his sad, sad, sad, sad, sad, mother, and I cried. Right there in fucking front of everybody. I just broke down and cried. She saw me standing there and tried to comfort me. Right there in the fucking hospital. I couldn't hold it back. I was crying before I realized it. Because he had brain trauma. Because he was gone."

"Wow, that's incredible."

"It was incredible. It fucked me up for a while. It still bothers me. I had to go to that hospital again a week ago because that's where they hand out blood pressure machines to guys like me who need their blood pressure monitored all the time. There were guys there who were learning to use a wheel chair or how to use a new leg. That's when everything really hits home. Sitting here, I can still see that guy as if it was yesterday, but it was a couple of years ago. And then I can't even talk you into filing a claim or going into the Vet Center."

"I've made it to thirty-one on my own. I'm sure I'll be fine from here."

"I'm sixty-three. If I had gone in the seventies and gotten some treatment, I'm not sure where I would be. But I wouldn't be in the position I'm in now. Maybe I would've lived a normal life without the anger. See, I'm not angry anymore. It took me accepting the fact that I did have PTSD and that it was me, not everyone else. When I did that, I was able to start coping with life on a different level. It was hard for me. It was hard to go. But I'm glad I did. I'm glad I went to the Vet Center for two years and actually talked to a combat vet who knew what the fuck I was talking about. That was the biggest thing, talking to a bona fide grunt. 101st airborne. He was a lieutenant down by the DMZ. A team leader. He knew what the fuck I was talking about."

■ ■ ■

The universal sign of a gas attack is simple. It starts with putting your hands over your head and pumping your arms up and down in a flexing motion while yelling, "Gas!

Gas! Gas!" This is practiced occasionally. When executed by even a single person, it spreads immediately along the line of sight to everyone who sees the motion being performed, sending them scrambling back to their respective tents to throw on airtight suits and masks and wait. For an entire unit to survive a deadly chemical agent, they need a process that turns thousands of individuals into a single cohesive organism, like a chameleon changing the color of its scales to match its environment. As each scale changes color, so too do thousands of Marines shift from desert camouflage to tricolor green suits with masks in minutes. When someone decides nothing has happened or the drill is complete, word is passed around that it is over. We all go back to our training evolutions.

I have to imagine that some colonel must look back fondly on the particular time of the week when he would find himself finishing his lunch in one of the tents at Camp Ripper.

An enlisted Marine waiting nearby clears his throat. "Do you want me to do it this time, sir?"

Setting down his favorite plastic-wrapped meal, he finishes the food in his mouth and shakes his head. "No, the honor is all mine. Hell, this is the most fun I'll have all day."

"Will you be calling a meeting with the company commanders this time, or just doing it the old-fashioned way?"

"When is it more fun to do things any way besides the old-fashioned way?"

He walks toward one of the walls of the tent, throws the flap back and steps out into the warm pulsing desert, squinting to adjust to a broader spectrum of light and movement. Looking around, he begins to smile at what he sees. His favorite part isn't the act, but the moments before the act. It's as if he can predict the future for every Marine in sight. He feels omniscient. Stretching his arms up, he yawns, shutting his eyes and tilting his head up towards the warm glow of the sun.

Bringing each hand down towards his shoulders, he keeps his elbows pointed out parallel to the ground, like a strongman would display his biceps. With his eyes still closed, he pumps his fists up and down. Moments into the movement, his smile goes from a closed-mouth smirk to a shit-eating grin. Yells of, "Gas! Gas! Gas!" echo in a circle, expanding rapidly outward from the point where he stands.

One day, someone starts the gas attack signal while we are in the chow hall line. Command never plans the drills during chow. The signal ripples hundreds of meters down the two lines of Marines that snake away from the chow hall tent. Each man stops talking and stands straight, echoing the closed-fisted flexing movement like a bird about to take flight. The line disintegrates as Marines scatter back to their tents to don suits, swearing and repeating the symbol, pissed off at missing a cherished hot meal but unable to stop the mechanical process. Someone probably started it as a joke, creating an easy work day for the cooks.

I am sitting in my tent with sixty other Marines and fighting the urge to drift off to sleep. It's not often we get downtime, even if it involves sitting in a tent in full MOPP gear. While propped up against my pack, gun in my lap, I'm able to doze without anyone noticing that my eyes are closed inside the mask. Every time I start to drift off, though, I wake up gasping for air. Eventually I realize that the mask only works if I'm able to force air through its filter mechanism, which isn't possible when I fall asleep and my breathing slows.

Lewis walks over and hits me in the helmet. "Keith, get up and get your shit off! The fake-ass gas attack is over and we have a brief in thirty minutes. Looks like we get to find out where and how you will pussy out in combat."

I remove my helmet and peel off the mask. Hayes has somehow managed to fall asleep, so I nudge him with my boot until he sluggishly begins removing his gear. "Hey, Hayes. We have a brief now."

"Okay, Keith. Oh – Keith, do you have your writing gear?"

"Yeah, do you have yours?"

"Of course."

"Hayes, I'm in charge, okay? Don't check if I have my gear. That's my job with you. I'm sorry you aren't the gunner, but don't push it, man."

"Okay, Keith. Don't keep forgetting your gear and I won't have to."

Luckily, Lewis and Miller haven't heard Hayes. Lewis reminds me daily that, if Hayes has to keep reminding me to bring my notepad, I'm going to get stuck carrying the bag of gun parts into combat. Fuck that. I don't want to give up the gun. But nothing seems to stay consistent in our squad. Preston just lost his spot as team leader to Luvs after their fight. If Hayes keeps showing me up with these little moments of superiority, it's only a matter of time before I'm running around like a jackass with the ammo bag myself.

The brief is short and to the point. Someone from battalion command has set up dry-erase boards with maps and bullet points. He waits until everyone from the two platoons piles into the tent and finds a place to sit before he begins.

"All right. It looks like we have about half of Lima Company in the room, and the other half is being briefed in the next tent over. We now know our mission. We will be broken off to work with Tank Battalion. While Kilo, India, and Weapons Company will be fighting Iraq's mobile infantry elements, Lima will be following the tank battalion into the showdown with Saddam's tank-mechanized units."

He drones on about strategies and formations. He talks about how we will be fighting primarily at night since the enemy doesn't have night vision capabilities at all and it will give us a clear advantage. I'm glad we get a tank army with us. Maybe this means the tip of the spear will involve 200 angry M1A1 Abrams.

"When Tank Battalion hits, they will hit hard and fast. Lima will act as a sweeper team, running behind the main assault to cut off resupply lines, flanking elements, or scattered pockets of resistance. This is the first time in the history of war that those actually fighting it will be given all of the information available. You should feel lucky. You know what the president knows. So, make no mistake, if you tell anyone from back home about our strategy for the invasion, you will be charged for disobeying a direct order and possibly for treason."

We wake up the next morning and run, then grab the guns from the tent and head out to the desert for gun drills. Lewis and Miller turn it into a competition between their teams and hours go by, the six of us going through the motions over and over again. Finally, Hayes and I walk back to the tents and stop at the line of stifling plastic bathroom stalls. Using them in the middle of the day is hell. You walk in clean and leave sixty seconds later, completely drenched in sweat.

Command orders us to make sure we don't leave any letters from our families in there, because some of the local employees on base are faced with real incentive to sell the info to insurgents who could use it to hurt our families. One day, a Marine shows up at my tent with a picture of my family. He is laughing because I left a letter, a picture of my family, and an envelope with their home address in the stall.

Later on, Lewis has something to say about that. "You okay with getting your family killed, Keith? You sure seem like the type who'd be okay with the people he cares about dying from a bomb in the mail."

I think about Lewis's words now, and how horrified and ashamed I was that day. Then I remember the night someone killed himself inside one of the stalls as I stood outside.

I heard the shots, a three-round burst. I was standing with another Marine and didn't move when it happened. The sound suddenly froze us in place. The guy looked at me, but I had already made up my mind to do nothing. Whatever had happened had nothing to do with me.

The other Marine turned and opened the door, looking inside the shitter. When his face reappeared and he ran off, I was glad it had been him and not me. Soon, a crane appeared. A Marine produced tape and ran around the plastic stall several times, taping the door firmly shut. Then the stall was picked up by the machine and carried off somewhere. I've always wondered where they took it. No one ever said a word, as if it never happened.

The constant pressure pushed some guys pretty far. I can't say for sure what that kid was going through before he killed himself. I can only guess.

Each night tantalizes him with the promise of an evening of peace, a peace that exists only in the glow of light spilling from the tent flap as Marines go in and out. The feeling grows as he plods towards the tent. He finally reaches it and pushes back the flap to look inside.

"Close that fucking thing!" someone yells, sick of cleaning sand out of his rifle. Others mutter in agreement or yell out in hilarity as someone runs by wearing nothing but a sock on his hard-on.

The kid finds his pack and lays down his rifle, unstrapping straps and fumbling with the gear until his sleeping bag is stretched over a thin green mat. He had cleaned the gun before he went to use the head, but already a fresh coat of dust clings to the excess oil leaking from the places where the metal pieces meet. Too much is just as bad as not enough, out here. He leans against his pack and cleans it again, nodding as he makes eye contact with some and avoiding the eyes of the rest.

The platoon sergeant returns from an evening briefing and disappears behind a neatly stacked wall of boxes of rations. Here, privacy is something earned only through seniority.

Mail call is announced each night. Whispers from their letters comfort and torture him. *We miss you so much. We love you and can't wait to see you.* If they could make it better, they would. They call him a hero. *Keep your head down and remember God and stay strong.* He cringes at that line. The only thing he prays for these days is a break from gun drills, humps, fighting holes, and the assholes he doesn't care to see anymore. Why couldn't he have imagined that it would be like this before it was too late? But that kind of individual thoughts is what gets people killed. He has to block them out. Fade into the role.

The pressure burns worse when he thinks about home. Maybe if he stops fucking up, he can get past this place and never talk about it again. Never tell anyone how scared he was, that they were right when they told him not to go in the first place. He is a Marine now, someone with less of an excuse for things like fear, weakness, and stupidity than ever before. The words of the letters remind him that home is there waiting and his family is proud of him. They make him believe that tonight will be okay, even though some day soon may not. They make him want to make it through this.

Maybe that night he receives a letter from his girl, opening it with relief and excitement. Maybe he finds a few words, awkwardly reorganizing the dreams he harbored and the hope he had been holding onto about what happens if he survives and makes it home. Instead of being surrounded by a wife and two or three kids someday, his girl will be gone. She can't wait any longer. She's moving to the next town over with another man.

Maybe, once the letter is opened and read, he looks up and out of the tent and changes a bit inside. Suddenly, there is no past or future surrounding him, and the present isn't even remotely the same. Getting up with his rifle slung across his chest, he walks to the tent flap. He stops to let a few words out, the last he has inside him, communicating to the Marine who is watching the gear or maybe to his team leader that he will be back in a moment.

I imagine his face is relaxed and his tone steadier than it has been since he left his home. All the doubt is gone, leaving him at peace. His team leader looks up from cleaning his rifle, surprised, not remembering a time this guy hasn't sounded burdened or confused. He mistakes the sense of peace for a sign of strength, not for what it really is. This man is already walking in the past. He is a ghost without a future, a kid without much time left in the memories of his friends and family as someone to miss or love or hate, to think of in a solid emotional present tense.

He isn't calm, but he knows that the weight of everything he has been facing is gone. He isn't exactly at peace, but he knows he doesn't have to worry about being away from everyone he loves anymore, in this horrible place where people treat him like a coward. He is supposed to be a warrior. Maybe that is what this moment feels like, in a way.

Now his pain is going to stop. Sitting in the john, he eases the gun off his shoulder and stares down the barrel. He puts the gun on burst with a couple of clicks and uses one hand to steady the end of the rifle between his clenched teeth. He takes in the smell of the blue shit solution in a stuffy box that has become all too familiar over the past six months. The taste of cleaning solvent from the gun's lightly oiled barrel gradually replaces the blue-shit smell, and he squints his eyes shut, pushing both out with the memories of smells from home.

He reaches down with his other hand to gently push the trigger. As he applies that tiny pressure, every version of him and the people he would have touched is suddenly and completely erased.

Then I am standing outside the stall, blinking, and wondering who the poor bastard was that isn't anymore.

Pressure is constant here. We are told that the enemy is training day and night. They are a little faster than us and hungrier for a fight. They won't back down or run, and while we sleep, they train. While we train, they train harder. We can only win if we become all around better at our jobs. We need to become better at being Marines, better men.

We run gun drills, and I hit the sand and sight in with the gun pressed firmly into my shoulder. I have no idea how any of this is going to make me capable of handling business in an actual combat situation, but it's what I have to do to get back to the tent and write home, then lose consciousness for a few hours. I bet that's why that Marine did what he did. Whatever he read in that letter or conclusion he drew inside his mind, he knew that if he went to sleep that night, he would have to wake up in this place.

At night, we patrol with our night vision goggles hanging off our helmets, dropping the lenses down over our eyes to see the environment in lighter shades of green. People practice moving around in the dark, using only the enhanced lighting from the lower spectrum made visible by infrared. I'm carrying the night sights for my machine gun in my hand as well, looking through them to gauge what kind of world I will see through this type of technology. While the infrared lens shows everything in greens picked up from low light, the thermals identify heat signatures. They visualize heat in more than one form. I can choose if I want the heat from living things and machines to turn up as black or as white. Clicking back and forth, I decide I am more comfortable with the white-hot signature.

One day, I'm running around base with Hayes, slamming open doors on the newly installed shower rooms. We run inside as Marines are shaving or showering, making sure to check underneath everything. I can't believe I've lost my load-bearing vest. My pistol, grenades, ammunition, and who knows what else are all strapped to it.

Things had been going well, too. I had started to gain a little confidence in training, while managing to fly under the radar for once, effectively avoiding abuse from Lewis or Miller. But when the showers were finally installed as the base grew, I finally lapsed back into the daydreaming state that had been known to rob me of common-sense decision-making skills. I did it to myself. Which is why I had laid out all my gear during a routine inspection, confident nothing was out of place or missing.

As Lewis walked past in a somewhat positive mood, he stopped and looked at my gear, slightly concerned. "Keith, where's your LBV and pistol?"

Panicking, I look everything over and blurt out, "I think I left it in the showers!"

"Which fucking showers?"

"I have no idea. They all look the same!"

"Well you better fucking find it right now! Take Hayes, and don't come back until you have it! No, fuck that! You better be back with it in five minutes, before Moore comes by and wonders why one of his fucking gunners can't keep his shit together for a routine inspection!"

Moments later, Hayes and I have made a full circle of the immediate area and are standing behind one of the tents, arguing about what we might have missed the first time around.

"Keith, do you think we missed one?"

"I have no fucking idea."

"Maybe we should go back and tell Lewis we tried. It will eventually turn up."

"Yeah. Just in time for you to strap on the pistol, take my gun, and give me the ammo bag."

"Keith, you're the one who lost your pistol, man. Don't get mad at me. I'm just trying to help," says Hayes.

Hayes decides to run in the direction of another section's shower area. He says, "Let's try the one over to the west. I think today we went there because we decided the other one was always more packed." He points at a white shower box in the distance as the sun drops further behind the berm, giving us maybe another ten minutes or so of unimpeded sight.

"Fuck, man. Okay, let's go," I say, as Hayes starts running and I begin to follow. "Of course," I yell up to him as we trot past rows of tents and smoking areas, "It would be a lot easier if my NVGs weren't strapped to my goddamn vest that we can't find!"

Getting to a shower box, we burst through the door, right in front of a bunch of senior Marines who clearly are annoyed by our presence. Apologizing and calling them by their ranks as much as possible, we look under the sinks. Eventually, Hayes yells me over as he pulls out a vest that no one around him is claiming. Pushing past a couple of people as they step out of the showers, I sigh with relief and hug Hayes.

"You did it, man. Thanks. If I've got to carry your ammo bag, at least it's because I deserve it at this point."

"No problem, Keith. At least we found it."

That night I follow Lewis and Miller out to an empty desert area on the base. We meet up with Green and Pickett, who have Foster and Fisher face down in the sand. The corporals are laughing while stepping on them in places. Lewis orders me down on the ground next to Foster and Fisher. Lying there, I feel the back of my head getting stepped on, and I squint my eyes shut while my face is ground into the sand. Lewis's boot jerks up and down.

"So, you don't want to learn from losing your driver's license; you have to go and lose your LBV and pistol? Good, Keith. I'm glad you've established how fucking retarded you are, bitch."

Walking behind me, Miller kicks at my legs. "Spread 'em, bitch," he says, as he lightly steps on my balls. I start to pull up off the ground, and Lewis kicks me in the side. "Did anyone fucking tell you to move?"

"No, Corporal."

Pickett and Green are giving Fisher and Foster similar treatment. Because we don't react as much as we used to, or maybe because this kind of game has become par for the familiar and monotonous course, their fun ends more quickly than usual and we return to the tents for the night. Green stalks around, laughing. "I love this shit, gents!" He says he's happy to be here. At least, he does until he winds up with a hernia and leaves for Kuwait before the invasion even starts, passing down his team leader spot to Flynn while Foster becomes the gunner.

Later that night I write home to Mom, not mentioning how ashamed I feel. I almost have to force myself to write to her. It's the last thing I want to do, but I know how much it means to her when she receives my letters. I write to my dad and Aunt Mary. I write home to ensure they will write back. Hearing about what is going on there matters more than anything here.

Someone in the tent one night is telling a story. Earlier that evening, he had been training with Tank Battalion out by the Kuwait and Iraq border.

"We know the Iraqi army has assembled somewhere across the border, right? Last night, India was practicing combat formations and firing at targets in the distance. Apparently, they saw movement further out across the border. When they looked through their optics, they saw that the Iraqi army was waving white flags in the air. Can you believe that?"

11

THE FIRST SERGEANT CHALLENGE

"You know, I heard of this one girl who shows up to hospitals and hangs out with vets to help them get out of their heads. I sold a phone at work to a guy who's friends with her. One time, there was this vet who was hospitalized because he was found in his home, starving himself. I guess he just sat in his house and avoided people and quit eating altogether. At the hospital, he didn't talk to anyone or let them help him. But she got through to him. After she started visiting him, he started letting the doctors and nurses treat him. He opened up and got a lot better, at least how this guy was telling it."

"How did she pull that off?"

"She showed up in her lingerie."

"That's amazing! What an amazing person. She made that guy feel normal."

"It's not like a requirement someone should start putting on nurses, but I agree. Just to exist in that moment makes her an amazing human being. I guess the hospital staff wouldn't let her in at first. Can you imagine how that conversation must have gone down? The Doctor would say, 'Excuse me, miss, but you can't take your clothes off in front of a patient like that.' Then she would reply, 'Really? So it's decent to send this guy to his death, but completely unacceptable to show him my tits?'"

"Man, you crack me up, nephew."

■ ■ ■

Our squad kneels in a half circle, somewhere away from the tents, the makeshift roads, and the portable bathroom stalls. We are out of sight where we can run a few gun drills in peace. Miller is detailing some of the basic maneuvers involving our gun teams and the 0311s. He uses his finger in the sand, drawing lines for roads and houses, and more lines to indicate where we will run or stack up against walls and where Second Platoon should theoretically maneuver.

"This is where we need to be very careful. When shit goes down, there's no guarantee the worthless 0311s won't run in front of our positions and completely ruin our fields of fire. Hey, Hayes! Fucking listen! You can fuck with your chin strap later."

"Yes, Corporal," says Hayes.

"Keith, I'm going to ask you a question." Miller turns to me, anger making his expression even more pouty than usual. "And when you answer, if it's not correct, expect to spend the rest of the night standing post even if someone else in the squad or Second Platoon is already doing it."

"Yes, Corporal," I say, nodding.

"How heavy is the M240G?"

"24.2 pounds, Corporal."

"Keith! Now that you've answered a question correctly for once, do you feel like you are on my level? Do you think you know what it's like to be on a real deployment? Don't forget; you don't rate shit until you've done a full tour in Okinawa like Lewis and me."

"And that goes for the rest of you pussies, too," adds Lewis.

"Okay, listen up," Miller says. "Our entire company will be competing as four-man teams in a massive obstacle course run. From the starting point, there will be makeshift stations spread out along the line of communication poles into Kuwait City. The poles run about a football field apart for fifty miles between here and town. Obviously, the race won't cover that entire distance, but you get the point. At each station, there will be a Marine with a specific team-building task that will have to be adequately completed before you can move on. We can't let the 11s show us up, so the machine gun teams better place high. Or at least we'd better not fall back on the list because of any of you bitches, got it?"

We all nod or give him the good old, "Aye, Corporal."

"Whichever team wins gets to go on a day trip back to a base camp in the rear. You know, where there are fast food and phone centers and shit," says Miller.

The teams are picked. A few are considered superstar teams and are placed in the front with the idea that the most capable teams should go first to avoid a pile-up at any of the stations. Moore and a few of his friends are considered one of the dream teams in our company. The one that includes both Bryant and Franklin is another. On the opposite end of the spectrum, Lewis, Luvs, Hayes, and I are laughed at as a team that is never going to win. It makes sense. We are capable, but average in height at most and thin, instead of tall and athletic. None of us have ever scored anywhere near some of the others on the physical training tests, and we never will.

We stand in our teams and wait for the Marines running the race to signal to us that it is our turn to start. Each team begins, and its start time is recorded as the little groups take off to the first telephone pole. In the distance, a Marine stands at each pole, waiting to give instructions and approve the team's performance before allowing them to run to the next station.

The fastest teams leave, and now it's down to midlevel teams. When it is our turn, we stand in line, waiting for the signal to take off. Lewis looks at us, saying, "You better give everything to this, fuckers. I'm not finishing last because people want to stack teams with talent. If any of you slow down or quit, you'll feel it from me later."

The Marine with the stopwatch yells, "Go!" We take off. The sun beats down, and the sand is soft as we awkwardly run to the first post and are told to drop down for team pushups. Once we complete them, we are told to run again. We careen forward in a line, Lewis in the lead. This is going to be a long run, and Lewis isn't pacing himself. He's running as hard as he can. We hit the next station quicker than we did the first.

This station requires two Marines to carry the other two for a hundred meters, then switch and be carried back to the station. We do this as quickly as possible. Lewis finishes first and drops Luvs, turning to yell at me as I struggle to haul Hayes back to the post. We finish the exercise and realize that this time we can see the team that started just before us. They are far ahead, but still running between this station and the next.

"Let's get those motherfuckers now!" Lewis yells as we run raggedly along with him. "Let's fucking go! Get a fucking move on!"

The little tan forms in the distance begin to grow from shimmering hangnails to a line of four full-sized Marines with their heads down, moving forward at a jog. "Let's go, motherfuckers," yells Lewis.

We pass them, and they realize what is happening only when they look up. It's too late for them to stop us. "Fuck!" one of them shrieks.

We complete the next task before the other team. Lewis points at yet another group in the distance, saying, "Let's get those motherfuckers!"

We run harder and pass more groups as they curse and try to speed up, but each time we pass one and scramble to the next station we are running less efficiently. Our bodies struggle to perform. Lewis screams at whoever falls behind to suffer and catch up now or suffer more when it's done.

We close in on another team, and Lewis says, "Holy shit! That's Moore's team!" We run as fast as we can but fail to catch them.

"Hey, guys," says Moore tauntingly. "You thought you could catch us, huh?"

For once, Lewis doesn't say anything. Our section leader and his handpicked team finish up at the station and run off like a bunch of gazelles towards the final station.

"We better catch those motherfuckers!" Lewis says, as we crabwalk towards a marker in the distance and then back before careening towards the last station. We are handed a sandbag that we carry in turns as we run towards the finish line in the distance. A group of the top teams is already there, walking off the pain of the event.

My turn to carry the sandbag comes. I can feel my head start to tingle with dehydration, and a panicky sort of nausea kicks in. I'm not sure I can take this pace any longer, but finishing strong is important. We might not win, but finishing a couple of seconds behind anyone else's time will drive Lewis into a rage.

We cross the line in the sand and finally slow down, then stop. We walk in a circle with our hands over our heads. Hayes stops to throw up. He gets yelled at to move away from where we and the other Marines are walking off the run.

An hour later, all the teams have finished the race. When it's over and the scores are posted, Miller approaches us. "Holy shit! Good job, guys. You beat everyone else in the company! I guess you get the free weekend, you lucky motherfuckers. Looks like three of the machine gun teams finished in the top ten, and the rest were pretty damn close. We showed those 11s who stands where!"

Lewis actually cracks a smile. Laughing, he says, "And they all hated on us. Shows those motherfuckers right."

Later, Pickett calls me over to where he is sitting in the opening of a tent flap. "Good job, Keith. You represented our section well today."

"Thanks, Corporal," I say awkwardly, not sure how to react to a compliment from someone who looks for every chance to pick us apart.

Shaking his head at the lack of strength in my response, Pickett says quietly, "How can you do something like that and still be such a giant fucking vagina? Huh, Keith?"

"I don't know, Corporal," I reply. He feigns distraction and returns to looking down at the rifle he's cleaning. "Go away," he says without looking up again.

The next day, we get the call to invade Iraq. Running to the track with our gear, we throw our packs down in neat rows in front of the armored assault vehicles. Marines are yelling and milling about their respective tracks, which are lined up in tight formation. Soon, we are boarding our track. We sit in silence as the gate shuts, closing us in.

An army Humvee with giant speakers begins playing music that we can hear through the metal walls around us. Its volume is intended to command enemy soldiers to surrender or be shot with rounds dipped in pigs' blood, or to warn civilians to leave areas of contention, but now the Drowning Pool song "Let the Bodies Hit the Floor" reverberates through the air. We slam the butts of our guns into the metal floor below us in unison to the beat, staring across at each other in a frantic wide-eyed delirium. We are going to war. Right now. There is no past or future until it is over.

The music ends and we sit in silence as the vehicle moves up and down, waiting.

JINGLE BELLS, MORTAR SHELLS, CHARLIE'S IN THE GRASS

"It's hard for me to express just how fucking miserable it was in that fucking hangar. It was corrugated steel on three sides and the top. I can't even remember if it had a concrete floor or not. It may have had a concrete floor, but the whole thing seemed like dirt to me. It was big, and it was hot. We were close to the equator there, so it was all tropical, and it was hotter than fuck and more humid than you can imagine. I had to get out of there. And, like I said, everyone treated each other like assholes. It was a real unfriendly fucking building to be in. To me, it seemed like everyone was always yelling at one another. I couldn't get my arms around it. That's why I had to get out of it. I was going nuts there. You didn't come out of that hangar without being covered in dirt and oil every day. When I finally got into a helicopter, I breathed a big sigh of relief."

■ ■ ■

After only six weeks, sooner than I had dared to dream, I get reassigned to Second Platoon; a helicopter platoon. I am finally out. The first day, I report to my new command.

They size me up, asking probing questions and looking for weakness, ignorance, or some sort of authority complex. The crew chief is big, mean, and has a huge mustache. He easily commands my full attention.

"You're going to be the door gunner."

"Yes, sir."

"Right now, we are assigned to ash and trash duty, bringing shit like rations and mail to the base. When we go up, learn what you can, because we will be going on combat missions soon enough. You will be sitting behind me on the M60, keeping the fucking dinks off our back. Is that going to be a fucking problem, boy?"

"No, sir."

"Well, anyways, we'll see soon enough," he says, sounding unconvinced but unconcerned.

My new home with Second Platoon is a wooden building, slat-sided and screened in, with sand bags stacked chest high around it. It comes with hooch maids. They are local Vietnamese women who keep the place clean. Our hooch maid is named Hoa, which sounds like "wah." She seems old to me, even though she is only thirty, but she is sweet and kind. She wears black silk pajama bottoms, thong sandals, gray and white blouses, and a round, coned hat. Her hair is always done up nice.

She has been working with the Americans for ten years and seems to understand us, even with all of our anger towards her country. She seems like more of an older sister than an employee to me, and we talk sometimes. I find out that she fell in love with one of the GIs who was stationed here. They had a baby together. When his tour ended, he left for home and never came back.

The first time I am taken up in one of the hueys, it's a test to see if I can handle the job. Either I will sit in the back on the gun with my mouth shut and shoot when ordered, or this won't be a place for me.

We climb into the helicopter, and I watch the pilots strap themselves into the front. I strap myself in behind them. They are flicking switches, turning knobs, checking dials. The rotors above begin spinning and pulling slightly. Suddenly, we are in the air, and the ground disappears. We are now in a different physical state. I'm part of it, somehow, but it feels like it's in the mindless way that an arm is part of a body.

The pilot drops the chopper down, and we appear to be careening towards the tree line. We abruptly lift just in time. Over and over, the pilots float us up and down, getting us as close to the ground as they can without dying. They are giving me the sense that yes, this is their world.

For me to survive in it, I will need to trust them and do what they say and not show fear.

Vietnam is a very beautiful country from the air. From a thousand feet up, the rice paddies are green and filled with water. Nui Ba Den, the mountain near our base, is huge. Flying by it is breathtaking. That first day, I have no idea that the mountain is honeycombed with tunnels full of enemy troops. To me it is nothing more than a gigantic rock covered with trees.

"Go ahead and shoot at shit! Get the feel of the gun!" The officer pilot yells to me over his shoulder as he flexes his wrist, pulling or pushing on the stick. We move and dip in motions completely unlike anything I've ever experienced in my life.

The M60 sits on a mounted swivel, angled towards the ground along the outside of the fuselage. I shot one during my helicopter mechanic training at Fort Rucker, but that only lasted a minute or so before I had to jump out of the seat and hand it off to another trainee. This is all new and completely different.

I aim at different clusters of trees, spraying them with rounds as the belt of ammo disappears in a rush, brass falling around my feet. The huey circles and weaves in sweeping motions above the forest. I try controlling the gun's bursts, but I seem to hit in sporadic patterns. I try to adjust, as if the helicopter and the gun are part of me, and learn what to expect. I let my eyes float and my muscles react to the huey's unfamiliar motion.

This feels good, in spite of the strangeness of it all. And it's cooler up here above the trees. I think to myself that now I've found a job I can live with. Without warning, the pilot pulls up. We are rushing toward the sun; nose pointed directly at the sky. A thousand yards disappear. The huey groans and rattles as it attempts to climb further. There is a sickening moment of impossible vertigo as the chopper suddenly shudders and stalls. We are dropping rapidly nose first, and my life flashes before my eyes as I look back at the officer pilots, realizing they are looking at me and laughing hysterically at my complete confusion and terror. All of my organs feel like they just floated up to my mouth and then fell like dice down to my feet.

As we gain downward speed, we level off and return to a stable state of forward motion. Later, I learn that this maneuver is called the hammerhead stall. I have passed my one and only test for the job. Eventually, I even begin to enjoy the hammerhead stall.

We approach Tay Ninh and finally land back where we started. I dislodge the gun and take it with me to the gun shack. Working with the gun means that it's my job to clean it as well. I haven't even held an M60 until this flight. I know there's a way to open these things up, but I have no idea what it is.

I am standing at a large metal tub filled with diesel oil, wondering what to do first, when the door opens and one of the veteran gunners in my platoon comes in. He is carrying two M60s, holding the buttstocks and letting the handguards rest on either shoulder. He tells me to move and I get out of his way. Without saying another word, he begins to take apart one of the guns. I stand off to the side and watch closely.

He asks me if I know what the fuck I am doing. I am honest and tell him that I don't have any idea how to take it apart and clean it. He lets me watch him clean his guns, and then helps me clean mine.

Missions blur together as I lose track of the days, a preferable state of being to finding myself stuck in the mechanic bay. We fly from point A to point B, picking something up or delivering something to someone. We fly to the artillery base where we drop off food, picking up mail and returning only to turn around and drop off supplies somewhere else in the jungle. One day, we lose one of our own as the team of choppers is departing the landing zone. He is shot from the ground by a fifty caliber enemy round that punches through his chest, exploding out his shoulder and killing him instantly. Command reorganizes the rank structure while we're still in the air, making me the new crew chief.

I get back to the base that day, not knowing what to do. I sit there, thinking about the bullet holes that dented the huey that returned carrying the dead soldier. I realize that up to this point I have been shooting when I am told, but at random targets instead of the ones that I was advised to engage. It's not that there are enemy soldiers I am actively choosing not to shoot, but the truth is that I don't have the intent to kill guiding my actions. Now, I realize that going through the motions might not be enough to protect myself and the others on board. Our flights have increasingly come under enemy fire. Some people have gotten shot, and the hits are close enough for shrapnel to cut people.

My first full day as a crew chief begins by dropping infantry soldiers into a landing zone. We pick up troops at one location. When we begin to land at the other, the pilots give the order to shoot for suppression. I lean out as far as I can, lighting up the treeline. I sweep the gun in a slow, steady motion as evenly as possible, putting as much lead as I can between the departing soldiers and whatever waits for them in the dark, forested nothingness.

I walk the tracers into the treeline. The infantrymen we are carrying appear as green forms in my peripherals, yelling and dropping down into the grass. I keep sweeping the treeline in unison with other gunners from the other hueys as we land in a tight jagged circle.

Then we pull away, back into combat formation in the air, above everything. We're a world away now, maneuvering low when possible to avoid any unneeded harassment. Sometimes we stay high to avoid small arms fire or pick spaces back and forth between ravines connecting neighboring mountainsides.

Every morning we awake before dawn. I either wake up to my wind-up alarm or am awakened by someone who sees me not getting my ass out of bed. The very first thing we do is get dressed. Not even a good morning piss is allowed before you get your boots on. The next step is taking a leak. Then, it's off to the mess hall for coffee and

C-rations. We eat powdered eggs and haul our equipment to the flight line. It is a mechanical routine.

By the time it's full daylight, the pilots are here, and the rotor blades are untied and ready for them to turn the chopper on and get us out of there. I rarely know where we are headed until we get airborne. We're never briefed much on the ground, but I don't care. I am along for the ride, for the thrill of it all, and to stay off the ground where the weather just sucks.

The first stop is to pick up infantry and drop them off, either close to or right into the fight. Huey slicks are used to carry grunts into a combat zone. Cobras are the heavy guns, the ones hitting the targets first. Once they believe the area is ready for an insertion of troops, we are cleared to land the hueys where we were told.

It's nearing midnight on Christmas Eve, 1971, and we're in the air when Jingle Bells begins playing poorly over the radio. It's cold and dark. The air is cold and dark. The metal is cold and dark. The huey gunship floats through the night, the other choppers alongside ours. I hang out the door behind my M60 machine gun, looking down.

Earlier today we dropped off an infantry unit in one of the landing zones below us. Now we have returned with big white phosphorous shells that will light up entire areas when they're dropped, and hopefully illuminate any enemy that is sneaking around or advancing.

In the jungle below, the outlines of a few random trees are lit up by tracers flashing back and forth in the sporadic open pockets. With all the lights turned off in the huey,

I can see for miles. There are many little battles between Army infantry and the Vietcong occurring at the same time, and in the dark, it looks like a small lightning storm spread out below us.

Jingle Bells keeps playing. I watch the tracer rounds dance back and forth to the beat of the soldier back on base who thought it would be entertaining to serenade us while we are out here, floating in the wind and watching lives wink out of existence below.

"Jingle bells, mortar shells, Charlie's in the grass. Take this merry Christmas, aaaaaaand shove it up your ass! HEEEY!"

12

IRAQ

"One general told us, in a speech before our second deployment, that we needed to go over there and be capable of handing candy to kids one moment and turning to shoot an insurgent the next. He said we needed to win hearts and minds. But we didn't have a degree in psychology. We were kids. That speech wasn't for us. It was for his friends and the American public. That speech was the same reason they sent us to Iraq, the same reason they said the Towers were attacked, and the same reason they do anything they feel needs to be done. It's because we can't handle the truth. They weren't conditioning us for combat. They were conditioning the American people. I have no idea what that general even meant. Do you think he ever had to operate in a combat zone under that kind of pressure? I doubt it. The world he believed he lived in was a lie. He was making everyone back here believe that lie. No one has those standards for themselves. But now they all treat us like we're somehow different. We slip off their consciousness, like when you watch a movie that's so pathetic you can't remember how it ends. Their thoughts are bullshit."

"It's war that's bullshit. We go over there to kill motherfuckers. Hearts and minds, my ass. It's going to get easier, Gabe. There is a light at the end of a tunnel, there really is. You're not losing your mind. Don't let these civilians get to you. They're idiots, just immature and idealistic. Let them talk. I know it bothers you because they believe their opinions are truth and because rationalizations can translate into actions even though you and I know they're just empty words. Then again, it's okay. They're not your problem."

■ ■ ■

The track rolls on for hours, carrying us into Iraq. I clutch my machine gun, propping my helmet against a knob on my gun that allows my chin strap to hold my head up so I can drift off to sleep. I wake up as the track jerks to a stop. Light peeks through the slits of the vehicle's metal top. For the first time, we are about to do something relevant to our job descriptions.

"There is a large element of Iraqi infantry advancing on our position," says our track commander from above.

"We have to hold them back so they don't flank the rest of the convoy."

Lewis takes control of the cramped metal space and announces that it's time to pray. He removes a wrinkled piece of paper from one of the pouches on his LBV and awkwardly begins reading a psalm from the Bible. I wonder when he found time to put that together. Everyone bows their heads, scrunching their faces closed and blocking off all senses except the sense of self-preservation through prayer.

Everyone, that is, except me. I am watching them all pray. I look at each of the other Marines. I can't believe this is happening.

Oh, God. Why can't I believe in God right now? I think.

The track jerks back into motion and speeds forward and around. It feels like we are going in circles, but we know the drivers are reenacting a drill designed to push them into a line with the other tracks. Then the vehicle stops, and our tracker at the door with a headset tilts his head, listening, then nods. The back of the track begins to drop. We all stare at its maw as it opens. We prepare ourselves one last time. I have two hundred rounds wrapped around my body, one end of the belt secured in the tray of my gun.

As the gate drops, we pour out into the desert and run towards a berm about fifty feet in front of us. I can hear and almost feel the entire company hitting the dirt around me with their bodies, slapping into the ground with a thud, guns aimed forward. All of us are straining to identify anything that might need a million bullets dropped into it.

Nothing. We are scanning, but it's quiet. No one is there. We push forward. Lewis barks to stay close. From the wide-eyed look on his face, this isn't a dream or some movie version of a heroic last stand. This is real, and we have nothing but whatever we have inside us and our guns.

"Lewis, come over here!" yells Miller, who is a little way off with Luvs and Preston.

"Fuck off, Miller! You come here!" Lewis yells.

We run to a berm further up and sight in frantically, waiting for what we were told would be a wave of attacking Iraqi soldiers. But everything is silent, almost sickeningly so. Staff Sergeant Kelly begins walking down the line at the base of the berm below us in a sort of staunch march. He says, "Marines! Hold your ground. Choose your targets well. Hold the line, gentlemen, and be brave."

How does he always end up in these epic moments? I think to myself, my brain struggling to disregard the thought and keep out other irrational or irrelevant observations.

Walking behind my position, Kelly recedes further down the line of his platoon and I look back towards the tree line in front of us again. Lewis is next to me. He asks, "How long are your bursts going to be?"

"As long as it takes."

He nods without shifting his gaze from the tree line.

"Lewis!" yells Miller again. "We need to get closer to ensure we adequately utilize intersecting fields of fire!"

Lewis barks to move, and we glide forward quickly to another berm. Lewis whispers under his breath, "Fuck that. He can move his dumb ass this way if he wants to die. Because I don't!" I'll never forget how insanely wide his eyes were then, or how comforting it was.

Still nothing. Now the entire company has pushed up, and we wait again. The tracks are behind us, their vehicle commanders stoically sitting in the turrets, heavy guns aimed at the tree line.

Tank Battalion was getting ready to engage and hit Saddam's mechanized forces, and supposedly there was a small contingent of infantry that broke off and was heading our way. Nothing happens.

Eventually, the commanders order us to board the tracks again. We drive on as the morning progresses and the day extends into the next night. We haven't eaten, and we are trying to preserve our water since we don't know when we will find more.

The following morning, we arrive at the mouth of a massive desert canyon. Command tells us to start digging fighting holes, so we spread out and begin digging. Lewis is drinking water and watching me and Hayes dig. The ground is hard and riddled with rocks. We are barely two feet down when people begin echoing a command along the line. When the message gets to us, we realize we are being told to move fifty feet to the right and start over.

"Fuck!" I yell.

"Shut the fuck up, Keith! And start digging again, bitch!" yells Lewis.

There are hills behind us and the open desert before us. Unless there is some army of Egyptian mummies that's going to magically appear to kill us all, none of us knows why we are digging in an empty environment.

I look at Hayes, who is more put together than me in some ways. He never forgets his gear, and he knows everything about the machine gun. But right now, he's breaking down.

I look over to where Luvs is digging and realize Preston isn't holding up that well either. Neither of them is putting energy into digging the fighting hole. Hours go by. We are barely two feet into the ground again when Miller walks off for a meeting with the leadership.

The desert has been quiet, but then the AAVs behind us begin to roar as one by one they turn on and begin circling around, then driving away in a single file line. I stop digging and look at Hayes, who is just as confused as I am. Then Miller walks back from his meeting. "Listen up," he says, a little more sheepishly this time. "We are going to be hit by enemy artillery tonight."

"What the fuck?" says Lewis, "Well, then, what the hell are we doing here?"

"Apparently," Miller says, as he looks up at the sky, "Colonel Rhodes or some other asshole believes that the enemy artillery is somewhere in front of us. But until they begin firing, we won't be able to lock on to their position."

"Well, how about we figure out a nice little math equation, or fly something around in the air - like, oh, say, a fucking jet - and figure this shit out," says Lewis.

"Good, Lewis. I'm glad we have you here to straighten out all the top brass in the Marine Corps. What the fuck do you want me to do?" says Miller. "We dig. Okay? That's what they're telling us. Apparently, the enemy's artillery is fixed in place. When they begin firing, it's only a matter of time before our superior artillery can drop Patriot missiles on their location, taking them out before they take us out, and freeing up the entire movement to continue into the country."

"Where did the tracks go, then, if there's a plan for getting us out of here?" asks Lewis.

"Well, command doesn't want to risk losing any of the AAVs, so they are falling back to a safer position."

"Great. But we are completely expendable. That's great. Fuck."

"Okay. So, Keith and Hayes, start digging faster. That goes for you two as well," says Miller, nodding in the direction of Luvs and Preston.

I've been digging for hours, and the sun has moved almost directly overhead. I look up and close my eyes as its heat beats down indifferently on my face. Lewis yells at me to keep digging, and I look down to realize Luvs is walking over to my hole.

"Hey, Keith."

"Luvs," I say, nodding.

"How goes it?"

"Not good. I can't get Hayes to do a fucking thing."

"Well, just make him dig. He's your ammo man."

"I tried, but he just picks at the dirt. And I want to fucking live, man. Lewis has been riding his ass, and he's got to carry Lewis's tripod on top of the ammo bag."

"Well, look what I have to deal with," Luvs says, as he turns back to his fighting hole. I follow his gaze and find an unfortunate scene. Preston is standing there with one hand on his hip, daintily tapping the e-tool into the dirt with his other hand. His face is contorted in discomfort as if a bad smell has made him unhappy about his task and therefore reluctant to try harder. Preston is very strong in some ways, but this kind of endurance is a weak point for him.

"Good luck," I say to Luvs, as Lewis yells at him to get back to his hole and I resume digging.

We dig the holes almost waist deep, then pace back about one hundred yards and dig rudimentary holes for secondary positions. They are unfortunately shallow, but if we lay down flat we are just below the surface. We keep digging as the day leaves and the night begins. Most of our canteens are running empty, but there's a clear bottle of water placed neatly on the edge of the fighting hole that Hayes and I have been digging.

"Hey, Keith, let's take a drink of that," Hayes says, motioning to the water bottle.

"I wish we could. Lewis said he would kill us if we did."

"He doesn't have to know!"

"How do you expect it to go when he gets back and sees that there's less water in his bottle? You know he checked the level before he left!"

"If we only take a sip, he won't notice at all. Or, at least, maybe he won't care."

"All right, fine. Go ahead."

Hayes unscrews the cap and hands the bottle to me first. I take it and fill my dry mouth with water – a single gulp. I hand it back to Hayes, and he takes it and chugs the rest of the bottle. I reach forward and grab it from him, yelling, "I thought you said we should take a fucking sip!"

"I'm sorry, I'm just so thirsty!"

"Great, now he's definitely going to have our asses!"

"What's the worst he can do, Keith? We already stand all the posts at night, dig all the fighting holes, and he still eats our rations and drinks our water!"

Realizing he has a point, I resign myself to more digging. The night thickens. Lewis returns and loses it as if we had stolen the water he had in reality taken from us to begin with. Explosions reverberate in the distance, far enough away to give us hope that this whole issue will be resolved soon without incident.

I'm sitting in the hole with Hayes when we are told to take off our MOPP suits and get the gun ready. I remove the night sight from its case and set it on the gun, then start taking off my gas mask and suit. I lean against the sandy side wall and exhaustion floods in. I realize how nice it is to rest for a moment.

I'm not sure why it happened, considering everything that was going on. Maybe I was tired. Maybe staying up for three days without sleep had something to do with it, or maybe it had to do with the lack of water and food, or the day spent digging. Regardless of the reason, I fall asleep next to Hayes as the evening sets in.

I wake up to the thunderous sound of impacting artillery rounds. They are closer than before, because now all I see in front of me is blinding white light that vibrates and pulses as it pounds the earth. The ground erupts in the valley, and I can see everyone down the line leaving their fighting holes for the ones dug further back. Lewis is screaming at Hayes and me to fall back now. As we start to climb out of the fighting hole, my legs stop. I fall forward. My gas mask suit is around my ankles where I left it, and my gun falls in front of me, losing the expensive night sights I had left unsecured on top of the gun.

Lewis leaves his hole and runs up to where I am, grabbing my helmet and jerking it around, so my face is staring up at his, blinding white light all around us. "What the fuck, Keith?" yells Lewis. "Get your fucking shit together, and get the fuck back. Now, now, now!"

I jump up, tear my gas mask and suit off, grab the sights and the 240G, and run back to the rear hole. I realize I lost my helmet and run back to grab it before dropping down next to Hayes in the prone position. Securing the sights on the gun, I place my head against the sand and attempt to fight sleep. The explosions roar closer and closer, but I'm unable to keep my eyes open.

When I wake up, I see only the dirt in front of my face, though my helmet props me a few inches off the ground. It's early morning and quiet. I sit up and look around as others begin to move and adjust along the line. I get up and walk over to take a piss in the trench dug by the Corpsmen last night.

Walking back, I head to where Luvs is standing, looking up. I follow his gaze again and see little white streaks moving across the sky followed by little cracking sounds.

"Are those the Patriot missiles?" I ask.

"Yeah. Our avenging angels of death," says a Marine behind us, as he walks back from a fighting hole further down the line.

The tracks return, and we board them again, resuming our trip towards Baghdad. That night, Tank Battalion engages the enemy. What is important to understand about tank battles is that our tanks are newer and better than theirs. They have a motley assortment of vehicles. For instance, T72s are common. Our M1A1 Abrahams are twice as fast and can fire rapidly while coasting across most types of terrain. Their T72s are much slower and can only fire if completely stopped. Even then, they have to turn the turrets in an agonizingly slow motion before getting on target, which is hard to do when ours can outrun the turning motion of their barrels. At night or during a sandstorm, they can only see out through a slit.

I remember climbing into a tank back at Camp Ripper during a sandstorm and staring out at a clear, magnified expanse of serenity. The tanks' night vision is excellent. Our tank rounds are deadlier and travel further. The enemy lines snake across the terrain in the distance, nose to butt - old, dead tactics with old, dead technology. Our tanks communicate through satellite radio, with the added bonus of forward-operating flying drones and a full set of infrared sights allowing them to see things far ahead.

I was never a tanker, but I imagine they coast up on the enemy and stop, taking their time to decide how to kill hundreds of tanks with forty of theirs. Maybe it looks something like mice versus cockroaches. All the while, Cobra helicopters are dealing death from above with Hellfire missiles.

During a battle, one of the Cobras accidentally hits an Abrams and the tank drives off. Lewis and Miller stand, yelling. "Did you see that?"

"Holy shit, over there! Look over there!"

"It's on fire!"

"It's still moving! Look, look! Get that motherfucker!"

Luvs tries to stand up and is yelled at to get back down. I'm perfectly content to sit, avoiding the off chance of taking a direct hit to the face.

The trackers yell, and Lewis and Miller drop down, joining the rest of us as the top metal doors are closed. Small pockets of gunfire boom sporadically in measured bursts or crackle into existence then out again. Shadows rotate quickly over lowered helmets and upright guns from Hellfire missiles hissing by overhead. Thunderous thuds into dirt berms and the sound of metal tearing come from somewhere in front of us, as the track moves and jerks around in mysterious mechanical maneuvers that will hopefully be effective.

One morning, after a battle I was in but never witnessed, I stand up and look out to see a peaceful farming landscape straight out of a cartoon. Every little hill has a tilled field, and the road dramatically slopes up and down the hills, connecting different plots of land. There are irrigation canals and tiny bridges in the distance that slope further towards the sunrise. The footprints of rolling metal beasts run crooked and purposeless throughout. It looks like a brutal ordeal. They must have milled about in maddening confusion as the chaos sent them into trees or up the sides of hills.

The tanks burn and smolder wherever they wound up. On some of them, the bodies of their drivers burn blue as they jut upright from the hatches or lean weakly from trapped hips. They must have popped the hatches to climb out of the burning oven of the tanks' cabins and emerged into another burning hell. I imagine their wide eyes catching first as they scream and claw into the night air. They die as the burning wick on a metal candle, sparked by incendiary rounds that burn on impact and keep burning as long as oxygen exists. They look like Luke Skywalker's aunt and uncle as they burned in the desert outside their home, smoldering and fossilizing into the ground on a lazy morning in a quaint farming village.

13

MILKMAN KILLER

"You know, my cousin who I'd been close to for years said she felt like she owed me an apology once I got out. She said she had been going to antiwar protests while I was overseas and felt guilty about it. I could tell she really did feel awful. To this day, it doesn't bother me. Whether she believed in the war or not, it had nothing to do with my decision to join the Marines in the first place. And I told her as much. There was one thing she said that I disagreed with, though. She said she had carried a sign with a picture on it of me in boot camp in my dress blues. My mom had sent it to her. On the poster, it read, 'I support the troops, not the war.' But she never supported the troops, and she doesn't have a right to say that. Most people don't. They put them in fucking boxes. I used to ignore the irony of empty statements like that, but it burns me up these days.

The proof was right there on her fucking poster and she didn't care to see it."

■ ■ ■

Inside the stuffy metal box, we sweat and wait. The tank battalion just broke up the main force of Saddam's mechanized unit, at least from what the trackers are yelling, but there are pockets of scattered vehicle convoys attempting to run away. If not stopped, they could flank our main force or resupply the little pockets of resistance that remain. The tracker sitting near the door tilts his head down as he concentrates on something being said through his headset.

"Hey, you guys are getting out soon. Get ready," he says.

We prepare and check our gear and weapons, tightening chin straps and sucking down a little water from camelbacks or canteens. The back door thuds into the sand and we move out into the dark. Quietly, we rush up a hill.

I drop in place with the rest of the squad and look through my sights. I click back and forth from black hot, the toggle that turns all heat signatures black, to white hot, which turns anything alive or mechanically so to bright white. That one feels right.

Being stuck in a metal vehicle with no windows is what will keep moments like this alive in the future. Now, I remember what everything looked like the second I jumped out, but nothing from a moment before.

All the tracks are facing a hill, which in fact isn't a hill at all. It is the base of an empty water canal. In the distance is a bridge. We sit underneath the canal, looking down the valley as it curves outward and then up, disappearing from view where it slopes back down out of sight again. The tracks are able to hide most of their metal frames under the canal, pushing up into the hill to create leverage and a stronger line of sight.

Through the filtered world of my sights, I see white dots cresting the hill in the distance. They grow into a convoy of Iraqi vehicles, mindlessly moving down the road, unaware their escape route is anything but a safe path.

"Corporal Lewis, I see vehicles. Should I shoot?"

"No, Keith. It's too far away, dumbass. Wait until directed. It looks like the tracks will be able to handle it unless they get closer."

Soon one of the trackers opens up with the 50-caliber automatic machine gun, and long white streaks begin lasering into the convoy. As the impacts grow, the convoy stops. I can see perfectly outlined smaller white heat signatures moving away from the bigger ones and running off the road, little white flailing spots. The white streaking bullets over my right shoulder follow their path, relentlessly cutting them down. In a matter of seconds, there's no movement. Everyone on the line relaxes a bit as we wait for what we are told will be a larger force that will soon come pouring over the hill.

A burning white phosphorous orb pops brilliantly overhead, illuminating the rigid metal of the tracks in stark contrast against the rounded hill. I can see helmets all down the line on the berm self-consciously dropping further down. The orb floats down, blessedly restoring us and our nakedness into the dark.

One tracker continues to fire from his turret, and our lieutenant runs over, yelling at him to stop. Later, others will say that the platoon commander of the AAVs was in the turret and refused to stop firing until he had walked his impacts onto the area he felt was responsible for firing the white phosphorous round that lit up our entire position. He grimly continues firing as the Lieutenant frantically yells and waves in front of him. After that night's battle, some Marines from the unit will go and see that he had not only killed the Iraqis that abandoned their convoy in the dark but also an entire unit of mortars that had locked in on our coordinates.

As everything becomes quiet again, I'm replaced on the gun by Hayes, allowing me to go take a piss further along the berm. As I walk in that direction, I come upon an interesting scene. Corpsman Cox is kneeling over a moaning body in the dark and talking to it. "The orcs of the third realm are the fiercest," he says in a soft but firm tone. "They are a randy bunch, only succumbing to a strong force such as the elven tribes of the third ward."

"Hey, who's that?" he asks as I approach.

"It's Keith. What are you doing?"

"This is an Iraqi soldier. He was shot when we pushed into the area. He doesn't understand anything I'm saying, of course, but I'm trying to keep him calm until we leave this place so he doesn't injure himself further. Can you watch him? I've got to take a piss. Try talking to him a little. If he moves around, his bandages will rip."

"Okay, sure." I reply.

"Thanks, Keith," says Cox. He walks off. I sit there and look at this Iraqi's form in the dark. I can't tell where he's been shot, but it can't be anywhere good since I doubt he even knows I'm standing over him. Cox returns, and I walk to the edge of the berm and take a piss.

When I go back to where my squad is sitting, word spreads to load up. We get in the track and move on in the dark. The tracker says we are going to hit a convoy again soon.

Some of the Marines in the tracks are playing with weapons that aren't ours, AK-47s they recovered from Iraqi soldiers. Our M-16s are well worn, but even so the metal and plastic looks uniform and competent. These AKs with their wooden components and jagged overlapping metal pieces look ridiculous. I haven't seen all that many guns in my life, so I grab one and turn it around in the dim red light. These fire bigger rounds than our M-16s, but with less accuracy and depth.

We keep the guns in our tracks for the rest of the trip. If we're capable of picking up anything deemed dangerous, we do. There's comfort in what we decide the weapons might be good for in the future. There's always the chance we could make a mistake and need to protect ourselves from going to prison for it, like accidentally killing someone without a gun.

There's a fuel truck intent on resupplying the enemy, and we are going to set up an ambush. Again the door drops. Again we run out. We feel naked and exposed, as we run with our guns towards a small rise in the dirt and drop in around each other in a crooked half circle. Securing the thermal sight to my gun, I push my eye into it and the white-hot heat signature kicks on. I kneel just below the top of the hill with the bipods buried in the dirt, stabbing the butt stock deep in my shoulder. I can't see anything because there is nothing to see. The blackness reflects back through the sight as I search with my eye and follow with my shoulder, which controls the barrel and regulates the potential path of the bullets.

A vehicle's front end, outlined in perfect white heat, turns into our area. A beam of constant white light starts pelting into it from every gun in the circle. I start shooting, adding to the stream, but can't see anything with the optics jumping so I stop and watch through the sights as the vehicle slows to a stop. Everyone eventually ceases firing. The vehicle remains brilliantly white. I look for any movement, and something catches my eye. I'm tired, so I say something dumb. "It looks like something's leaking!"

"What?" says Lewis.

"I don't know - I think it's milk!" There was hot fuel leaking from the gas tank, but what my eyes saw was its white heat signature.

Looking away from the dripping fuel, I see movement on the ground on the other side of the cab. It had been hidden by the fuel as it rushed out, but now feet are moving on the other side, approaching the front of the vehicle.

"Corporal, I see someone!"

"Good, then fucking shoot!"

As a man turns the corner of the vehicle, I see one arm rising as if to throw a grenade. I aim center mass and pull the trigger as his body fills my optic lens. The picture jumbles with the release of the ammunition burst then clears as I stop shooting. The man reappears off the nose of the car in splendid white light as he spins around like a top, his arms flailing up and around before he ultimately collapses.

"I got him, Corporal!"

"Good. Fall back!"

"Yes, Corporal," I say as I run back. An 0311 is kneeling as security, and Lewis yells at him to get out of the way to let me post up. I sit there on the gun and wait as everyone in the area jumps into the tracks. I'm the last one to jump in. There isn't any room on the benches, so I sit on the floor.

Everything makes sense now. I get why we sit and point and click at empty targets and fake enemies. I understand the concept behind gun drills, why we run and set up the gun and sight in over and over again, why we clean our guns with little cloths and long metal utensils until we can't find any dark unwanted blemishes. If this is killing, I am going to be okay, because I can do this long enough to get home. I didn't freeze or hesitate. I might as well have signed my name on a piece of paper or tied my shoes with my eyes closed.

As the track starts up and begins moving again, I realize someone is sitting on the ground directly in front of me. "Oh, girl," Preston says to me, in his way, in the dark.

That night, we park somewhere and sleep in a jumbled heap under a large piece of material that blocks the wind and keeps dirt off the guns. The tracks are parked in a circle around us, guns facing out. We sleep with all our gear on, but for once we're not cramped in a sitting position. The next morning, we continue on.

Lewis grabs the 240 from my hands. Then he slams his rifle into my gut. "So, you want to be a worthless little fuck and the only one with a fucking kill, Keith? Well, you didn't deserve it. And now I'm going to get mine, bitch."

I'm quiet, feeling the weight of the rifle. I know he'll hand it back when it gets too heavy for him, which will be soon.

"Well, bitch, do you think because you got a kill you don't have to address me by my rank?"

"No, Corporal," I reply as we board up into the tracks.

The tracks jostle us around as they position themselves into formation and get back on the road. Lewis is standing up, looking out at something.

"Look at that. There's the guy you killed, Keith."

"Can I see, Corporal?"

"All right, fine. Get up here. Just this once."

I scramble up to stand on top of the metal bench. I blink as my eyes adjust to the morning light and the openness of everything. An old truck with a big tank sits awkwardly just off the road. The tank is painted red and sits inside the wooden-framed bed of the truck. The cab is also red. Sprawled out near the nose of the vehicle is the man I killed, wearing a flannel shirt and jeans.

I find out later he took a bunch of shots to the body but was able to fall out of the vehicle as the majority of the impacts cheese-grated the cabin. He stumbled around the nose of the truck towards where I was waiting.

Preston would have shot, but his belt of ammo was in backwards. Another Marine with a SAW tried to pull the trigger, but his gun jammed. He watched as the man turned the corner, raised both hands to surrender, and was dropped by a burst from my gun.

Someone I knew from boot camp was on the team responsible for picking up bodies. He told me later that when they recovered this body, the torso was wrecked with 5.56 rounds and the head with 7.62. Only Preston and I were shooting with that caliber that night.

I don't know why everyone remembered this guy. Maybe because it's rare to see someone die so close to you in combat. Maybe because on that deployment we didn't kill that many people, or because he was one of the first we killed. Of course, everyone will remember that I'd said there was milk draining from the vehicle, and a nickname will eventually circulate.

"There he is, guys," someone will say later on as I walk by. "There goes Keith, the Milkman Killer."

14

WASTELAND

"I'll tell you why I struggle with the idea of valuing most Americans, when I hear their strong opinions about Iraq. If someone held a gun to their head and told them to describe what an infantry Marine's job entailed over there, they would be forced to let the man blow their shit off. The same would hold true if they were asked about any combat-related job in the Marines, whether it involved tanks, Cobras, tracks, corpsman, or any of the supporting roles. They don't even know what we did every day, but they have strong opinions about specific things that they're convinced happened. Whether they think we are fighting a true war or wasting our time and hurting civilians, they don't know what is going on, and they're okay with that. They're okay with having opinions about America's involvement in Iraq, but they have zero frame of reference.

They ask me how many people I killed. They tell me we should be over there. They tell me we shouldn't be over there. They believe we are freeing the Iraqi people. They believe we are oppressing the Iraqi people. They all have computers, but none of them have ever Googled what the Marine Corps infantry does on deployments in Iraq. Why would they need that information, when they have movies to give them metaphors and symbolism to dictate what they feel is right and wrong about the world?

In my entire life, I've never seen so much misinformation on a single topic. Do you want to know why we don't talk about our experiences? It's because what we experienced is not what is considered real. The story we need to tell in these pages doesn't make sense, or it isn't portrayed in the proper context. Everyone is set on picking one of two sides. Glorify the military and the government, or demonize them. Believe we are fighting a war to preserve our way of life, or that we are simply cold-blooded first-world warmongers."

■ ■ ■

We travel for two weeks in the tracks while sounds of gunfire ebb and flow through a sea of hours, of nights, and of days. I don't think most of us know what is going on or particularly care. I know I don't.

I wake up, looking at Preston, and wonder why he's staring at his wrist. Maybe some shadow is playing off his hand from moonlight seeping through the crack in the metal doors overhead. I can't tell. Suddenly equilibrium shifts and the wall I sit against becomes the ground. Preston falls, landing against me, our gear slamming together.

We unlock the back hatch and crawl out into the cold night air of the desert. I look around and realize that we had been following the track in front of us along a make-shift road that skirted the edge of a small ravine. When our driver fell asleep, he kept going straight when the road curved around to the left. We careened off the edge, roll-ing sideways down a hill. We board another track to keep going.

Days pass and we are sitting in the track when the con-voy slows and the track commander yells down that we are stopping to clean up the vehicles. Lewis proclaims that anyone who hasn't seen time in Japan will get out and post up as security while the convoy stops. Outside the tracks, a vicious sandstorm eats at everything. Even our hands disappear if we hold them out far enough. We turn off the road and get out to lie down in the sand with our guns fac-ing outward. That close to the ground, the sand kicks up in my face, wriggling past my gear and into my orifices. I try breathing in and out softly, but it makes little difference.

Coughing and choking, we wait until the track com-mander yells at us to return. I climb inside. When I turn around to sit down, I can see one of the other Marines who has yet to climb back in. He's taking instructions from someone, saying, "Yes sir, no sir," about something. When he looks back in, it's at me. Staff Sergeant Morgan is in the track behind us and wants me back outside. The other

Marine squeezes into the track as I squeeze past him, back out into the sandstorm and the snaking convoy of vehicles.

Morgan is standing in the track behind ours, his upper body projecting from its hatch. He towers over me, leaning over the nose of the metal ship and yelling into the wind. "Take those rounds off your neck before I come down there and remove them along with your head, motherfucker!"

Looking down, I realize he's talking about the belts of ammo that I've wrapped around my body in a looping X over my shoulders, across my chest and under my arms.

"You better have gotten enough fucking pictures trying to look like a fucking badass while those belts become even more doggone dirty and incapable of shooting! Get that shit off your neck now! Fucking now!"

"Yes, Staff Sergeant!" I yell back, taking the ammo off my body in coils and holding it under my arm as Morgan leans forward over the jutting metal front end of the track. He completely overshadows me as I wait for the ass-chewing to finish.

"Get out of my fucking sight," he snarls, and I take the cue, jumping back into the track where Miller is waiting.

"It's okay, Keith," Miller says. "For once, you didn't fuck up. That guy's an idiot. How else does he expect us to get all of the shit we need from point A to B if we don't have ten arms and legs?"

I cram back into an open spot as people curse and squeeze in next to each other. When I jumped out just now, I realized my feet were burning. We've been sweating and moving through wet environments with complete disregard for our personal hygiene. I haven't taken my boots off for a week now. Something is definitely wrong.

The Marines around me are complaining about pain, too. When they remove their boots, a dark greenish-brown substance clings to their feet. It looks like compressed moldy bread, and it smells awful. Later, this will get even worse and I'll wish that I'd taken the advice someone gave me to piss on my feet.

We keep pushing through the desert and stop at a bridge. On the other side is a small town. Popping open the track's little door, I climb out into the tall grass on the side of the road. I limp over to a small rise and drop down to one knee with my gun. I can feel others thud into the soft dirt around me as they get into position. I sight in on the far end of the bridge, but one of our tanks creaks forward and stops right where I am aiming. I move my sights a little inward towards the town and wait.

The Army Humvee with the loudspeakers begins booming out statements in Arabic, telling enemy soldiers they won't die if they surrender to the military and leave the city. It continues, letting them know that if they don't surrender, we have dipped our bullets in pigs' blood and won't stop until they are all dead.

Explosions ring out in the city, and another tank rolls over the bridge next to the first one. We are poised to invade. Slowly, people trickle out of the city. We pat them down for weapons and let them walk on their way. Some Marines are frustrated because they believe many of the young men leaving the city are soldiers who have taken off their uniforms and will eventually find more guns and attack us later. We are confused when some of the town's dwellers remove their shoes and point at them, repeating Saddam Hussein's name each time. The symbolism is lost on us.

After we have established a checkpoint and screened many of the Iraqis who walked out of the city, an Army convoy approaches. Whether water trucks or mobile satellite stations, the vehicles are all tan and heavily armored. They drive over the bridge and on past the city. Once they are gone, we continue north.

Days and nights pass, and other bridges are secured without incident. Lewis and Miller sleep in the track while Hayes and I are posted on checkpoints for security. They open boxes of rations and comb through them for the best ones, then pick apart the ones they plan to give us. Hayes is stuck eating the same main meal from the same ration every day and is getting sick and malnourished.

Corporal Gibbs, the big, jolly Marine who is always happy, becomes sick. He leans against everyone in his row on the track, moaning deliriously. The other Marines curse and push him in futile attempts to get him to sit his giant frame upright instead of on top of them. When we stop on the side of another road, he is the first one to get out. His feet drop onto the sand in front of the track's door, and so do his pants. He drops into a squat with half-lidded eyes, taking a giant shit. On our way out, the rest of us jump over it, or cling to the side of the track and attempt to hop to either side.

"Keith," Gibbs says as he approaches with a sad look on his face. "What's that?" I know he is referring to the crackers I have just found in an MRE. Gibbs made it clear that if any boot had any crackers, they were his and he would take them.

"It's my food," I say to him, wishing I had waited until he was moaning and passed out in the track again before pulling them out.

"You know the rule. Give them to me," he says.

"No," I reply. "You have like ten packets of crackers in your pouch. I can see it right there." I point at his pouch, which is bulging with thin packets of rations. "I need food, too."

Gibbs swings his hand up to grab at my neck.

"Here you go, fuck!" I say as I push his hand away, throwing the crackers on the ground. As I walk away, I realize that he isn't reacting at all to what I said. He is intent on following the path of the crackers from my hand to the ground. He bends down to pick them up, laughing about how he has crackers now.

Back inside, I attempt to sleep, or at least to allow my consciousness to wander. First, I must find a position that hasn't yet made me sore from maintaining it for hours. Whether I lean to the left or right or forward, I prop my helmet on the edge of my gun's gas cap, allowing the chin strap to hold the weight of my head in place. It blessedly breaks the seal of the material between my helmet and my head that holds in heat and sweat. It keeps my head above my body without requiring help from my neck. It frees my mind until we jolt to a stop and run out and out and out again and again.

I wake up in the night. Gibbs stands over me. He kicks me accidentally as he jostles to balance himself on the bench, and I look up to see what he's doing. Piss sprays down on my face, and I hate Gibbs just a little bit more for it. I swear and wipe my face with my sleeve.

Miserable and sore, my feet burning from the un-checked fungal infection, I drift off to sleep while we bounce along. The track has stopped when I wake up, and one of the trackers yells down, letting us know he will have to use the rest of our water supply to cool down the engine before it overheats and leaves us exposed in an open field.

"Fuck you, you will use the rest of our water!" yells Lewis. Everyone laughs.

"That's a direct order from our commander, and if you don't listen you will be court-martialed!" yells the track commander.

"Fuck your commander, he ain't ours!" Lewis yells back.

"Fuck my commander? You are out of line, Marine!" the tracker screams.

"Come down here and say that!" shouts Lewis.

"You come up here and I will, then, asshole!"

"Come down here, and I'll do more than that, you POG-ass bitch!" yells Lewis. The engine is quiet, and so are we. Moments pass and the engine must be cool enough for us to continue because our driver backs down from the argument and starts up the engine.

I open my eyes as light pours in through the small hatch at the end of the track. Staff Sergeant Kelly, unflinching in the sand and sunlight, looks in at us with one hand on the door. "Marines, this is it. We made it to Baghdad. I'm sure you have heard by now that a sniper was killed trying to defend Sergeant Major Wolfe when they were pinned down by enemy fire the other day. Well, that man was my friend. Let's keep him in our hearts as we take the fight to the enemy, and end this war once and for all."

Leaving our track, he moves on to another one. I think to myself how epically Kelly just delivered that speech. As I watch him strut over to the track behind us, I realize he must have had time to practice it.

Before we go into the city, they let us jump out and stretch our legs one last time. I look around at the landscape. The tracks are positioned in a big circle, the gunners in their turrets facing outwards. The sand is washed flat for miles. It looks like a gigantic beach, with no physical characteristics except for the sand and dirt stretching on and on. What will happen now? The track door has dropped more times than I can remember, and each one is different. Will the next few end in blood? Next time I might run out into the burning sun, confused and disoriented for one maddening moment, and find my feet taking me left when they could have carried me home if only I'd scrambled to the right.

I imagine Mom's SUV again; this time parked a little outside the circle of tracks. She held me when I had seizures and couldn't talk. She stared into my eyes, and even though it was futile to will my lips to move, we knew that we loved each other. If she were here now, she would take me home.

But these are useless thoughts in a useless place. I jump back into the track on command, waiting for the final battle ahead.

15

TAKING BAGHDAD

"I think it's important for me to get my arms around the war I was in because I don't think I have been able to wrap my arms around it yet. And I think it's important for you to wrap your arms around the war you were in. It's hard to do that. I think the similarities between the experiences that you and I experienced as enlisted guys in the middle of it, in the fight, display a lot of commonalities.

"I got married after being home for two weeks. I was nineteen, and so was my girlfriend. Her dad had paid for everything, and I didn't want to disappoint anyone. That poor girl had no idea what was going on in my head when we got married. She looked at me and saw the kid she knew, but I had become something else since she last saw me. I need to make sure I find out what that was. My story really is about winding up on my parents' steps in

Port Washington, dressed in my fucking uniform, pissed off that my mom spent all my money when I was overseas and wondering where the fuck I'd been and where the hell I was now because yesterday I was in Vietnam. That's what my story is really about. It was a hell of a struggle for a PTSD guy trying to pull off blending in. That's why I didn't say a fucking word for twenty-seven years."

"Hey, Uncle Rick, I'm honored you're in my life. I know that the one thing I can be proud of, from all the bullshit I went through over four years, is that you and your generation of warriors consider me one of you."

■ ■ ■

We roll into the outskirts of Baghdad. Some of the Marines shoot at a couple of soldiers who stuck around for the invasion. The majority of the forces left are Republican Guard. They were Saddam's Special Forces unit, a much smaller group of fighters and considered more determined.

Gibbs sprays brass down from the top of the track. Some of it catches under the neck of my flak jacket, stinging my skin. Flinching, I flick it out and prepare myself, tightening down on the 240 at its pistol grip and bipods.

The gate drops, and we begin a methodical push through the city. Miller yells at me to clear around the side of a small shack in the middle of a field in front of the town. I run forward, popping around the side and sighting in on the doorway to an open courtyard beyond. Others run in around the area, slamming into walls and flopping down on dirt mounds or piles of rubble.

Teams and squads sight in, locked on any opening that someone might look out of or run through, while other teams and squads rush forward, stopping once they have covered a little more ground and secured a little more of the environment. Rinse and repeat, we close in squad by squad, getting nearer to the inner city of Baghdad. It is a painfully monotonous and inexorably repetitive process.

The tracks and tanks position themselves along roadways and in courtyards. They use their more powerful guns to punch bigger holes over longer distances than we can deliver. Cobras circle overhead. We don't see much shooting, though. Most of the areas we clear are empty. Shots reverberate in the distance and our radio man keeps us informed about areas where firefights are happening, but none of it seems to find us.

I run forward through a courtyard and find myself alone in front of a house. I push forward, knowing that the quickest way back to my squad is on the other side of this enclosure. The gate through a low-built wall is smashed shut, and I kick it open with my machine gun at my hip and a belt of ammo around my neck. I swing the gun around in a half circle as I enter the backyard, looking frantically around for any movement. Then I see a massive puddle of blood on the ground. I freeze before I press on, deciding to skirt around the side of the house. Better to avoid whatever is inside, whether it's the bodies of people other Marines have killed, a waiting ambush, or nothing but shadows that will threaten my tenuous hold on my sanity.

As I move along the house, more smears and little pools of fresh blood dot the ground. I turn a corner into the backyard and find a big cow looking at me, her eyes bulging. Her udder is bleeding. I find out later that some of the 11s had shot her and other livestock.

I leave the backyard and head out through the gate, rejoining my squad as the company continues pushing forward. We come upon a gated military base. One of the tracks tears down the gate with a chain and we pour in, posting up on outer walls and a crude make-shift barricade. We run past big, dead tanks, archaic remnants of other wars long gone.

Big hangars are lined up in two rows. The tracks continue ripping down doors. Hayes and I break off from our squad, running from one hangar to another.

"Hayes, let's go back!"

"Fuck you, Keith!"

"Seriously, man, this is the kind of shit that gets us in trouble!"

"Then go back!"

"Fuck," I swear under my breath as I chase after him. We continue clearing corners and moving through doorways. Hayes runs past a corner, his gun facing down the new expanse as I careen past him, aiming my gun in the direction he'd been looking. My barrel clears his profile, and I aim forward, taking a knee behind a block of concrete

and dipping behind an adjacent wall. We pull open draw-
ers and put anything interesting in our pockets, breaking
mirrors or stopping to stare at weird pictures on the wall
only to abruptly careen into another room, looking for
something. Anything. We are supposed to be looking for
intel on nuclear bombs or terrorist activity, but being nineteen also means we are curious. This is new.

Near the far end of the base, we crack open one of the
hundred or so crates that we've seen scattered throughout
the compound. We look inside and find ourselves staring
at a giant red missile cradled in packing material. As we
look up and see all the other boxes, the possibility that
huge numbers of missiles could be strewn throughout the
base becomes self-evident. Other crates are broken open
and it turns out to be more of the same.

The missile I'll never forget finding is behind a door
that we post up on as a squad. Miller orders Luvs to give
him his pistol and aims at the lock on the door. Pulling the
trigger, he misses. He shoots again and misses.

"Fuck, Miller, get out of the way," says Lewis, who
takes the butt of his gun and hits the lock a few times
until it breaks. As he pushes the door open, we all aim
inside. The door swings aside to reveal a squat missile, just
about the size of the door, sitting on its base. We all look
at Miller as he stares at the missile.

The day slips away, and the night starts to set in as we
approach a bridge on the Diyala River. We run up a massive sandy hill. Lewis instructs us to set in, and I look out
at an interesting scene. Off the massive berm where I'm

lying, there are houses packed along the edge of a drop-off that leads down to the river. A bridge that once connected the two sides now stands with its middle blown out. We are finally staring at the city of Baghdad, but with night setting in we've stopped for now.

"Hayes, get the fuck over here," says Lewis, who has been more angry with Hayes than usual for the last three days. Lately, Hayes has been getting caught sleeping on post. Every time someone busts him, he is forced to spend more time on the gun, which causes him to fall asleep more and more. This wouldn't happen if Lewis or Miller stood any post at all.

"Last night was the last straw, motherfucker," Lewis unloads on Hayes. "You're horrible at your fucking job, and all you have to do is what you're told. Is that too much to fucking ask for? Huh?"

"No, Corporal," mumbles Hayes.

"Well, obviously it is. You're fired. Get out of my fucking sight," Lewis says. I stare across the river behind the gun, scanning.

Moments later, Miller crouches down next to us. "So, we are on line along the Diyala River with the rest of the battalion right now," he says. "There's a bridge just a little ways down that will be the main attack point for the unit, but we will attack here as well, dividing their forces and drawing them across a larger expanse. Since we are dealing with the Republican Guard, these motherfuckers won't fade away. They are here to fight. This is where shit is going to get real, so don't fuck it up, Keith." He pauses. "Where's Hayes?"

Looking around, the three of us realize that Hayes is gone.

"Lewis, where is your ammo man?" Miller says.

"I don't know! I fucking fired him; then he walked off."

"You fucking fired him?"

"Hey, I didn't know he was going to take it literally!"

"Well get him back here. Or you can explain it to the Colonel when Hayes gets himself captured and fucking killed on TV," Miller says, as he crouches down behind the edge of the hill, skirting the safe side towards the other team. Below us, on the other side of the berm, the rest of an old army base is spread out with barracks and an armory for gas masks and weapons.

"Keith, find Hayes and don't come back until he's with you," Lewis orders, grabbing the gun from my hands.

I get up and realize I'm soaked in a cold sweat. All the running today burned me out. Now, as night approaches and the chill sets in, I hunch forward a bit to keep the shell of my flak jacket close to my body for warmth. I have my pistol out, and I make my way in the dark back towards the AAV. Hayes is there. He's climbing up the side of the track and digging for something in his pack, maybe a letter from home or some food he had stashed somewhere.

"Hayes," I hiss at him, whispering like we're contentious brothers trying not to wake their parents with an argument. "Get the fuck down here now! Miller is pissed, and we've got to get back."

"Fuck off, Keith," he says.

I grab at him. He drops down and grabs me by the vest, yelling, "Keep your fucking hands off me, motherfucker! I've had enough of you, you piece of shit! Don't you ever fucking touch me, bitch!"

Swinging his rifle up, he jams it in my flak. I smack the barrel away. "You going to shoot me, huh, Hayes? I'm trying to help you, man. Get your shit together. What the fuck?"

I push him back against the track. Hayes begins to cry. He stumbles off again, though this time in the direction of the berm. Looking up, I see the tracker is staring at us.

I run after Hayes. When I find him again, he is crying and sitting just off the path on a rock. "Keith, I'm sorry, man. I can't believe I just did that. I consider us brothers. I would never be able to live with myself if anything happened to you because of me," he says, as he wipes his face with his sleeve, sniffling and shaking. "Someday, I'm going to visit you in Minnesota, and you're going to show me around that mall."

"It's okay, man. Let's just go back."

"No, it's not okay. I could've killed you!"

"Yeah, but you didn't. You wouldn't. It's okay, let's just go back."

"Okay. And I'll tell Lewis, that way he can hear from me. Maybe he won't think I'm a coward because I came clean about it first."

"No, it's okay, Hayes. Don't say anything. It doesn't matter. I shouldn't have grabbed your foot. Let's just go back, come on."

Hayes stands up and takes a deep breath. We jog back to the berm, run up the three-story dirt mound, and rejoin Lewis. He leaves Hayes alone but gives him a longer shift that night.

The next morning, we push forward to a set of houses overlooking the riverbed and the city beyond. We climb up a ladder on the back of a one-story house and set in on the roof. The only cover is a one-foot lip along the edge of the surface, so we lie in the prone, sighting in along the bridge as support in case anyone attempts to cross.

That night, people on the opposite bank of the river begin lobbing rockets and small arms fire onto our side. This is mostly ineffective, landing a safe distance in front or behind us or off to either side. Each time a light trail flares up from the clustered houses along the city's edge, tracers from our side lace into the dark, searching with lead for the specific window or doorway where it originated.

When it's my turn to stay awake, I watch the bridge from behind the gun. If soldiers make a run for this side, I'll cut them down and alert Miller. He won't let me fire back at anything lobbing missiles from the city, though. He believes it would needlessly give away our position, and we are dangerously close to the bridge as it is.

I begin thinking that there is an upside to standing post half the night. While others sleep, I think about what my options would be if something shot from the other side finds our rooftop. I would have a moment to jump and save myself. But then, what side should I choose? The missile might weave randomly to one side or the other. What if I jumped in the direction it landed? In the end, sleeping through the explosion seems less maddening, even if it means risking the possibility of never waking.

Further down the river, an RPG hits the dirt next to Flynn and sand blasts into his eye. First squad fires at windows that light up with enemy muzzle flashes. Pickett is ruthless and chooses not to hold back. Miller, however, stays cautious. Somehow, we wind up crouching and waiting until the next morning. The exchange over the river ends as daylight restores our advantage.

An odd-looking tank arrives. It moves across the first section of the bridge to where it ends in a charred broken mess. The tank's mass of metal begins unfolding itself into two parallel metal arms, which arch up into the air and reach across to the other side of the damaged bridge. It unhinges its main body from the arms as they set down, and I can see that it has detached two perfectly spaced support beams, just right for vehicles and infantry to traverse.

A lone tank approaches, driving over the bridge and posting up on the other side. A Marine visibly mans the turret, a 240G of his own locked down in front of him. Only a blast shield stands between him and the city. I watch and wait in the prone on top of the house. Everything is quiet. I never know why we wait or why we go. I just move and stop as ordered, losing time for days.

As I sit and stare forward, I see people emerging from a doorway into the open field between the town and the opposite riverbank. They start walking, then pick up the pace and begin running at the tanks. They hold white material like flags, waving it above their heads. It looks like about ten people, maybe a family. Maybe more fleeing soldiers.

The gunner on the tank opens fire, dropping the faster ones in front. The rest turn back, but the gunner keeps shooting. None make it back to the city's edge.

Heavy silence returns until an old lady emerges from one of the houses, screaming and wailing. She stumbles down the embankment away from the tanks and the bridge. She thuds to her knees at the water's edge, muddying her black dress, her head swiveling as her throat projects indecipherable sounds of pain.

She knew them. Maybe they were family. Only moments ago, they might have been clinging to each other in a room, her son holding his wife and kids close as they clutched him back. He might have looked up from his family to her imploringly. He had been the man of the house for quite some time now, but he needed direction from his mother again, like he had so many times in the past when he was only her child, not yet a father or husband. Here and now, in this place, he had no answers. Did they not hear the sound truck telling everyone in town to leave, days ago? Why stay when everyone else had left?

Maybe it had been this woman who made the decision to gather as much white material as possible. Perhaps she sat there with the other adults as the morning light crept into the room, instructing the children on how to wave the pieces of material over their heads effectively, telling them that it would save them and they would be together forever and everything would be okay. She might have looked outside to see the tanks on her side of the river and the soldiers looking in their direction, and wondered about the life they would start together if they could just get out of the noose that seemed to be tightening around the neck of the city. They had survived last night. Now they were here, and freedom was so close.

Did she run with them then, as they careened out towards the tanks in the morning sun? Or was she too old? Did she hold back just enough to see the shooting start, capable only of clutching the wall of the house her family had left for the last time in this world and screaming as they died in front of her?

Her screams and wails continue as we look on from the other side of the river. A rifleman positions himself next to me and implores Lieutenant Oliver to let him take a shot at her. "Sir, I have her dead in my sights. I can take the shot," he says over the radio.

"Don't take the shot. I repeat: Don't take the shot," Lieutenant Oliver's voice replies.

"Fuck! Guys, I made a fucking bet with someone back home for a case of beer that I would get a fucking kill," says the Marine to the rest of us on the roof. "This might be my last chance at it. Fuck if I came all the way over to this shithole for nothing!"

Getting back on the radio, he sights in again as he relays another message. "Sir, she may have bombs strapped to her chest under all that material. She is moving down the hill towards our position. I'm going to take the shot. I repeat, I'm going to take the shot." He finishes the message and looks back down the barrel, one leather-gloved finger tightening on the trigger.

"Do not take the shot. That is a direct order," Lieutenant Oliver responds.

"Fuck!" The Marine lowers his gun. I relax and exhale, only then realizing that I had been holding my breath.

In time, the woman stops wailing. She sits slumped over on the bank of the river. Eventually, she begins to shift around and stands up, aimlessly wandering back up the hill and out of sight.

That night, the shooting from both sides begins again. When I'm awake on the gun, I stare, trying to gauge the path of each rocket fired. I tense as it leaves the far side and relax as it impacts harmlessly on this one.

The next day, I'm delirious and not sure what is going on. We are ordered off the building and I walk down with all my gear and ammunition to a short berm, directly in front of the bridge. Other Marines fall in against the berm, and I realize we are getting set in formation. Behind us, the tracks are lining up. A tank moves past our position and rolls over the bridge, joining the other tank on the far side. We have reached the moment when we will take the bridge and invade the city itself.

I lean against the hill and watch others in the company line up behind and in front of my squad. About two hundred of us wait to file over the bridge. Once we are all in position, the tracks begin rolling out single file. As the first one passes us, the Marines in front start peeling off the hill and walking in a staggered formation on either side of the tracks.

I move forward. Miller walks to the other side of the next track that passes us, and I stick to the right side of the road and wait for him to get a few paces ahead before turning the corner and following Lewis towards the bridge. My eyes float in a painfully overheated and agitated daze, looking back and forth at the first set of houses across the river.

I'm comforted by the heat emanating off of the giant metal AAVs. They creak forward in between us, slowly but with relentless urgency. Looking up I can see two Cobra helicopters making continuous figure eights in a lazy dance just over the river ahead of us. As I reach the edge of the bridge, shots ring out on the other side. Instantly, the world turns into rapidfire chaos.

The 50s and the automatic grenade launchers mounted on the tracks begin firing as the tracks themselves kick into a higher pace, moving forward with an increased clacking of mechanical will. The Cobras overhead complete a figure eight with precise accuracy, and as they turn about to face the city, Hellfire missiles hiss out from underneath their fuselages. The missiles impact with heavy whomping sounds, causing a heat wave and fiery explosions. Now, I'm running over the bridge. I can see other Marines slamming into any cover they can find on the other side.

When I clear the bridge myself, I post up on a wall. I follow Lewis as we move ahead to the next building. In the middle of the road, a little way into the city, I see a Republican Guard soldier curled up in the fetal position.

He's seared black all over and looks childlike in a brutal sort of way. I wonder what he saw when the gates of hell opened up in front of him. Did he hope that this would be some sort of epic last stand, or did he think his little ragtag band of resistance had a real chance here? Maybe he believed it was better to die fighting for his government's cause instead of risking his family's death if he chose to defect and hide somewhere safe. Or it could be religion that kept him here, the dream of some beautiful place to come once a switch turned him off in this world and on in another.

He's out of sight, only a memory as I careen around the side of a stone-walled structure and turn the corner, running through a courtyard and into a building. It's a pool hall, and I run into the public bathroom and begin kicking the doors in one by one. I aim my gun from the hip each time I kick in a door, but there's no one there.

Random areas of sniper fire are flanked and taken out. We keep pressing forward. As we move up to an open area with a tall building in the distance, I can see someone firing out of it. The unit avoids going through the open expanse, choosing to slink through a narrow alleyway instead. We run through a big, walled enclosure, and I can see the giant metal doors across the courtyard punching in violently as impacts chew them up.

Running forward, I squeeze through a gate. There's a tank completely engulfed in flames, spitting shrapnel in all directions. Someone is yelling at me to keep moving. I turn and run towards the next set of buildings.

Whether we post up on a wall, along a berm, or in a window, we sweat and blink away the burning sensation, anticipating enemy movement.

Moving up to an intersection away from the road, all three platoons meet at once. I post up just off the road as Miller, Pickett, and Perry find each other behind me. I turn and look at our three squad leaders' faces. They seem relieved.

"I think we might all make it out of here," says Perry.

"Yeah, this wasn't so bad. I thought these Republican Guard faggots were supposed to be tough," says Pickett. They talk for a bit, then return to their platoons.

We press forward again, this time moving into an area that is distinctly the Beverly Hills of Baghdad. A Marine with the self-appointed moniker "Sniper Bait" sings at the top of his lungs and walks ahead of us through the city. We walk down a winding road lined with artificially designed landscaping, palm trees, and grassy yards. The houses are still brown sandstone, but they boast multiple stories and look ornately designed. They are spaced out along the road, some with balconies and driveways.

This is the first time we have walked on a sidewalk in Iraq. We take turns breaking off the road and running into front yards, pouring into empty mansions and gliding up balconies with guns aimed upward and through rooms. Our eyes are always searching rooftops and alleyways and inside the doorways and balconies. In one mansion, I stop and look at a massive tapestry of someone's kid sitting on Saddam's lap and then turn into an office room. I make sure to kick over the chair before rifling through the desk for paperwork or any trinkets that will fit in my pocket.

The nice houses give way to an urban environment.

But I don't remember how I got to this point.

Maybe it took hours.

Maybe it happened right then.

Maybe it didn't happen as I remember.

The pace abruptly relents like a giant, maddening bubble suddenly popping. Explosions seem further away than before, and everyone slows down. We have been moving on foot all day. Now we are approaching the heart of Baghdad, an area that has yet to be walked by American troops.

Unlike in the wealthy suburbs, the people here haven't left the city. We walk in staggered formation down the road as they watch us from doorways and windows. It feels inappropriate, making eye contact with strangers from such a different world. The patrol stops and starts as we creep along.

The men in front stop and I take a knee next to a wall placed as a median to divide a fork in the road. I wait for the formation to continue. A lady smiles at me, and I smile back. She leans down and whispers to a girl who stands just behind her. The girl skips out of the doorway, burdened only by two small sandals and her little dress, until she stops about a foot in front of me. Her face is almost level with mine, but even so, she is still closer to the ground.

I'm looming over her, dripping in sweat and tired from the weight of all of my gear and the weeks of hell I've spent here in her country. The kids are all small, and we generally misjudge their ages. She looks five, but she's probably closer to ten. Uncomfortable from the stress of leaning on one knee, I begin adjusting my machine gun. I stop when I notice her smile faltering as she sees the movement of my gun.

Her smile returns slowly. Moving her hand out from behind her back, she hands me a flower. I nod and smile. I realize I can't carry the flower, but I feel compelled to keep the gift. I look down at my gear, dropping the stem into a crevice among my various pouches, which prompts a little giggle from the girl. She covers her mouth and turns, running back to the lady, who lifts her arm in a wave as her daughter finds a place to cling amongst her skirts. The child looks back at me, and the mother lightly rests her hand on the side of her head as they both stare down the road.

When people from home ask if I believe in the Iraq war or not, I think of that little girl. It makes me wonder myself.

More little boys and girls run out of doorways, handing me flowers. I put them in my gear and continue on. An hour later, Miller stands in front of me, his face riddled with an odd mixture of anger and confusion.

"Keith, what the fuck are you doing? You look like a goddamn gift basket! Get that shit off of you before you inspire the Iraqi army to retake the city. For fuck's sake!"

As he walks away, I brush off all the wild flowers. I make sure to fold one of them into a piece of cloth I carry, placing it carefully in my pocket for safekeeping.

Our patrol continues on. Eventually, we stop to set up checkpoints and begin searching every vehicle and their owners as they attempt to leave the city. I sweat profusely in the heat. We started out in Kuwait in February. It's now April, and the sun beats down relentlessly as summer nears.

Lewis walks over, grabs my neck protector, and with a flick unstraps one side. He lets me know that I need to let my gear breathe a bit, because we will be here until Marines a few blocks away finish taking down Saddam's statue.

SAPPERS

"Another Vietnam vet came by here today. He is one of those guys who haven't talked about it at all. All of a sudden, the war is the only thing he can think and talk about. That makes two guys this week. It's good and it's sad that it happens this way. It's good that they are able and willing to talk about it, and sad that it took over forty years for them to get there. Wish me luck. All of a sudden, I am the wall for them to lean on."

■ ■ ■

At night in Tay Ninh, there is tracer fire. We load our guns with tracers for every five rounds, and thousands of them go everywhere, up in the air in every possible direction. There are mortars coming in, and at the same time the sappers are coming through the wire, looking for us. Even so, some of our guys are just firing blindly at the dark.

And then, there are explosions along the flight line. Really big explosions, some of them. Helicopters blowing up. One night, they even blow up the ammo dump. It doesn't happen all at once. But once the Vietcong start walking those mortars in, it provides the sappers with a huge distraction. They sneak up on us, running through our base and blowing shit up. It's suicidal. They know it, and we know it. They sit outside the wire at night and get loaded up on opium, staring from the tree line at the claymore zone and concertina wire that are just waiting for them to creep through. There are no lights, so we can't see them. The perimeter is guarded by Vietnamese soldiers who are on our side. When the sappers get past the claymores and the wire, they kill the Vietnamese on their way into the base.

The sappers go after the helicopters first, because the choppers are what tear them up during battles. They get pretty close sometimes, though usually we stop them by the time they get past the perimeter and cut through the Vietnamese soldiers.

There are these leaflets called Chew Hoy that the Air Force drops over towns and forests, telling the Vietcong to surrender. The first time I ever see one of them, it is outside our company area, tacked onto the flagpole right next to the company clerk's office. The papers we send to them, telling them to surrender, are left for us as a brutal and costly way of telling us to take our own advice.

Another night, some guy comes running into my tent. He almost knocks my bunk over as he yells about us getting attacked. I grab my gun, run out to a hole with sandbags around it, and wait. The sappers make it to our hangar, which is where we get them. It's a firefight. It's dark, so we can't see anything, but we shoot anyway. The next day I see the guy we lit up. His body looks like a wax doll, chewed up with holes from our M-16s. He still has C4 strapped to his hands.

In March of 1971, our company is involved in a multi-company assault into Cambodia. The first insertion goes well.

The second insertion is when all hell breaks loose. There is so much enemy fire coming into the flight from what seems like all directions that the infantry soldiers on the helicopters are falling off the ship dead before we touch down. At one LZ, they refuse to get out of the chopper. My gunner and I have to get behind them and push them all through the door.

Scared and panicking, they tumble out of the helicopter onto the ground in a pile. Later, I hear that ours wasn't the only ship that had to physically push them to get them to move. Once they are all on the ground, the pilot pulls pitch leave before I can even get back to my seat and get behind my M60. We leave the LZ as fast as we can, being shot at and missed all the way out.

On another insertion, everything seems normal on the way into the LZ. When we are just feet off the ground, an enemy machine gun opens up right in front of me from a concealed bunker. I let go of my gun and instinctively curl up into a ball, thinking to myself, "I'll wait until the bullets hit me." None of them do. I can't figure out why. Maybe it has something to do with God.

During that same week, I get relieved one day. I stay back in the company area. We are given updates on that flight, and find out that they are returning with one wounded. Quite a few of the helicopters have bullet holes in them, and it sounds like the whole flight has been shot up. We all go out and wait for them to come in and land. When my ship finally sets down on the ground, I am horrified to find out that the guy who took my place is the one who was wounded. He was shot in the leg and hip. I will never exchange a day off again.

We insert about six hundred troops into the LZ in seven days. Less than sixty of them walk out, and those only by permission of the enemy. At the end of day at the end of that week, I make it back to my bunk. I throw my gear down and am sitting there in a daze when my platoon sergeant walks over. He throws something onto my bunk, saying, "Here is your fucking air medal." I will never understand why he was such a prick about it.

We hold a memorial in our small company area in honor of two of our guys. The CO speaks first, and then the chaplain. When the chaplain says, "Please bow your heads for a moment of silence," I look down and realize that I am sitting on an empty 50-gallon drum. There are a couple of sandbags piled on it for comfort. Sitting there with my legs hanging over isn't bad, but it isn't comfortable either.

I sit there in silence, staring at my feet and trying to deal with the knowledge of the instant deaths that day. I am still shocked by it all. It feels like the Grim Reaper really got into our faces that day, and it is hard not to let a different kind of fear creep into my soul. I look up for a moment and see the rest of the company standing all around me, silently looking down at their own feet, still in shock. Then, like me, they accept it. They know that sleep is needed. It is only sleep that will let our brains work on it alone until we wake up in the morning and let us go off to do it again.

The CO concludes the hasty little gathering, and we all head back to our hooches, or to the shower, or to the club for some alcohol. Nobody is talking, just solemnly walking back to our own areas. I feel like I am in a dream, floating back to my own little area. I am still trying to absorb the hit all of this had on me.

16

THE HOUSE

"They have all these opinions, but all they do about it is go watch a movie or think of some other social issue they want to have feelings about. Because that's what I am to them, a fucking social issue."

"Gabe, listen. They don't have a clue. It's not their fault. Listen, I know what I'm talking about. Believe me, when I got home in 1971 I just wanted to get away from people. So I give them a pass. My real friends are veterans. So I listen to what you say. I'm proud of you, and I respect what you did. But the people who didn't serve don't belong in our world, and we don't belong in theirs. The difference between me and you right now is that I'm not angry anymore. I'm not pissed off. I mean, really, it sucks walking around being pissed all the time. It's all about perspective. One tour in a combat zone changed the way I am, just like it did you. I'm telling you as your uncle, and your fellow combat brother, you got it too. It's nobody's fucking business but ours. We have PTSD, and it's okay."

"I'm sorry, but that's not the box I'm going to allow anyone to put me in. I don't care if that's going to make it awkward between us. I'm not going to be that guy with mental issues that people avoid. I might be a monster in my head, but it's not the kind of monster they imagine. It's hard because I had this idea of what I would be when I grew up. Then I went into the Marines, and nothing happened the way I thought it would. I've had to live with that, and with all the ignorance from people and their opinions about everything I experienced, since then."

"Well, I think you're normal. I really do. We are normal. You're a survivor, and I am too. Getting our arms around this PTSD thing takes a lot of time, a lot of thought, and a lot of dialogue. Maybe no one will tell you this except your uncle, but you have PTSD, and until you accept that and get help you are going to struggle every day. Now, if you want to think I'm crazy and get off the phone right now, I'm okay with it. But you're going to hear me say it until you get help like I had to. I agree, you should move here and we'll finish the book. But the first thing we will do is get your sorry ass in the truck and go to the VA. I don't care if they think you are faking your back pain, I'll stand there with you and we can put in a claim together. Who cares what those people think?"

■ ■ ■

Second Platoon and all its attachments, including my gun squad, stay in a house that night. Now that we have taken Baghdad, this is it until our unit decides what to do with us.

Lieutenant Oliver pays one of the locals to fill his car with cold beer and back it into the driveway, right up to the side door. The boxes are unloaded and the bottles handed out. Someone hands me a beer and I look at it, realizing I've never had a full beer in my life. I turn the bottle in my hand. It's tall, and the liquid glows through the glass, unmolested by labels of any kind on the outside or any imperfections on the inside. I drink the beer, glad it isn't warm water even though I don't care for the taste, and walk around the house.

I'm unsure where Lewis and Miller have gone. The 11s have taken over security for the night, and for once I don't have to stand post. I walk up to the roof with only my pistol on my hip, feeling lighter than I have in a long time. One of the 11s hands me a can of Pepsi.

"Ever tried whiskey?"

"No, Corporal."

"Take a pull. It ain't Jack, but at least it's better than the shit water we've been sucking down."

I look at the can in the dark, put it to my lips, and take a sip. I ignore the taste like I've been ignoring the taste of warm stagnant water and the smell of burning shit and sand.

"It looks like things are over," the corporal says as we stand on the roof.

"Did you see the guys they've got downstairs?" I ask.

"Did I see them? I brought them in!"

"What did they do?"

"We think they were shooting at us from a building. They surrendered when we started to return fire. Hard to say. I was providing security, so I was focused in another direction when it happened."

Someone hands me another beer, and I begin floating through the house. It feels like I've been forgotten for once. Dust stands in the air. Marines sit quietly at windows or lie asleep in the rubble, low talking and tired laughter coming from the places where more than two congregate.

Ordered to clear a room for holding POWs, a bunch of Marines begin moving everything out of the biggest room on the first floor. Corporal Gibbs orders me to help, but as he looks at me in that unlit third world house, he stumbles a bit. I leave. When I find Hayes and my gun, I lie down, glad that the last couple of days are dead forever.

The next day, I stand post on the roof with a group of others. We share the rumors of the day. Saddam got away. We'll be coordinating a giant movement to cordon off the entire city of Baghdad. We might be going home. We won't be going home.

Lieutenant Oliver sends a squad to the market. They patrol out from the building beneath me as I sit with my gun on the roof, scanning. They pass through the gate and ease their way out in two rows towards either end of the street. Looking out to other points where platoons have posted watch on houses, I pick out the occasional Marine on a rooftop or in a window. I can see one in a house further down the road, on top of a roof with a railing. The glass on his scope reflects back to me in the sunlight.

On the first day my parents moved the family from the city to the suburbs, we noticed the absence of traffic sounds, though in the city we'd almost forgotten their presence. I realize, like I did that day, that for the first time in a while there is no background noise of gunfire and explosions. Hours pass. The day gives way to the falling sun, the return of shadows bringing a heightened awareness of what might be hiding within them. The squad that left returns with pita bread sandwiches, filled with lamb meat and vegetables.

We operate out of that house for a week, guarding the perimeter of the building while squads conduct patrols. The house is small for us, and sharing it with prisoners is hard. It doesn't take long for the zip-tied Iraqis to become comfortable with us. As they sit against the walls, facing the door to the room, they stare with contempt at their guard. He stares back, confused and unsure what this means. They commiserate quietly in Arabic. In the past, when the Marine on guard told them to be quiet, they would stop and look down. Now, they keep talking.

Soon, they will see a side of us they didn't know exists. We are kids with guns. That alone isn't dangerous in a conventional sense. But never underestimate the potentially destructive nature of kids. If you hurt their feelings, they became capable of anything.

"Keith, can you go into the haji room and stand there with Lee?" asks Corporal Trent.

"Sure, what's going on?"

"The hajis won't stop glaring at him, and it's gotten to the point where it looks like he barely has control in there. I'll be in in a moment. Just going to round up some others first."

The Iraqis mutter and glare at me as I walk in. "Look away," I say to them in an improvised lower tone. "They really aren't afraid of us, are they?" I laugh to Lee.

"I guess not. It's getting creepy. One moment they sit there looking sad, and the next they won't stop looking all mad at me."

A bunch of Marines files into the room, squaring off with the disheveled bunch of Iraqis. They still don't get it. They stare up at us in some sort of patronizing unity.

"What the fuck are you looking at? Yeah, I'm not glad to be here either, you fucks," says Trent. Stepping forward, he places the barrel of his gun against the forehead of the apparent leader in the group. While the rest of them seem to cower a bit despite their silent protest, this one doesn't flinch away.

As the barrel of the gun digs into his forehead, the Iraqi breathes a little harder but continues to glare. We aim at the others that are still looking at us. We aren't smiling anymore, but curious to see how far we will have to go to get them back under control.

"This is what you need to understand, you pieces of shit," someone starts in. "Angry looks can't save you now. Just because you think you're right and we're wrong, it won't change the fact that we win and you lose. If we catch you disrespecting any of us again, this will go from a peaceful demonstration to you getting fucked with. So keep it up, motherfuckers."

Staff Sergeant Kelly storms into the room. "What the fuck is going on here?"

"Staff Sergeant, some of the hajis were eyeing Private Lee, so we were –"

"You were committing war crimes, is that what you're telling me?"

"Not exactly."

"Yes, exactly. We are not here to humiliate them. Look at his face, all of you. Look. He doesn't seem scary, does he? That's because you can see him. He's sitting in front of you. But there's a good chance he'll be set free to do whatever he wants to do. He could decide to go home and become a farmer. Maybe he'll choose to get married and carry out the life of a good and peaceful Muslim. Or maybe he'll remember how badly he was treated here and decide to pick up a gun and do something about it." Kelly pauses. "Where will you be then? Maybe home, maybe not. But someone will be here. Hopefully he's not looking in a different direction when this guy makes his move. What happens then? Did you think about that? No, you didn't. And until I give you the order to think, you will do what I say. And I say leave them alone. If they are guilty of anything, they will be tried and convicted later. We aren't the judge, jury, and executioners, Marines. If you have a fucking problem with that, then too bad."

"What do you want us to do with them then, Staff Sergeant?"

"Blindfold and separate them. If they can't see each other or us, it should break up any sort of little mutinous nonsense they come up with."

I move forward and grab the one who thinks he's angrier than I. He tries to maintain eye contact. I wonder if he thinks he's been through as much in the last couple of days as I have in the last six months. Not possible. He's overweight.

I wonder what type of poetic justice he is wishing down on me as I spin him around, dragging him by his shirt to the far corner of the room. Grabbing two points on the shirt, I rip it off his body in a few jerks and tie it around his eyes. It must be filled with his sweat. Immediately, he starts shaking his head and yelling in pain. Others are getting a similar treatment. They begin wailing and crying as well. Somehow, this works better than guns.

Lee and the rest of them leave me in the room to take a turn watching the now blindfolded and separated group of wailing Iraqis.

"Shut the fuck up!" I yell at one, who begins to cry. He continues, so I slap him in the back of the head, hoping he will stop. The sound of his yelling and my slapping only sets off the others.

Someone else walks in to help and grabs another Iraqi by the shirt, only to realize the man he grabbed has defecated all over himself. As everything continues to escalate,

I look over at the other Marine. He looks back at me, both of us unsure of what we should do next.

Kelly runs in, grabbing the loudest Iraqi. He spins him around, rips the blindfold off, and presses the barrel of his rifle into the man's sweat and hair-covered forehead in one fluid movement.

"Shut the fuck up, shut the fuck up, shut the fuck up!" he yells. The Iraqi goes quietly along with the rest. The room is silent, except for whimpers and the sound of shifting bodies on the concrete floor. Then, like the ebb and flow of a wave, it begins again. They start yelling and crying back and forth, louder than before.

"Okay. Get five others and meet me back here in five," orders Kelly.

Kelly puts the blindfold back on the Iraqi and places him in a corner. He has the six of us stand back to back in the center of the room. Our guns bristle outward as we wait for his next move. Kelly begins counting down from five. When he finishes the count, he loudly commands, "Make ready!"

In unison, we rack our rifles and pistols. It seems to work. The Iraqis may have thought we were about to execute them. Maybe they were simply tired of the game they started. Either way, the drama ends. After a day and a half with them, a truck arrives to take them away.

That night, Lewis is checking my gear to make sure I have everything I'm supposed to be carrying on the patrol, nothing more, and especially nothing less. Hayes is stuck carrying the most since I have the gun and Lewis won't carry anything more than his day pack and rifle. Whenever we go anywhere as a gun team, Hayes is stuck carrying most of the ammunition, the ammo bag with the spare barrel, and the tripod. None of that extra gear is designed to be carried easily, but he manages somehow. Sometimes he gets lucky and the tripod isn't necessary. Then he only has to carry ammunition, and he's even allowed to leave behind the bag with the spare barrel and the attachment that connects the tripod to the gun.

It's dark as we file out of the house and move across the street, a squad of 11s leading in the front and following up in the rear. I keep the Marines in front of me in clear sight, waiting for commands to stop or take cover to be quietly passed down the line to me so I can relay the message and follow suit. Sometimes, when people are talking in the street or inside a window in Arabic, we are commanded to halt. I shrink quietly to the side of a house and aim down an alley or at a window, waiting for the order to continue on to be given, and our patrol is resumed.

Loud clacking sounds from an AK-47 rattle out in the night, and we run forward. I have no idea whether this is good or bad. I run up to Miller where he stands, waiting for Hayes and Preston to catch up to the rest of us.

"There's a sniper somewhere up ahead. Clear through this area and cut him off," Miller says. Lewis pushes past him and begins moving along the side of a building. "Lewis, get back here!" he yell-whispers at Lewis's back.

"Fuck!" he adds. Then we are off, moving past a few buildings as the other squad of 11s peels off down an alley and circles around so we can both approach from the same direction.

Miller yells at Lewis to come back as Lewis yells at us to follow. He is running down an alley; gun focused in on rooftops as he disappears from a courtyard that is filled with unobstructed moonlight.

I freeze in the open courtyard with the rest of the squad, unsure who I should follow. Suddenly more shooting starts, and Miller screams at us to get down. The clacking of the AK-47 mixes with maddening snapping sounds as bullets pass overhead. I drop down to the ground, one hand still on my gun. I stare straight at the pavement a few inches away from my face, waiting to be hit, waiting for my frantic thoughts to be put to a hard stop by unimaginable pain or unending nothingness.

Then the 11s close in with covering fire around us from the outskirts of the courtyard. They are chewing up a two-story building somewhere. My helmet blocks it from view. I hear Miller yelling over the gunfire and pull my legs back underneath me. I follow him out of the moonlight, safely slamming into the wall of a house on the other side of the open space and willing myself to push the crowding thoughts of nothingness away.

The snapping of the bullets yields to the AK's clacking. Miller yells again and we move, dropping into the shadow along the side of the building. The cat and mouse game ends. No one is hurt on either side.

The next night, I'm on post at the top of the building when I see muzzle flashes on another rooftop in the general area of one of our platoon's patrolling squads. One of the 11s on the roof with me begins radioing intel on the shooter's location. We are dug in around the area where the shooting is happening, so the unit getting fired upon is instructed to avoid friendly fire by moving into the house. Then they can take out the shooter at close range. By the time they get there, whoever had been shooting at them is gone. I watch the other Marines pace the roof in the distance.

17

THE EGG, THE AMUSEMENT PARK, AND JOE THE CAMEL

"I'm glad I'm not the only one that feels like America is based on empty symbolic pride, not principle. If our country believed anything I did was important, addressing my back would be important. Most Americans would never go over to a desert and risk their lives for an idea, but they talk about the importance of their ideology like it's a tangible part of who they are. They think their ideas protect them from being ignorant, but all that's accomplished is protecting them from being real human beings. It gives them a license to float through life. It justifies them in pointing at the anger behind my words as proof that I have issues, instead of looking at the meaning and the experience behind those words long enough to judge whether my issues are based on something real. Something fixable.

"But then I have to look at myself and what I did over there that first time. I killed one guy. He was surrendering, and already dead on his feet. But I'm the one with PTSD? I think I'm the one who failed, and one way or another I have to figure out a way to get ahead in life. Otherwise I'll never forgive myself, or forgive anyone who ever called me a hero and felt better for it."

"The thing that fucks us up is our ideals, Gabe. They go out the window when you go overseas. It's simply a mind fuck. You're raised one way, then in less than a year you're questioning everything. They're ideals, Gabe, and they're gone. We need to accept it. We need to move on."

■ ■ ■

Saddam had a zoo. It was gated and held many different types of animals. The one I remember most was a camel called Joe. We built sandbag bunkers at key points around the zoo, including outside Joe's gated enclosure. He would lean his head over the gate to where we stood or knelt behind our guns, and we would turn and feed him rations from our MREs. Someone fed him cigarettes. Joe ate it all, using his long neck to thrust his big head with its half-lidded eyes directly into our bunker. He made this post the most coveted during that time.

Now that there are specific places designated for our entire platoon to watch, Hayes and I don't have to split up the entire night on post. One morning, right before my turn to sit behind the sandbags with our faithful camel, Lewis gives me instructions for the day.

"Keith, here's some Iraqi dinar. When you get on post, wait for that sand-nigger with the alcohol. Buy the shit shaped like a tear drop. Got it?"

"Yes, Corporal."

"Don't fuck it up, unless you want me to give you Hayes's shifts tonight," he says. He picks up his sleeping bag, rolling it up and tucking into his pack.

Joe the Camel holds his head over my shoulder as I scratch under his chin, looking out at the road in front of the zoo. The Iraqi was sitting on the other side, his random assortment of alcohol, food, and trinkets neatly arranged around him in a half circle on a couple of thin blankets.

"All right, Hayes, watch my back. I'm going to get Lewis's worthless ass his breakfast of champions."

Hayes nods, handing me his rifle as he positions himself behind my machine gun. He unwraps a piece of candy and slips it into his mouth. I step over the sandbags, looking around for a moment before running across to the Iraqi on the side of the road. I get to him and take a knee, pointing at the tear-drop-shaped bottle as he begins counting on his hands to let me know the price. I hand him the proper amount of dinar and grab the bottle, then turn and run back to the post.

The next day, I hear about what Lewis and his friends did with the tear drop bottle of liquor. They got drunk and stumbled into the zoo, where they started tearing the place apart. Lewis grabbed a little pig called Babe and strangled it to death while his friends looked on, laughing and cheering. Other animals were hurt as well.

Fisher and Foster from first squad share a post with us, and we exchange rumors and stories from around the unit.

"So there's rumors of us pulling out of Baghdad early and going home."

"Shit. That would be fucking fantastic."

"Yeah, but we're up against a couple of other units in our regiment. Getting to Baghdad first might not mean a damn thing."

"Did you hear about Lewis and Pickett and the others? How they killed Babe?"

"At least they are passed out right now and will leave us alone for a few hours."

"I hear you there. I wonder when these fucks will stop treating us like we're still in boot camp."

"You think Miller and Lewis are bad? Pickett is probably lazier and more fucked up. He punched Foster in the face the other day for no reason, like he was just trying to prove a point. All we do is work hard for that motherfucker, and he never does anything other than fuck with us."

After the zoo incident, the officers tighten down on the lower enlisted ranks. It was clear that they'd given us a moment to breathe, and now that moment is over. We rotate the barricades along the perimeter of the area we are securing and change the shift schedules, trying to stay unpredictable and therefore be less likely to get caught in a firefight during shift change. This also forces us to dig more fighting holes under the scrutiny of Lewis and Miller.

We move to a broken-down amusement park. We patrol through it, feeling slightly nostalgic. This place feels more like home than anything we've seen yet.

Next to the crooked merry-go-round and assortment of rusted-out rides is a gigantic monument dedicated to the Iraq and Iran war. Imagine the Vietnam Wall in Washington D.C., and the impact of seeing every small space inscribed with the names of dead soldiers who died for their country. Then you can begin to imagine this towering structure. It is shaped like the two halves of an egg.

I walk up to it and run my hand along the Arabic words inscribed in its blue stone, realizing they are names. I slowly look up at the massive half-shells, trying to comprehend the scope of the war that could have led to this monument being built. I find out later it is called the Martyr's Monument and was built in 1983, the same year I was born.

As I stand there staring at their names, I am glad these men are dead. Better that than shooting at us here and now. Then again, they might have been farmers, forced to fight or sacrifice the safety of their families. Probably there is a little bit of truth in both.

Hayes and I dig a fighting hole next to the river along the side of the amusement park, across from the egg monument. As I dig, I feel nauseated from hunger. I pull out a packet of charms, deciding I might as well eat the candies this time. I sit there with three of them in my mouth, enjoying the sugary taste and drinking warm water from my canteen to ensure they don't get caught in my throat.

Lewis sees I've stopped digging, and walks over. "Hey, Miller, come over and check out Keith! I just caught him eating charms! Oh good, Keith, you want to eat charms," he says. "How many did you finish already? You know that's an hour of post per bad luck candy you've eaten?"

"I don't know, but when I finish the pack, I'd say it will be about ten."

"You better show some fucking respect!" says Lewis, as he takes a step closer to my fighting hole. I don't care anymore.

"What are you talking about?" I say. "You make me stand post all night while you eat all the food. I dig all the fighting holes. I never complain. And when the only thing you leave for me is charms, I can't eat them because it's bad luck? You're actually mad that I'm eating the only food you left me?"

Lewis is quiet for a moment. Then he walks over to his fighting hole, yelling the whole time. He jumps into it and begins throwing food at me. He must have been stockpiling it down there.

"You want food, huh, Keith? You worthless fuck! Here's some fucking food, bitch!"

I realize he's pelting me with all the best shit. All kinds of food that I haven't seen in a month rattles off the sides of my fighting hole and into the dirt. I'm excited, but trying to be careful not to show it. I reach down and grab pound cakes, chicken breast rations, protein shakes, and everything else he's thrown at me. I can't wait to tell Hayes about this later. I'll share all the food with him. He won't believe it.

"You happy now that you have your food, bitch? Huh, Candy-ass motherfucker?" Lewis shrieks. I block him out and focus on breaking open a main meal I haven't been allowed to eat since we crossed the line of departure. I eat it quickly before Lewis changes his mind and forces me to give everything back.

Later, I tell Hayes about what happened. We share the food, filling our stomachs for the first time in months. Afterwards, I sit up half the night, watching our surroundings and trying not to fall asleep. It's important that I stay awake, though more to avoid punishment for getting caught sleeping than out of any real fear of being attacked.

Stories start pouring in about more hit and run incidents in Baghdad. We had hit them hard at first, and everything was extremely peaceful. But then it wasn't. Shooting erupts at night, sometimes accompanied by yelling.

One night I'm awake, sitting behind my gun against a berm and looking out at the empty desert. There's half a night in front of me before I can wake Hayes up for his turn to stand post. I hunker down against the cold breeze and look back at the two lumps that are Lewis and Miller.

Standing up to shake off thoughts of sleep, I take out my pistol. I aim at one of the lumps, knowing it's Lewis, running the sights from his middle up to his head. I hold my aim there, thinking to myself, "It's too bad he hasn't gotten killed yet."

The lump shifts in his sleep, and I drop the gun to my side.

I'm playing video games with Flynn at his apartment in St. Paul, years later, when he tells me that he didn't flinch as he stood over Pickett one night. He aimed his rifle at his squad leader's head, wishing Pickett would wake up and anticipating the flinch that would force his hand.

More stories surface. I hear one about Wagner and the other gunner in third squad. While attached to Third Platoon, they set up a vehicle checkpoint to stop all traffic leaving the city. One day, a lone car with two unarmed passengers drove towards the checkpoint, not slowing down or making any signs of stopping. As Wagner sat behind the gun and sighted in on the vehicle, Iraqi civilians on either side of the road waved frantically as the car rushed past them, trying to stop what would soon become the inevitable.

As the car approached, undaunted by the crowd of flapping arms or the Marines with guns at the finish line, Perry gave the order to open fire. The gunners obliged, punching out the windshield with lead, tearing up the metal hood, and sinking the two front tires into the ground. Jerking to a stop, the vehicle sat there, a wheezing broken mess.

Wagner dropped the butt of the gun out of his shoulder and arched his head up to see what happened next. Getting out of the car on either side were two men. Both had been shot. They weakly pulled at their Muslim garb and revealed white material, attempting to surrender in the way they'd been taught we understood. This time, the peace flags were red with blood. They deliriously stood there, fanning out bloody clothes. Moments later they stopped, walking away down an alley.

Wagner said that he followed with a squad, but even though there was a clear trail of blood, they never found the pair. Does he still wonder why they ignored all the signs, the waving crowd, and the guns pointed at their car?

18

DYSENTERY

"When my friend Flynn got out of the Marines, he moved back to Minnesota. He left with his honorable discharge and good conduct medals, and had held a leadership position the entire time he was in. They turned around and called him back. There were a bunch of officers who weren't in the infantry, who had never gone overseas, and they were reading off names from a list of people who were being recalled. They were laughing and saying shit like, "Your number was called, I guess you're going back!"

"When they called his number and he went up there, he asked them what was funny. They said, "Well, it looks like we called your number." So he asked them if they had gone over there. And they were like, 'No. No, we haven't.' Then he said, 'Well, I've been over there three times, and I don't really know what you think is so funny about it.'

"They almost went after him for it! They tried to say, 'You can't talk to us like that. We're officers.' They treated him like shit because of his rank. Because he wasn't an officer. Because they had this list in front of them. No idea what he endured to get there.

"The doctor who had the final say, sitting there in front of Flynn with two stamps and his service record, saw that he was a junior in college and had already served three tours, so he let him go. He realized Flynn had done his time and didn't want to make it any more difficult for him back in the real world. He just wanted to start going to college and live his life. He just wanted an education. The civilian world is where, in the end, he'll have to prove himself. That's what everyone has to do.

"At the end of the day, the civilian world is where you make it or break it. Not the military. That's just something you survive to get to this other place."

"You hit it. You hit the word: Survive. A lot of people go, 'I was a victim.' Well, no, you weren't. You're a survivor if you're here. That word has special meaning to me. I survived my war by the skin of my teeth and so did you. It does a number on your brain. That number on your brain has got to get fucking dealt with, and the sooner you get it dealt with, the better at dealing with life you'll get, too."

■ ■ ■

The tracks leave us for good one day, replaced by seven-ton trucks that take us out of Baghdad and drop us off somewhere outside of the city, in a place called Diwaniya. They leave us in an open area of sand and churned-up mounds of compacted earth from past tank wars.

The back gate on the truck drops for us as we blink and file out into the sunlight, stretching the moment we find room to move. The place is nothing but a mechanically churned dustbowl. Tracks and tanks drive by, some dropping off groups of Marines while others continue on to a different section of dirt. The leadership ranks move out for a brief, and the few of us left from second squad can see first squad standing in the distance. We walk over to them.

Preston, Luvs, Hayes, and I stand across from Flynn, Bryant, Fisher, and Foster. We are covered in dust and sweat, our camouflage worn down and crunchy from the repetitive process of getting drenched in sweat during the day, frozen solid at night, and ground against the elements during the grueling push to Baghdad. Bryant nods at me, and I nod back. I shake Flynn's hand. Foster smiles and nods at me. Everyone finishes greeting each other and we stand there, waiting for someone to yell us in a direction.

The dust swirls around and bounces off our skin. We have been cycling through a continuous process of sweat-washing and sand-dusting for weeks without the chance to get clean. I run a fingernail down my neck, pulling a dollop of brown butter off my skin and playing with it between my fingers as we wait.

Soon all of the privates, privates first class, and lance corporals are ordered to line up. "Look for golf ball-sized metal objects," they tell us.

What they mean is, "Walk all over this godforsaken place until someone steps on something none of us want to step on. Or until nothing happens and we decide we can safely walk around as much as we want."

After trudging over the entire area, we set in. We dig fighting holes along the tank-made berm and wait. The Navy Corpsmen dig latrine trenches for us a little way off. Between stints of digging, I walk over and squat down, dropping my pants. It hasn't taken long for flies to find the shit trenches, and as we shit over and over again, a gigantic swarming mass of them shifts like a dark mist. As I lean over the moving mess, the flies swarm upwards, coating my anus. It feels like ten pairs of fingers struggling for any small opening to probe my taint. The act of shitting only stirs up more flies, an ominous buzzing chorus.

The trucks leave and we settle in further. Holes are dug deeper, shit trenches buried and re-dug. It is a brutally simple process when the dysentery begins to settle in. We defecate into the trenches. The flies swarm. Later, as we eat, they leave the shit and find our rations as we put them in our mouths.

At first only a few Marines become sick. Over the next few days, everyone starts puking and shitting their brains out. One night I'm on post, feeling sick but maintaining better than most. The nights are quiet, broken only by whimpering or the demonic sound of retching, mixed with the splattering noises from others who have managed to scramble to the trenches. As I stand, leaning against the side of my half-dug hole on the side of the berm, a Marine runs up on line about fifty feet away. He pukes over the side. The violent nature of his sickness makes the fluids leave his system in such a way that it creates an eerie, otherworldly shrieking sound. I watch him as this happens every thirty minutes for most of my shift, wondering how he keeps finding the strength to run, or even to stumble back to where he feverishly sleeps.

The Corpsmen cover up the old holes, digging new ones, trying to deter the disease-carrying flies. One night, I wake up dry heaving as warm water runs down my leg. I have shat myself. Stumbling to my feet, I make my way as fast as I can to the shit trench. I am shaking as I undo my belt and drop my pants, squatting over the hole, feeling weak from being sick.

Lewis appears out of the dark and squats down.

"Keith."

"Corporal."

"Fuck."

"I think I shat myself."

"Yeah, good luck with that."

He leaves. As I pull up my pants, I fall forward. The spins kick in, and I throw up into the sand in front of the trenches. My eyes bulge. I try not to breathe in the mud on the edge of the trench, smeared with shit, puke, and piss from two hundred sick bastards.

The next morning, I look around and realize that the ugly churned dirt on the ground is almost the same color as the sky. Then, I think of home. I think of my parents' three-acre backyard and dinners with friends and family. Like so many times before, I think about certain things I would give anything to be doing. I would love to be wearing jeans and a T-shirt, walking around in flip flops, no gear weighing me down or creating a shell of heat. I imagine staying inside when it's cold or finding shade in the heat, sitting or resting when I'm tired. Avoiding assholes, playing video games, reading books. Peace and quiet. Silence for days. Gentle interactions with my environment and the people in it.

Most of us recover, more or less. The trucks return and carry us on to another area. This one has a cluster of old Iraqi Army buildings. The low-ranking Marines line up and walk the entire stretch of the environment for land mines like we did before. Tents are put up, and the rest of us unroll sleeping bags in the buildings or outside on the stone walkways against their shells. We dig fighting holes and new shit trenches. This time, the trenches are further away.

Captain Potts assembles us in the largest of the clustered buildings on this random plot of desert blandness. Everyone in front sits, the ones in the middle kneel, and the rest stand in the back near the empty window frames and doorways.

"All right, Marines. First off, I want to say good job on not getting killed or making any serious mistakes. We did our job, and we're going home. Looks like you will be awarded the Presidential Unit Citation for taking over Baghdad as quickly as we did and pulling down Saddam's statue. Of course, we all know none of you were there for that but enjoy the ribbon. Also, enjoy the combat action ribbon, even though you didn't do anything. Don't get it in your head that anything you did these last four months mattered. The reason no one died is because you really had nothing to do with the main effort. When we get back home soon, we're going to turn around fairly quickly. We will be the unit sent to replace First Battalion Seventh Marines in Okinawa, Japan. All right, stay sharp. And don't pay too much attention to any rumors you hear. We were the first unit here, and, at least for the moment, it looks like we will be the first unit sent home."

That evening, I walk out to a fighting hole on the perimeter of the environment and replace the Marine who is sitting there. He's excited to go back to camp and eat or sleep. He chats with me for a bit, then leaves. I stand in the hole. My helmet and flak jacket are weighing me down, so I lean against the side wall, picking at the dirt and occasionally creating little runnels of sand that cascade down, powdering my boots and getting under my fingernails. Eight hours of this passes. I think more about home. I think about the conversations I'll have with people, the girls from high school I'll run into. I'll talk to them this time. I think of all the things I need to say to my friends and family.

A platoon runs by me. One of their men is trailing behind. A few others flock around him and yell as he cries and stumbles, weak and tired or just giving up like most shitbags do.

There's a certain type of Marine that never should have joined. Every platoon has one or two. They are infamous for their ability to be completely dumb and physically inept. They talk funny, fall asleep on every post, fall out of every run and every hump. They break mentally and embarrass themselves constantly. Others avoid them like the plague because, through association, people respect their friends less.

Kennedy was one of these guys. One day, he kept forgetting his rifle in the sand or against a building. He carried a light machine gun called the M249 Saw. Out of desperation, his team leader tied a little rope to the gun and attached it to his flak jacket. Kennedy walked past a group of Marines, the rope trailing him and his gun dragging behind as he plodded along, one of the dumbest people on the planet and a United States Marine.

As I sit in the hole, the sounds of people training and running around continue. There's a pit in the distance where trash is dumped. Smoke billows and the pit occasionally spits shrapnel when a round overheats, turning heads with a pop and a ricochet. We burn everything, creating a thick dark cloud. The key to throwing trash into the pit without injury is to run towards it, toss whatever rubbish you're carrying into the hole, and back away quickly.

We are all hoping to avoid becoming the poor sap who survives getting shot all deployment only to take a bullet from the garbage pit.

I hear two Marines approach in the dark. Someone is bringing my relief for the night. I attempt to make as little sound as possible as I rewrap my flak jacket, re-snap the chin strap on my Kevlar helmet, and attempt to create an image of studiousness on post. Corporal Jensen reaches my position and taps his night sights. He's letting me know with one subtle motion that he has been watching me fumble around in the dark, trying to situate my gear and hide the fact I have lost all composure by the time my eight-hour shift comes to an end.

I climb out, walking back to the buildings. Light from lanterns and flashlights emanates from within. As I approach, my imagination takes over. I recreate the way the base must have looked years ago before Saddam's army invaded Kuwait, when places like this might have been well staffed.

The light inside the buildings glows as Marines walk back in from post or the trenches. Others talk quietly inside. The dull, painted stone is fairly well lit, pushing the shadows a few feet outward. Electricity isn't nearly as common here. I can imagine Iraqi soldiers, living on the outskirts of a city where many grew up or migrated when they were recruited into the Iraqi Army. Staying quiet, they talk about the war with Iran, or politics in the Middle East, or maybe religion. Or maybe never religion.

The place grows from a scene in the distance until it becomes my own. I wonder if this is what Iraqi soldiers had done, returning to these buildings to escape the wind and eroding sand for a night before getting up to do it again the next day. I step onto the stone walkway and look around, wondering if Saddam ever visited shitholes like this when he was in power, wondering where he is now. Someone walks by and I jump, coming out of my trance. I return to where my gear is laid out next to my squad and pass out for the night.

The next day, the machine gun section begins training together again for the first time since we left for Kuwait. We grab our gear and guns and walk out to an area not far from the tents. Moore gives us our first brief as a section.

"Okay. As you guys already know, no one got killed or even hurt from Lima Company. A few did die in the other companies, but no one I knew, so I can't really talk about that. What I do know is that there are a lot of rumors floating around about when we will officially be getting the hell out of here. We are going to keep running gun drills and cleaning our weapons until the moment we board the plane. The war is over, but shit could still happen. And I don't know about the rest of you, but I plan on going home," he says.

We pair up in teams and practice taking the gun apart and reassembling it as quickly as possible, running the drills against each other. This drill doesn't end once the gun is put back together. The moment the last pin is dropped into place and the gun is racked for confirmation, the gunner has to stand up and spin in a circle a certain number of times before running past the officers' tents.

Once past the tents, he turns and runs back, crossing the makeshift finish line in the sand. The key is to avoid falling onto an officer's tent.

Second Platoon trains a little way off. I can see they have made a circle, and in the center two men are about to grapple. Lee approaches Carlos, grabbing for a bear hug. Carlos grunts and says, "Damn, retard, strength," gasping for air between clenched teeth with every word.

That night, Wagner walks past me as I begin to settle down on my sleeping bag.

"Hey, Keith. Do you know if anyone has tried using the phone tonight?"

"No idea. Why, are you going to?"

"Uh-huh. You want to go?"

"Sure. How do you call from that thing?"

"You haven't done it yet? Oh, man. It's a pain, but as long as we crank it and type a few numbers in, we can call home just fine."

I place the gun next to Hayes, strap on my pistol, and follow Wagner out to a cluster of big green plastic boxes with a crank phone sitting on top. Overhead, a canvas cloth is tied and stretched to cover the electronics.

Wagner sits on one side of the phone, and I on the other. I watch him explain in frantic excitement how to use the little portal to home. He clutches it in his big hands and tells me the tricks of how to make it work, what to do if certain problematic scenarios happen, and how long I can expect to talk to my family. He cranks it up and types some numbers into the device. Then he asks for a number I would like to try. I give him my parents' number. He hands over the receiver as he finishes typing it in.

Mom picks up and we talk for the first time since I was on a connecting flight from somewhere in America on my way to Kuwait. That was nearly four months ago. My dry eyes fill with tears as we talk. I had forgotten how real being home was and how much I missed it.

The next day, I'm standing in formation next to Lewis. Looking over, he punches me in the groin. I resist the urge to drop to my knees, relaxing the muscles in my face to avoid showing pain.

"Just want to make sure you don't get too comfortable, Candy-ass. Maybe you'll think twice about smiling in my direction next time, bitch."

We go on a morning run as a section. As usual, Hensley falls out. Getting yelled and screamed at, he struggles in the back of the formation. He is unable to keep up, and emotionally unable to handle the added pressure of getting yelled at after falling back so quickly at the beginning of a run.

Like Hensley, I was always bad at running. Flynn would tell me later that I ran like an ogre. Even though I was thin like most of the others, I slammed my feet into the ground and kept my head down. I was going to finish every time, just not gracefully.

During the day, it's too hot to train. We look for places to sleep or talk in the shade. A few of us pass out against the side of one of the buildings. I wake up hours later, my stomach in the sand, my back burns from the heat of the sun and my stomach is drenched in sweat. This is the most sleep I've had in a long time. My feet have finally healed up, with only traces of weakness left as proof of the dysentery a couple weeks ago.

The mail trucks arrive with sacks of letters and boxes of different shapes and colors with different handwritten addresses. Two of my uncles sent CDs. One decided to send old songs that he thought I would like, and I do. The other sent popular music from my generation he thought I would appreciate, and I do. Aunt Mary sent me letters typed in single-spaced font that were pages long. I love them. Dad wrote letters in cursive on expensive paper, and Mom wrote hers on the kind of stationary I remember walking past in places like Borders or Barnes & Noble.

Uncle Rick sent a letter for me as well. I haven't talked to him much over the years. I know he lives in Florida, and that he had been in Vietnam, or so my mom says. I read it through, interest piqued. It is a letter like most of the rest, really. He tells me he hopes things are okay, that my family is proud of me and he is too. He said he hasn't seen me in a while and he'd like to meet up at some point when I get back.

He says I am doing a good job. I look up from the letter. Maybe he doesn't know. I am sure he had, in fact, done something better a long time ago. At the end of the letter, he says I am part of the brotherhood now. He says to keep my head down while I am here, but then keep it up once I get home.

Signing off, he calls me his "little warrior brother." In the envelope with the letter, is a Native American bracelet made out of leather strips and beads. He says it's a warrior's bracelet, given to him by a Native American friend who had served in the Special Forces. I sit there that night, playing with the beads, glad that my uncle who fought in Vietnam is proud of me but unsure what I will say to him if he ever asks me what I did or didn't do.

The trucks return, and we load up back to back on the benches that have been placed in the middle. We face outward. Driving along, we zone out like little military bobble heads, staring at the terrain as we pass. It's comical, really, thinking about us as kids staring out for any movement that might be a source of entertainment as we zoom past villages and farmers out with their flocks of animals. Kids giggle and wave, jumping around while pushing each other out of the way. Hours go by. The dirt road turns into pavement, then eventually into multiple lanes of traffic complete with a median and highway signs.

We approach a base in the distance. All of our heads swivel to the front to see the gate as we approach. The trucks drive in and we get off and into formation, counting off our weapons and gear, cursing the sky every time the count is broken. This requires us all to hold our guns over our heads until they're accounted for.

All we can think about is food. The blessed chow halls hint at the past glories of our lives before the military, hopefully foreshadowing future meals with families and friends. It is a religion of sorts. We are about to enter the temple, and everyone can feel it.

We walk into the chow hall and a captain yells at us to stop. "Get the fuck out of here until you are clean! You look like shit, soldiers!"

"Sir, actually, we aren't soldiers. We're from Third Battalion Fourth Marines, and we need to eat," one of us, who is a little more daring than the rest, argues.

"Eat when you are clean. Until then, go."

We shower, then head back to the chow hall, looking around in disbelief. There are so many fatties here. It's unbelievable. Their skin looks clean and soft, not burnt tan or dry. Their faces are relaxed. We look at them, wondering why they wear uniforms like us, why they even have rifles or pistols. We sit there like feral animals at a tea party.

Then we see this girl. She is beautiful. She sits across from a group of us and stares at her plate, maybe praying, but maybe just young and uncomplicated. She is tall, with long blonde hair. Maybe somebody is waiting for her back home. Or even here, maybe another Army kid she met at training or in her unit. A group of girls drop down around her, their cafeteria trays slapping the table in a quick and finite clattering that ends as the talk about boys and dating begins. They all start chattering about who they are dating on base, the gossip afforded to people with a lot of free time and not a care in the world. We have been gone for months, long enough for the Army to push up behind us and set up this gigantic base. It's filled with people who carry out administrative jobs, like they did back home on bases like the ones in 29 Palms.

When I get home, it's going to be this kind of military veteran that is interviewed by the media, given standing ovations in stadiums, or packed into venues in Kuwait for troop-oriented entertainment. It's not entirely a bad thing. They are much more appropriate for the camera. They use words like 'honor' and 'warrior spirit.' If someone had interviewed myself or any of my friends back then, I would be terrified to find the recording. I might delete it before watching, if I could.

We leave the chow hall and walk back to the area of tents where we dropped our gear. Two Marines from our platoon are in the tent, watching all the machine guns. We pick up the guns and walk back to our different sleeping areas, cleaning them and chatting. Word is passed down that in the next couple of hours, we'll be turning in our weapons.

The unit that has arrived to replace us sends their weapons platoon over to our tent, where we hand off the guns. They inspect the weapons before signing for them. We watch and wait. Looking across at these machine gunners, I can see the weight they carry. They look serious and distracted at the same time. Maybe they are thinking of home, a place they know is still there, though it already feels like a dream. Maybe each of them is wondering to himself if that dream will soon be taken away.

I'm handed a Coke, gifted to us from someone on base with connections. I walk about ten feet into the desert outside the tent, looking at the can. It is a stark contrast, an object of such extreme familiarity in a still-foreign environment. Cracking the top, I put it to my lips and drink. The sugars shock my system. I'll never forget how cold and sweet that taste was, and how the simple act of drinking created a bubble of time-defying clarity I still carry. I'll never forget standing there outside that tent, realizing how lucky I was to be almost out of this place.

We stay on the base in Kuwait, milling about and waiting to go home. We aren't sure why they are keeping us here, but are told it's a sort of detoxification, a way for us to relax before leaving. They make us attend classes all day with a checklist. They stress us out by saying that if we fall asleep during the class we won't receive a checkmark, and if all the classes are not checked off, we won't be allowed to travel home. The pressure forces us to fight back drowsiness while listening to the rambling speeches about reintegration back into family life and normal living.

I am sitting in the tent across from Harper, and he is looking at my face with barely contained anticipation. He is one of the Marines I met in SOI, but we haven't talked much since then, even though we were attached to the same platoon. In front of us is a chess board, placed carefully on a box of rations. On the armrest on his right is an underlined word, "wins," with rows of neatly drawn marks below. On the right, is the word "losses." Below it, there is not a single mark. Harper points this out to me before we begin. I remember he has told me, "I am the undefeated champion and chess master of Kuwait."

We begin playing. Right away, I can tell he is a much better player than me. He moves a couple of pieces around the board, forcing my hand so that I have to adjust my pieces accordingly. Instead of creating a strategy like he has done, my half of the board becomes chaotic and undisciplined. Harper is enjoying a scene he has created probably fifty times already before closing in on yet another victim and an additional mark for the left armrest.

With miraculous luck, I find a way to trap his king. He is four moves away from taking my queen, but only three from checkmate. He stares for a while, then tips his king. He looks at me, smiling even though his unbeaten streak is over and that first single mark on the right armrest probably feels more like twenty. He shakes my hand and scratches a lone mark on the losing side of the chair. He is a good friend, and in this moment, he exists. In this moment, he is thinking only about chess and his fiancée back home.

Harper was not physically gifted in the way some Marines were. He was thin, and didn't have enough weight to win grappling matches against anyone. He approached obstacles with his mind. He had trained in aikido for his entire life, and with a staff, he could wreck the confidence of the biggest man in the company if they met with weapons instead of fists. He was there with me in that moment, though he wouldn't be in a year's time.

Finally, trucks show up to pick us up. We head off base to Kuwait City's international airport, where there are real jets instead of military cargo planes with stacks of weighted-down supplies in the middle and chairs squeezed in on the wall of the fuselage. The monotonous journey back to the States feels close to being over as we settle into our seats on the plane. We yell and cheer, smiling out the windows or mugging next to each other in front of disposable cameras. We all know something now that wasn't real just moments before: Our futures exist again.

Our first stop in America is in Bangor, Maine. The first thing I remember is walking off the plane onto the jetbridge and thinking that the smell of corporate carpet cleaning formula never felt so much like home before.

We shuffle out of the walkway and into the terminal. Up ahead, there is a sea of old people crowded around a space that has been roped off for us to walk. They wear WWII, Korean War, and Vietnam memorabilia, along with an assortment of American pride shirts, belts, and pants. It's like looking at a collage of old-school patriotism. They peer down the walkway, holding little American and Marine Corps flags. My eyes tear up unexpectedly, and I fight it back in order not to cry in front of my friends as we walk out. The older vets look ready to cheer, but they are quiet as they look on. We are quiet as we look back.

Someone touches my shoulder. "Do you need to call home, son? Here, use my phone," he says, as he hands me his cell. I can see other veterans handing phones to my friends, along with money to buy food at the airport. They don't ask us any questions or call us heroes. They just smile, and say things like, "Welcome home." They somehow found out that we were the first troops returning and made sure they would be the first people we saw in America, here at this random waypoint on our journey back to 29 Palms.

I call home, and Dad picks up. "Hello, this is Chris."

"Hey Dad, it's me, Gabe."

"Hey, son! Hey, Patty - get over here, it's Gabe! Where are you, son?"

"We just flew into Bangor, Maine. We should be making it back to base by evening."

"Well, praise God. That's great to hear, son. Do you know when you will be coming home?"

"No, I don't. But probably soon, I'll let you know when you need to pick me up at the airport once I find out when I'm coming home and have the plane tickets in my hand."

"Don't forget to bring your uniform. We are planning a welcome home party."

"I'm definitely not going to wear my uniform, Dad."

"Why not?"

"I don't know. Because I won't have to?"

"Well, you're my son. If you have a problem with a small request from your dad, you can keep it to yourself while you're staying under my roof."

"Fine, but I'm not wearing my uniform."

"Then find somewhere else to stay."

"Okay by me."

Mom cuts in on the back and forth. "Chris, shut up, shut up! Gabe, stop it. Are you there? Shut up! You're coming home! We'll see you at the airport, son!"

I get off the phone and hand it back to the old vet. He takes the phone and asks, "How was the flight?"

"It was good, sir."

"You don't have to call me sir. I'm sure you've done enough of that lately."

"Sure feels like it."

"Where are you from?"

"St. Paul, Minnesota."

"I have family up there."

We continue talking about family and various parts of the country where we've both been. I look around and see a man wearing a Vietnam veteran hat. He hands one of my friends a cell phone and doesn't say anything at all. He offers his phone and money for lunch, then smiles and looks down at his feet, pacing a little away from my friend and letting him talk to his family alone.

We board back up and fly towards the West Coast and the Air Force base where we initially departed. Traveling anywhere as a unit is a fairly involved process. On our way out, we carried gear and guns, filing from one tent to another and sometimes mooing to emphasize the feeling of being led like cattle from one corral to another. This time, by the time we have flown all the way back home and are getting onto a line of buses, the level of excitement has built up to a frenzied, maniacal zeal.

The bus driver is old, and gives us a little speech before driving us back to the base. Most of us will soon be two hours away from seeing the friends and family who have traveled from wherever home might be to see us. He tries to explain that we should treat him like an officer and show respect, but finds himself heckled into a sullen silence. He yells back at us a couple times as the busload of Marines sings songs like "99 Bottles of Beer on the Wall," counting all the way down to zero and then all the way back up to pass the time.

We drive back into the town surrounding our base. People are outside all of the little outlet malls and gas stations, cheering and waiving as we drive down the small main road. Moore stands up with Diego. They laugh and point at a girl who is standing outside, holding onto the hem of her shirt.

"She's going to do it!" yells Moore, as he pulls on Diego's collar. Both pairs of eyeballs bulge in gleeful anticipation out the window. Then, as if on command, she rips her shirt up and begins jumping up and down, flashing us as we drive by. Moore high-fives Diego.

Back on base, we get off the bus and are given our safety brief for the weekend. The brief is short, and we drive back around the block to where the families wait. A crowd of people are cheering and waving American flags on the grinder.

I get off with everyone else. My family wasn't able to make it out this time, but it's okay. They had been there after boot camp, and soon they will be waiting at the airport when I arrive home.

After people get settled down a little from the excitement of their first initial meeting, smaller family groups walk off with their own Marines. I find Flynn. He invites me to spend the weekend with him and his parents at a hotel off base.

His parents are nice people, Minnesota nice. It feels like a piece of Minnesota, and I enjoy every moment of it. They take us out to a restaurant. Real food never tasted so good.

Flynn and I sit and watch TV that afternoon. The Minnesota Twins are hosting another team in a live game at the Metrodome. "Look, Keith. Those are all Minnesotans. Every last one of them," says Flynn.

HOMECOMING

"When I was told I did a good job, I couldn't believe it. I thought I was the worst crew chief in the history of crew chiefs. But when a guy out there who I respected said that, it made me realize I've been my own worst critic. I don't have time for that kind of guilt any more. Write it off as self-preservation or whatever. I came home feeling ashamed and guilty that I didn't do a better job. Well, we all think that. But the truth of the matter is we all did our best. I needed to let a lot of self-loathing go to keep moving forward. We all do. You did better than you think. You are harder on yourself than anyone else. You were a good Marine. I'm real proud of you. I know you did a good job. You did the best you could, and that's what matters. You probably did a lot for a lot of people and didn't realize it, because that's how life is."

■ ■ ■

All of it overwhelms me, from my very first day in the Army until the very last one. By the time I get home I am all used up, a burnout who's angry at the world. Nineteen and numb from the experience, I stand on my parent's front steps, still in uniform. My clothes haven't even arrived from Vietnam yet.

I realize I'm broke. I feel so fucked over and so fucked up, and I'm not sure what to do. I just know that I have to get away from this house where there is always so much meaningless drama. I feel crazy being around it. I need quiet and I need it bad. I call a high school friend and beg him to let me use his motorcycle for old times' sake. He brings it over and says that I can borrow it, but asks me to make serious promises about its safe return. I make the promises and thank him. Not wasting a moment, I jump on the Honda 350 and head west on a local highway. I have no destination, only a desire to escape the chaos at home. Winding through the hilly terrain, I begin to feel better. I travel west, going through small towns and smaller villages. At times, I give the bike a hundred percent throttle and go like a bat out of hell. I smile, finally enjoying myself.

I pass through a certain small town that invokes all kinds of memories. I used to be familiar with this place.

Dad moved us here years ago, when I was a kid. I was comfortable here once.

On the way out of town, I am at a one-light intersection of county roads when I notice a VFW on one of the corners. Then, it hits me. It is a VFW.

I need to stop and rest, and I also want a cold beer. I am nineteen, but beer was not something that was ever denied me in Vietnam. As I pull into the lot and park the bike, it doesn't even occur to me that there might be a problem.

I walk up the steps and open the big brown door. I step into a dark room, where the only dim light comes from sunlight seeping through the dirty windows behind the bar. I'll never forget the woodwork in that place. It was dark and heavy looking, something from the early nineteen hundreds. Something from another world.

I stand in the doorway, scoping the place out, there are a couple of older men sitting together at the end of the bar. The bartender in his white shirt is leaning against the bar close to their seats. Seeing me, he breaks his stance and walks over to ask what I want. I step up to the bar and ask for a beer.

I am still in my dress uniform with the medals and the wings, obviously a military man. If that weren't enough, my attitude likely gives away the fact that I have just returned from war.

The bartender looks at me and asks how old I am. I tell him I'm nineteen and a half, and that I just got home and need a beer.

The two old guys stay hunched over their midday drinks, but they begin to turn, looking towards us. The bartender looks over at them and then back at me. "Get the hell out of my bar," he sneers.

I am in shock. I can't believe he has said that to me. "Why?"

"You are nineteen. You are not old enough to drink. At least not here. So go, before I throw you out."

"You're a real rotten son of a bitch!" I say. "I just got back from the war. I'm a veteran of a foreign war. Just give me a beer and I'll leave."

He is angered by that. "You haven't even served in a real war! It was just a police action over there!"

I look down to the end of the bar, where the old guys sit in their overalls and engineer hats. They are nodding their approval of the barkeep. He begins to come around the bar, so I leave.

19

HOME

"That 18-year-old kid needed anger to survive and get back home. The person you are now doesn't need it any more, Gabe. It's just not useful any more. I failed a couple of times in Vietnam, and when I got out I swore I wouldn't fail again. I became very intense. I want you to realize you are normal. You really are. It's fucking normal. All your combat brothers out there, and there are millions, are all normal. If we could, we would all live in the same community. We really would. I think what they call it is readjustment therapy. How did I go from being in a combat zone to working in a factory and being married? What an adjustment. I did not do well. But guess what? You and I are still here. Regardless of all the bullshit. We are still here, and that means we can let it go."

"When I can only write hate, when all I have in me for this story – for everything – is hate, I call you, Uncle Rick. You talk me off that cliff, man, even though we barely agree sometimes. I go back and erase whatever I've done. Then I write something that's hopefully better. Maybe hopeful, or helpful. I don't know."

■ ■ ■

I wake up in my own bed, in my old room in the basement. The sunlight laps against the wall. The breeze is pushing the blinds that hang level with the ground outside, revealing dew on the freshly cut grass. Someone is mowing the lawn, or maybe the neighbors'. I hear cars on the highway, or maybe someone driving up the driveway. None of these things are more than details here. Hot showers, homemade pastas and breads, and people I care about are just outside my door. Right now, I can choose to go in any direction I want.

A world of rough-cut materials, harsh patterns, and pure functionality has been replaced by one that is full of soft colors and pleasant tones. The process of checking gear, cleaning weapons, and coordinating efforts with at least twenty others before so much as stepping outside has been replaced by donning a t-shirt, shorts, and flip-flops. It is never hot or cold, only comfortable. I can choose whatever posture I want. If I see somewhere nice to sit, I sit. If I want to look at something for a long time, that is okay. I can hear nothing but music, or conversation, or nothing at all. I have no cares. No assessments. I can cancel plans and stay in if the weather is bad.

I have ten days of this bliss, then we are training again. But I push that thought away, shut my eyes, and fall back to sleep.

"Wake up, Marine!" Dad yells, slamming into the room, happy to have me home. He isn't afraid to show how much he cares. "It's time to get up and face the day!" he says, smiling and reaching for my blanket.

"Dad, go away! I'm trying to sleep!"

"No son of mine is going to waste the day away in bed!"

"Dad! Leave me alone! I'm not getting up yet!"

"All right. Well, I expect you upstairs soon, son. You said yesterday you would go into work with me and meet a few people who have been praying for you."

He leaves, and I get up. I go into the bathroom to shower, then pick out clothes and go upstairs where my mom is reading. She is happy to see me. I go to work with Dad and shake hands with some of the contractors he does business with. Many of them have known me since I was a kid.

My parents still have the '85 Oldsmobile they gave me in high school, and I drive it to meet Jon. His dad was the pastor of our community, and he has been my friend for my entire life. Jon and I played Superman and Superboy, or Davy Crocket and Daniel Boone as kids. Our families lived down the block from each other in the early nineties until my parents moved out to Stillwater. Jon has a big family, too. I see their pictures on Facebook. They look the same as they always have, one big happy bunch. I've always been impressed with their ability to continue on together like that.

We are adults now. Jon, who went off to college the year before I graduated from high school, meets me at his parents' front door. He yells at me and opens the door, wearing a huge grin.

"Hey bro, how've you been?" he says as we hug.

"Good, man. How are things?"

"Pretty good."

"How was it over there?"

"It sucked. Glad to be back."

"Glad to be out of that heat, huh?"

"And the cold."

"Yeah? Is that sarcasm?"

"Gets pretty cold at night, actually."

"How cold?"

"About fifty or so. I was never really sure."

"That's bad?"

"It can be."

"Hey, my parents want to say hi."

Walking into the house, I hug his mom and shake his dad's hand. Mrs. Sutton was as much a mother to our community as she was to her family. One night, during a normal childhood sleepover at Jon's, I woke up having a seizure. My arm and head were shaking uncontrollably back and forth, and all I could think was that this thing would never go away. Once the involuntary movements stopped, I walked to her room, crying. She hugged me until I calmed down and put me back to bed.

Jon and I are part of the first generation of kids that left their parents' homes in our community. Mr. Sutton knows this and wants to check up on me, to get a handle on how I'm doing. I sit down at the dining room table where Mrs. Sutton has laid out some food for guests who arrived before me. I serve myself from one plate or another, enjoying another round of home-cooked food, trying to experience it in the present and not focus on storing it away in detail for the future.

Mr. Sutton is talking with his friends. Apparently, he had mentioned earlier that I just came back from Iraq, sparking a conversation about war.

"Well, James," one of the guests says to him, "It's an interesting situation. We are going over there, presumably, to fight an enemy that has come here before and will possibly come over here again."

"When I saw people in war-torn countries in Africa, it was interesting to look at their faces. They seemed distant and numb. It was nothing like I'd seen on the faces of people here. I wondered what they had seen, and what about it had changed them."

"Yes, but what ideals are we maintaining as a fighting force over there? Or anywhere in the world, at that? I believe we do need to go over there to stop them from coming here. But if they didn't have nuclear weapons in the first place, are we fighting the right enemy? And with what sort of philosophy do we guide these decisions?"

"Well, if we are going to fight an enemy in another country, how can we know for sure if we are winning? Or if we're doing the right thing to begin with? There have been other wars in the past that have never felt resolved."

"Our soldiers are over there, and it's not clear what purpose guides them. As Americans, we need to be careful about the policing of other countries without proper discourse. It's like we are the schoolyard bully."

As the conversation progresses, I'm glad they aren't asking my opinion. With some conversations, all the answers are implied by the questions. That's a game I will never really know how to play when talking about Iraq.

I get up to leave, wondering what these people would think if they really saw the fighting force they so eloquently attempt to decipher, using words like "us" and "we." What if I opened the door for Staff Sergeant Morgan right now and he strode into the living room in a black rage, or if they could watch every day of my life over the last five months? They don't know the infantry.

They talk about fighting as a general term, something that is no more tangible to them than the metaphors they are using to describe it. I wonder how they would look right now if this table, with all its insight and objectivity, was placed squarely in the middle of Baghdad when we crossed into the city.

Mr. Sutton looks up at me and smiles as I move towards the front door, stopping me to say goodbye. We set a time to meet up for lunch. I walk outside and look around. People drive past. Others are walking their pets, and some stand on porches talking to those who walk by. I smile, walking down to the sidewalk and turn past my car. Two blocks down, across from my childhood house, the Deckers sit on their front porch and wave at me in surprise as I walk up.

We talk on the porch, and they tell me Tom is inside. He grew up across the street from me. We had sleepovers and talked about girls in school who we never talked to but thought we caught stares from. Sometimes we analyzed the little comments they made and attempted to decipher their meaning like it was the code to their souls. We've always shared this history of nerdy over-analysis like it's an inside joke. While my parents wouldn't let us kids watch television or play video games that had sexual references or negative humor, Tom's didn't want him near four-wheelers or chain saws, things which my family braved with reckless and sometimes comical abandon.

Tom and I walk around the block, revisiting the Catholic Junior High on the next street. I went there for seventh and eighth grade. Some of the equipment on the playground conjures memories of drama from a decade ago that seemed bigger than life back then. Tom is a year behind me, so as I'm just about to finish my first year in the Marines, he'll be starting college soon.

Mr. Sutton picks me up at my parent's house, taking me to a family restaurant he says he enjoys. We order food and talk. "So, how are you, Gabe?"

"Good, Mr. Sutton."

"I'm worried about you and need to know you are okay. Now, did you see any fighting while you were in Iraq?"

"A little."

He sits there, looking at me intently, maybe trying to read my body language to gauge some inner truth. He cares about everyone in his community, and I can see his concern on his face. "What was your job over there again, and what did you actually do?"

"Well, I was in the infantry. I was a machine gunner. We were on the border of Kuwait and Iraq. When we got the call, we pushed up behind Tank Battalion until we got to Baghdad, and then we took the city."

"How many people did you kill?"

"Well, there was one guy."

Sitting back, he sighs and says, almost to himself, "Well, good. That's not much."

Even though he was someone from a different world in that moment, Mr. Sutton was one of the greatest men I have ever known. He was notorious for having a very shrewd sense of humor. He enjoyed watching people develop as human beings who strive to become something else, to overcome their fears.

Our families met one time at Camp Snoopy in the Mall of America. The parents gathered around the tumbler ride, waiting for the ride's attendant to unhook the chain and allow the older kids in the group to file onto the platform. The ride looked terrifying. It involved a bunch of arms extending from a mechanical base in the center. At the end of the arms were little fuselages built to hold two bodies. When the ride began, the fuselages would lift off the ground and propel forward, rushing up and down as the ride moved around in a circle. It generated a lot of force for a little kid.

All of my friends were mad that I wasn't getting on the ride. Our parents stood around, waiting for the older ones to be done so we could move along to another entertaining enterprise. Mr. Sutton approached me, leaning down to my level. "You know, Gabe, the ride is really not that bad. It's actually more relaxing than anything," he said, as if he had accidentally happened upon this tidbit of helpful information.

Feeling reassured, I walked up, letting the carnival attendant swipe my armband and lead me to an open seat. I shifted around, testing the straps with my weight for reassurance as I waited for other kids to find their seats. Mr. Sutton approached, walking over to my spaceship of doom. "Gabe, I lied. This ride is terrifying. You might not survive. I'm sorry. Good luck, son."

A wave of terror and resentment washed over me. "It's too late now!" I thought to myself.

The ride was thrilling. I laughed and laughed as the plastic and metal bubble at the end of its flailing metal arm moved up and down, forward and back. It felt like light shining into the empty dark corner of a room, a place I had imagined was filled with unspeakable creatures that were now fading from existence, as if they had gone forever before I arrived. Or, as if the old, fearful version of me was now gone forever.

Driving around town, I meet up with Wendell. He also grew up with me and Jon. While Jon went to college and eventually earned a graduate degree, and I joined the military, Wendell went down a different path. The three of us had been close for years, but Jon and Wendell stopped being friends over each other's choice of company and pastimes.

Wendell planned to go into the Marines with me, since his dad had been in the Marines himself. But a previously botched knee surgery as a kid was identified at MEPS and Wendell was rejected. Coming face-to-face with his inevitable mortality at that age didn't help anything. He never had an easy path. He only cared for others but never himself.

I'll come back from future deployments to visit him in the apartment where he lives, now a repo man whose days are full of guns and weed. He jacks cars when he needs cash, and smokes weed, playing video games when he isn't letting friends in to stay and relax or party. I like Wendell's friends because they like to have fun and they like anyone who wants to have fun with them. They are a closer group than most. In the way that Jon is the natural leader of his group of friends, Wendell is even more so in his. People look up to him because he enjoys telling his friends they are awesome. For years, he pays for everything. He still does.

His friends meet at a coffee shop that stays open late. They drink gourmet sodas and talk. Wendell tells his friends that he would never fuck with me. Beyond going to church together every Sunday for the better part of two decades, we attended grade school together at King's Christian Academy. He stood up for me when I ran out of words, stepping in to let other kids know their place.

He is a great story teller. He gives the impression of a young mob boss, welcoming home a friend who is returning victorious from a mission to hit a warring family. He never asks questions, and is always glad to see me.

"Gabe! What up, buddy?" Wendell smiles. We are meeting at the coffee shop with his girlfriend and friends.

"Not much, bro. Good to be back. How are things?" I ask.

"Good, man. You know, just chilling. Hey, nice tan."

"It's only from the wrists and neck up, brotha."

"No way," he laughs. "Really?"

"Oh yeah. I wore my uniform all day and all night."

"In the heat?"

"And the cold."

"It was cold?"

"It was a lot of things."

"Got to feel good to be back in Funapolis. You remember Michelle, right?"

I went to school with Michelle's older sister, who was hot. She wasn't as hot as Michelle, who sits here, young and happy to be a big deal.

We sit around the coffee house on chairs moved out from the round wooden tables. The cool damp air from a stormy day, now over, wafts in whenever someone opens the door to enter or leaves to the sound of a little bell.

We close the place out. Wendell revs his engine next to my car, Michelle laughing in his passenger seat as I sit parked. I start up, hitting the gas and dropping into drive, zipping out and past him. He always gave me moments like that. I wish I could thank him for it. I wish he'd be able to hear it from me, if I did.

I go home, walking in a little late, but am quiet enough to not bother the parents. When Dad hears someone walking through his house at night, he never considers that his kids might appreciate a certain amount of discretion in the event they've brought home friends. He walks downstairs, a big man with crazy curly hair, unaware or just uncaring that he is standing nearly naked, wearing only a pair of whitey-tighties and a look that demands an explanation.

The next day is Sunday. Mom and Dad move through the house, waking up the kids. We eat breakfast, shower and change, and pile into Dad's F-150 and Mom's Ford Explorer. Seven kids in all, we head out to a church where I have never been. Since I left for the Marines, my parents have begun attending a different church than the one where I grew up.

Three projector screens face each side of the giant curved room. After the sermon, the preacher begins updating his congregation on the church's current events. I am zoning out for most of it until I see my picture from boot camp on the screens.

"And returning from a deployment to Kuwait is Colonel Thomas. If you could stand up and be recognized,

Colonel, that would be great, sir. He's here with us today, along with someone else who has just returned from a deployment in Iraq with the Marine Corps Infantry. Gabriel Keith, could you stand up as well, sir?"

Everyone smiles and claps. I am adrift in a sea of strangers. All of them mean well, but it's a lot of attention to handle, considering they've been staring at my face for the last four months and I have met them only in the last few minutes. When the congregation is released after the service, everyone begins leaving their seats. Some of them come over to where I'm standing to shake my hand and thank me for my service. A little girl stares up at me in awe as I reach down to shake her hand. Her mom, standing next to her, says, "You know you're shaking the hand of a real live hero, don't you, sweetie?"

I look over at Dad. He smiles, raising his hands to flex at me. In a way, he's telepathically delivering the slogan I grew up hearing him say to his friends when he would throw parties in the backyard, armed with spatula in hand, "I'm two hundred and twenty pounds of rompin, stompin dynamite!"

Thank God, these people don't know about the milkman. I leave the pew, walking towards the door and out into the rain. I find Dad's green truck, but the keys are still in his pocket inside the church.

I wait for the rest of the family, remembering how long it takes to gather seven kids and catch up with friendships shared for just a moment once a week after the service. As people begin filing out of the church, I realize they are walking out to me. They begin shaking my hand in the rain.

One man, who looks to be in his mid-forties, approaches after most have walked up and left. He looks at me and shakes my hand. I nod, wanting to apologize for forcing all this to happen in the rain, but decide against it since it would only make the moment more awkward. He looks at me, head tilted back a bit, expression cryptic though he is clearly thinking about saying something. Instead, he chooses to curtly smile and walks away.

Dad comes out with the rest of the family. We pile into the vehicles and head home. He isn't happy that I left the way I did, considering that all the people who were there have been praying for me this whole time. He reminds me that people just want to show they care by thanking me for my service.

The next day is day four. I have six left. Every morning I wake up and realize I'm almost done with this dream. My time in this place that I try my best to view as the present but that already feels more like the past. It is fast becoming no more than a chain of memories, jumbled in with the rest that have slipped through my fingers since the moment I joined the Marines.

For the next couple of days, I sleep a lot, staying in my room, coming out only for food or to drive to a movie with friends. I know I should be eating healthy and running every morning, but without the screams and the threat of losing my cherished weekends, I fall into a rhythm of fast food and passive pastimes.

One day, Mom pulls me aside.

"Son, your brothers and sister aren't happy with you, and I thought you should know."

"Why?"

"They feel like you don't have to do any chores and it's not fair."

"Well, I'm on vacation, and I don't live here anymore, Mom. Did you tell them that?"

"Yes, I told them. But I wanted you to know firsthand that they might approach you about it."

"Okay," I say, not really caring either way.

My parents throw a big welcome-home party that feels like I'm graduating from high school all over again. Friends and family arrive and park alongside the road. A big poster of a platoon patrolling through Baghdad has been printed off and hung in the garage, where food and drinks are arranged on tables. When my parents couldn't communicate with me, towards the end of my time in Kuwait, they clung to pictures or short videos of my battalion that surfaced on the internet or television.

Mom thought the pictures were of me, because one of the kids in both of them looked like me. It might as well have been me, but it never was. We all looked the same in matching gear, a bunch of thin white guys with no regard for sanitation or personal space, lacking the presence of mind to pose for a picture.

I overhear Mom talking to a friend at the party. She recounts her experience of watching the Iraq war kick off on national television, an experience she says later she will never forget.

"Well, Jenny," she says, "It was the most surreal experience of my life. It was a full-on broadcast, complete with a preview show that said things like, 'tune in tonight for the invasion,' and 'don't miss one important development of the war with our twenty-four-hour dedicated coverage for our viewers.'

"That must have been scary, Patty."

"It was. I didn't even know what was going on, and it was so dramatic. It was saying the fighting had begun and that troops were engaging as they pushed up into Iraq. I didn't get to talk to Gabe before it happened, so one day he calls to chat and the next I'm hearing on the news that this thing is happening. I was terrified as I watched. For all I knew, I was about to watch my son die on TV. I'm not sure if I've ever felt so helpless to protect one of my children. But me and Chris are glad he's back. We missed him a lot."

I only have a day left, and my family is finishing dinner. They leave the dishes for my fourteen-year-old brother Jake to clean, a massive chore involving nine sets of plates, cups, silverware, and all the pots, pans, and dishes used to prepare the meal and display it on the table. We have a dishwasher, but only half of the dishes fit. The rest have to be washed by hand.

I hadn't eaten with the family that night. I stay in my room while Jake cleans. Ignoring his obvious glares at me, I drop my plate in the water and leave. Jake follows me into the living room.

"Hey, where are you going? Aren't you going to help do dishes?"

"No. I'm meeting some friends."

"It's our turn, man. I'm not going to clean all this up by myself. Stop being so lazy. You haven't done anything the whole time you're here, and we do the dishes together in pairs."

"I'm on vacation," I say to Jake, turning around to face him as he stands in front of Mom's flowery cushioned chair.

"Oh, do you think you're special because you went to boot camp? No one gives a shit," he says, laughing.

I slam my hands into his chest, dropping him into the chair. Then my arm is pressed to his neck, pushing as hard as I can, trying to make him disappear into the fabric.

"Done yet?" I press harder. "Well?" I don't want to hear another word.

I slowly realize he can't speak, as he wheezes out the word "yes" in a soft exhale.

I let him go and he looks up, holding his throat with tears in his eyes, still mad and probably about to tell on me. I walk out the front door and leave. This time, I am meeting another friend I used to see at church every Sunday before going with her to see a few others.

The next day, Mom asks to talk with me alone. We walk out to the porch.

"So, I saw a bruise on Jake's neck. And he wouldn't tell me what it was, but when I had him take off his shirt, there was a long mark halfway down his chest. It's like all the blood vessels had burst on either side of a bruise. It took me a while, but he finally admitted that you did it to him. What happened?"

"Nothing, Mom. He followed me around and wouldn't leave me alone about helping with the dishes. I'm about to leave and go back to base. I don't want to spend any of the time I have left washing dishes."

"Okay. But next time, explain that to him."

"I don't care what they think. There's nothing to explain. I understand that washing the dishes is important here. That's his problem, not mine. Trust me, I wish it was my problem."

We talk it out, and I apologize, but not to Jake. We leave each other alone until I go. Dad drives me to the airport.

"Hey, Dad?"

"Yeah, son?"

"You know how, when people die in the military, there's the whole military funeral? Well, I don't want to be remembered like that. I don't want the full-gun salute thing, or the flag-handing ceremony, or pictures of me in my uniform. If they take my life, I don't want them to take my soul, too."

Looking at me carefully, he says softly, "Well, when we die, son, it's not really going to matter. When it's over for one of us, the funeral is more for the people we leave behind. It isn't our decision at that point anyway."

He was right, but I wish my dad and I had had more grace for each other. I wish I had understood how he was raised for just a moment. His dad would talk about the weather to his kids and was always a pleasant human being, but emotionless. Grandpa never told Dad he loved him, even though he did. But Dad said he loved me all the time. He had done everything he could to provide for me over the years, and I should have forgiven him for moments like this.

Now, I think back to the unburdened kid with his dad who I'd been only a handful of years before, when we would take trips up to the Boundary Waters. We stood in front of Dad's massive map of Minnesota's entire northern quarter. It was neatly wallpapered in big yellow sections from a book that was meant to be flipped through, not precariously tacked like a big puzzle in connected sections to the wall outside his office. Dad would let me pick our entry point, or at least he would graciously allow me to believe I had made the final decision.

We never really liked to fish and we were never any good at it. But we would try, together, in a canoe miles away from civilization, laughing and enjoying each other's company. The only sounds apart from ours were the constant slapping of the water as it played against the side of the canoe and the occasional loon call, somewhere in the distance but not too far away.

I wish I had remembered those times and talked about them. Instead, I was quiet and didn't talk to him for the rest of the trip to the airport. It should have mattered more that he loved me more than anything in the world, in a way that I couldn't understand but that was no less real for it. Instead, I focused on how little he understood about my life, not even a year removed from his. Then I thought of my Mom and how she cried when I left, and I resented myself even more as we pulled into the airport.

I hug Dad goodbye, missing my family already and hating myself for going back. I thought I had all these things to say to them. I had fondly rehearsed the moments I would share with them over and over in my head, but I couldn't find the words when I had the opportunity. I couldn't find any words at all. Now the whole trip is in the past. So quickly, I have gone from dreaming about those moments becoming present to finding myself back at the airport.

I hope that Jake doesn't hate me, but that is his problem. When I get back to base, I tell Wagner about it. When he asks why I didn't just do the dishes, I have no answer.

The old man at airport security says he's jealous that I'm flying to Las Vegas. Others pleasantly laugh around us. I see a music video playing on the TVs as I walk to my terminal, a rapper flopping a shiny handgun about on an undisciplined wrist while others jump in excitement around him.

At the terminal, I sit and wait. A kid in his alphas walks by with stacks of ribbons and medals on his chest, including a combat action ribbon and some other combat-related awards. As I approach, he stops in front of a magazine rack in the middle of the walkway and I ask him about the medals. He admits that they haven't been awarded to him, but says they are the medals his unit earned and they'll be awarded to him soon anyway.

I return to my gate, waiting for the flight to begin boarding, stuck in between worlds once again.

They tell me I'm a hero, but they have no proof. I tell them my back hurts. MRIs and X-rays show that it's true, but the VA tells me there is no proof.

I want to go back and fuck up Lewis. I want to go back and load a gun, to aim it at the recruiter just as he drives up my parent's driveway and make it a true kill. I want to become a better Marine. A more capable version of the one I was, the one I will always remember being. I know that this is an American story, however un-American it feels, at least because I am allowed to tell it.

You are too far removed, so they – your family – wait for you, even more when you are close, or in the next room. They need to see you when you listen to their day. They need to feel you, when they touch you at the end of the day. You went in to be a pack animal. Consider being one now.

I look back at the memories holding my regrets and wonder about their nature. I wish I had never left my family, but I don't celebrate with them now. I miss my friends, yet I isolate myself. I know I need to let go, but my back hurts and I can't sleep from the pain.

I need to hug my family and shake my head, accepting the journey and where it has taken me. The moments pushed are past. I need to make new memories warmer, replacing the old. Frame pictures of friends from the

Marines, but without the guns and gear. Knowing old soldiers from the past would approve, and let go of the rest.

There will always be a level of ignorance, always a level of bliss. The truth is something beautiful. Life is short because it's what we make of it, only here and only now. And we are here, destinies intersected for a moment before ending forever into forever.

Our world is each other's world. So even now, let it go. Even if you say no, it is still okay. They won't all understand, but the ones worth loving might.

Made in the USA
San Bernardino, CA
11 June 2017